Reimagining the Humanities

Electracy and Transmedia Studies
Series Editors: Jan Rune Holmevik and Cynthia Haynes

The Electracy and Transmedia Studies Series publishes research that examines the mixed realities that emerge through electracy, play, rhetorical knowledge, game design, community, code, and transmedia artifacts. This book series aims to augment traditional artistic and literate forms with examinations of electrate and literate play in the age of transmedia. Writing about play should, in other words, be grounded in playing with writing. The distinction between play and reflection, as Stuart Moulthrop argues, is a false dichotomy. Cultural transmedia artifacts that are interactive, that move, that are situated in real time, call for inventive/electrate means of creating new scholarly traction in transdisciplinary fields. The series publishes research that produces such traction through innovative processes that move research forward across its own limiting surfaces (surfaces that create static friction). The series exemplifies extreme points of contact where increased electrate traction might occur. The series also aims to broaden how scholarly treatments of electracy and transmedia can include both academic and general audiences in an effort to create points of contact between a wide range of readers. The Electracy and Transmedia Series follows what Gregory Ulmer calls an image logic based upon a wide scope—"an aesthetic embodiment of one's attunement with the world."

Books in the Series

Reimagining the Humanities, edited by Barry Mauer and Anastasia Salter (2022)

KONSULT: Theopraxesis by Gregory L. Ulmer (2019)

Exquisite Corpse: Art-Based Writing Practices in the Academy, edited by Kate Hanzalik and Nathalie Virgintino (2019)

Tracing Invisible Lines: An Experiment in Mystoriography by David Prescott-Steed (2019)

The Internet as a Game by Jill Anne Morris (2018)

Identity and Collaboration in World of Warcraft by Phillip Michael Alexander (2018)

Future Texts: Subversive Performance and Feminist Bodies, edited by Vicki Callahan and Virginia Kuhn (2016)

Play/Write: Digital Rhetoric, Writing, Games, edited by Douglas Eyman and Andréa D. Davis (2016)

Sites

Gregory Ulmer's *Konsult Experiment*: http://konsultexperiment.com/

REIMAGINING THE HUMANITIES

Edited by

Barry Mauer and Anastasia Salter

Parlor Press
Anderson, South Carolina
www.parlorpress.com

Parlor Press LLC, Anderson, South Carolina, USA
© 2023 by Parlor Press
All rights reserved.
Printed in the United States of America on acid-free paper.

S A N: 2 5 4 - 8 8 7 9

Library of Congress Cataloging-in-Publication Data on File

978-1-64317-344-3 (paperback)
978-1-64317-345-0 (PDF)
978-1-64317-346-7 (ePub)

1 2 3 4 5

Electracy and Transmedia Studies
Series Editors: Jan Rune Holmevik and Cynthia Haynes

Cover image generated by DALL·E, hosted by the OpenAI project. Output © 2023 by Parlor Press

Copyeditor: Jared Jameson
Book design: David Blakesley

Parlor Press, LLC is an independent publisher of scholarly and trade titles in print and multimedia formats. This book is available in paper, cloth and eBook formats from Parlor Press on the World Wide Web at http://www.parlorpress.com or through online and brick-and-mortar bookstores. For submission information or to find out about Parlor Press publications, write to Parlor Press, 3015 Brackenberry Drive, Anderson, South Carolina, 29621, or email editor@parlorpress.com.

Contents

Digital Compendium — *viii*
Acknowledgments — *ix*
Preface — *xi*
Introduction — *xiii*
    Barry Mauer and Anastasia Salter

Section One: Theorizing — 1

1 What Good Are the Humanities? — 3
    James Paul Gee

2 Of Literacy, Community, Texts, and Technology: Rethinking Literacies from a Text and Technology Perspective — 22
    Kirk St.Amant

3 Ethical Considerations in Digital Culture Research — 44
    Cassandra Branham and Jennifer Wojton

4 Traversing Theme Park Stories: Towards an Expansion of Transmedial Narratology — 67
    Carissa Baker

5 Not Quite Virtual: Technē between Text and World — 90
    Erik Champion

6 The New Poetics of Computer Animation: Selective Augmentation and Animated Realism (Digital) — 109
    Nathan Snow

Section Two: Teaching — 111

7 Co-Constructing Authority in the Classroom Chora — 113
    Jessica Kester and Jessica Lipsey

8 Metacognitive Experiences, Dialogic Pedagogies, and
   Designing Video Feedback   127
   Dan Martin

9 Classical Education and Partnership Networks: A Model for
   Higher Education Innovation   145
   Meghan Griffin

10 Pedagogy of Play: Fluxus in the College Classroom   165
   Marci Mazzarotto

11 Life in the Megapocalypse (Digital)   186
   Kenton Taylor Howard

Section Three: Experimenting   *189*

12 The Cowboy/Gypsy Boot: The Wide Image as Method for
   Humanist Inquiry and Action (Digital)   191
   David Matteson

13 "The Deserters:" Activist Critical Making in
   Electronic Literature (Digital)   193
   Laura Okkema

14 Citizen Curation (Digital)   195
   Barry Mauer

15 Good Times Post-Pandemic: A Dyn-O-Mite Method?   197
   Craig Saper

16 The Hypertext Years? (Digital)   218
   Stuart Moulthrop

17 The Cheshire Diagrams   220
   Gregory L. Ulmer

Contributors   *235*
Index   *241*
About the Editors   *255*

This book is dedicated to the past, present, and future students of the University of Central Florida's Texts & Technology PhD program.

Digital Compendium

While most of the works included in this book are essays intended for print, several of the works are fully born-digital and are introduced and discussed in the print volume but presented fully online, taking advantage of the platforms available to us for scholarly making, while others include augmentations and additional resources demonstrating the digital practices and thinking engaged within the text. The volume thus engages with questions and challenges of activist pedagogy, theoretical and methodological rethinking, institutional and administrative shifts, and applied, "maker"-driven work. These reflections are situated in practice, with scholars reflecting on their training and preparation for the work they are engaged in now and scholars pointing toward the need for more engaged self-evaluation in the work they hope to do in the future.

Access the digital compendium online at https://bit.ly/reimagining-humanities or follow the QR code.

Acknowledgments

We thank all the contributors to this volume for staying with us through a long process made longer, and more challenging, by the pandemic. Editing a book is a marathon, and we appreciate the efforts of our editors at Parlor, including the support and guidance of David Blakesley and Cynthia Haynes. Thanks to all at Parlor who made it possible to release this unusual volume with its hybrid and moving parts.

This work was shaped by insights from our research communities, including the Modern Language Association, Association of Internet Researchers, Electronic Literature Organization, and many others. And of course, thanks to our support networks, including our families; our friends; our faculty group-chats; and our colleagues in both English and the Texts & Technology program. Our profound gratitude goes to Michael Bonner for proofreading and to Lindsay Ashton Scott and Jared Jameson for copyediting.

Special thanks to Stuart Moulthrop, who originally suggested this volume should exist.

Preface

This volume was started prior to the pandemic, with a call that circulated at a different (but perhaps no less dire) moment for the humanities: we first circulated the call to authors in September 2018 and envisioned a relatively traditional collection in form. First drafts were completed prior to the start of the pandemic, and so many of these chapters were conceptualized at a moment before what would so often be called an "unprecedented" moment, and shifted with their authors through the process (and inevitable delays) of the pandemic's transformation of the university and society at large.

The impact of the last several years is evident across humanities publishing. Peer review timelines are shifting; volunteer labor is difficult to find in the face of collective overwork and burnout; editors are facing both supply chain and production challenges along with their own cuts and labor fatigue; and authors are working under the pressures of contingent positions, decreased staff support, and increased care-taking challenges made worse by university funding cuts and political scrutiny. This volume was transformed by these challenges, and we particularly regret the loss of some voices among our contributors as a result of changes in their own lives that made it impossible to continue – we note that this impact is felt most strongly among those already marginalized in higher education, and thus is a loss not just for the collection but for the humanities at large.

There are also changes in the volume that reflect shifts in our collective understanding of the importance of hybrid work: the conversation around digital scholarship, as reflected so strongly by the work of venues pushing the boundaries such as *Kairos: A Journal of Rhetoric, Technol-*

ogy, and Pedagogy; Textshop Experiments; Hyperrhiz; and *The Digital Review*, has been ongoing since before the pandemic, but demands renewed attention at a moment when so much of our scholarly endeavor has been transformed by technology. This volume is a partial (and as such preliminary) response to those shifts, and thus includes a supplemental digital component that exists on the web. The works included in this section reflect a range of voices, from experienced to relatively new creators of digital scholarship, and are documented in the print edition through abstracts pointing towards the full online versions of the works. We hope these serve as a model for continuing to think about the form and function of our work as humanists, though we note that while the work included was built to endure on web-based technologies, some of it may prove ephemeral with the shifts in platforms and structures that lie ahead.

We can imagine that the work of edited collections in the humanities can and perhaps must shift further in this direction, and that indeed our adherence to the centricity of print (and perhaps even to the traditional structures of the edited collection) can amplify existing inequities. It is our hope that this volume includes works to inspire conversation around this changing discipline, as we offer three lenses —theorizing, teaching, and experimenting – in the humanities.

Introduction

Barry Mauer and Anastasia Salter

As we struggle through a period that will be defined by COVID-19 and marked by a new and intense interest in the impact of online education and the intersection of text and technology in shaping every part of public discourse, we propose to look back at the models offered by the emergent, sometimes self-contradictory, space of the digital humanities for those seeking to imagine a humanities that can endure this difficult future. The study of the humanities involves a core research question—"how do we live a life worth living?"—that sets it apart from other fields—such as the sciences—because it requires we reckon with ideology. Ideology is the set of beliefs, values, and behaviors we use as our interface with reality and social life. We inherit ideology from our nurturing institutions—such as family, entertainment, school, disciplines, careers, and church—and our ideology has profoundly real consequences, both for us and for other people. The #MeToo and Black Lives Matter movements confront ideologies—patriarchy and white supremacy—that attempt to legitimize abuse and sustain impunity for the abusers. The goal of our reckoning with ideology is to attain wellbeing—both individually and collectively—and to learn from tragedies such as fascism, climate change, epidemics, mass extinctions, financial collapse, nuclear war, and genocide. The humanities' confrontation with ideology shares similarities with the process of therapeutic counseling, which aims to break through denial, recognize choice, and accept responsibility. The processes may be different, but the aims are similar.

To say the humanities is in crisis is exhaustingly familiar; the economic disaster of 2020 has already taken a disproportionate toll on humanities departments with "studies" programs that focus on race and gender particularly struggling in the face of cuts or closures. Likewise, Donald Trump's executive order of September 22, 2020, particularly sought to disrupt the teaching of critical race theory and anti-racist, anti-misogynist pedagogy and highlighted the Smithsonian Institution as an exemplar of the type of teaching now prohibited:

> A Smithsonian Institution museum graphic recently claimed that concepts like "[o]bjective, rational linear thinking," "[h]ard work" being "the key to success," the "nuclear family," and belief in a single god are not values that unite Americans of all races but are instead "aspects and assumptions of whiteness." The museum also stated that "[f]acing your whiteness is hard and can result in feelings of guilt, sadness, confusion, defensiveness, or fear." (Whitehouse.gov)

While President Biden revoked this order in 2021, similar restrictions are being passed in states governed by Republicans. Several works in this collection engage directly with questions central to these restrictions, while others look more generally at the need to challenge hegemonic structures, particularly in education and pedagogy. Stuart Moulthrop's work particularly reminds us to be suspicious of technological solutionism and evokes the role of social media and hypertext broadly in the culture wars. Meanwhile, Laura Okkema's experimental hypertext puts those same systems to use to amplify a multigenerational narrative of immigration, suggesting a framework for "activist critical making." Her work complements other works in the collection that draw our attention to the need for global perspectives in digital humanities' works, such as Carissa Baker's examination of methods for studying situated transmedia narratives through theme parks around the world.

By bringing simultaneously a lens of suspicion and optimism to the technologies supporting our reimagination of the humanities, we draw upon and acknowledge the pivotal work of scholars reshaping the field of technology studies more broadly: Safiya Noble, Andre Brock, Ruha Benjamin, Kim Gallon, and the many others who have cautioned against the potential consignment of humanist inquiry to algorithmic means.

The task for digital humanists is to update our methods for engaging with ideology in an electrate age. We ask what counts as knowledge (e.g., the true-false axis) and how we align our activities with our values (e.g., right-wrong axis) within an increasingly libidinal (e.g., attraction-repulsion axis) economy. We understand that shifts in information technologies facilitate different ways of knowing and that it is our responsibility to invent humanist methods for conducting research within these emerging technical-ideological apparatuses. Most importantly, we ask how these understandings must be addressed differently through transdisciplinary humanist education at a time when disinformation is dominant in the technical landscape shaping our classrooms and communities.

Grammatology identifies our age of electronic media as the fourth information apparatus, following orality, alphabetic literacy, and print literacy. Apparatus theory posits that human communication relies upon institutions and that apparatus shifts result from inventions across technology, institutional practices, and human subject formation. One apparatus in particular—education—trains people in literacy, critical thinking, self-knowledge, and citizenship. How should the educational apparatus reinvent itself for an electrate age?

To cite one example of apparatus shift, the invention of print technology led to inventions in information practices such as the textbook (Ramus 1543), essay (Montaigne 1570), newspaper (Carolus 1605), novel (Cervantes 1605), and encyclopedia (Diderot 1751). Print also led to the regularization of spelling, grammar, and typography and textual practices such as footnotes, bibliographies, and indexes. These inventions accompanied shifts in human subject formation, including the concepts of authors and critics, the experience of an inner self—an effect enhanced by reading—and the notion of democratic citizens of nation states. The resulting explosion of knowledge, which apparatus theory understands as a memory prosthesis, has profound historical effects. Movements such as the Reformation, the scientific revolution, and the Enlightenment are difficult to imagine without the invention of print.

Gregory Ulmer's heuretics work, which inspired this collection, identifies methods of discovery and invention to address the problems posed by our current shift from print to digital media. Heuretics investigates the consequences, characteristics, and modes of electronic literacy and conducts humanities research not only about but also within electrate modes of textuality. To that end, this project has an online component built as a hypertext, incorporating both linked and augmented works in a preservation-friendly HTML5 format.

Inventors of method—from Plato to Roland Barthes—have produced forms of writing, broadly defined, for research and teaching appropriate to their disciplines and to the information technologies they employed. Similarly, many of the projects documented herein experiment with methods designed to reinvent contemporary humanistic practices. Without abandoning critique and hermeneutics as they are practiced within the academy today, heuretics augments them; heuretic practices—borrowed from the avant-garde arts, the sciences, entertainment, and theory—include new genres of research within the academy and the production of new critical and creative works within these genres.

This anthology investigates, theorizes, and demonstrates emerging forms of humanities education and research within texts and technology—or the digital humanities, broadly construed. It addresses ways in which the grammatological shift from orality, alphabetic literacy, and print literacy to the electrate age of networked and electronic media changes our understanding and practices of memory, research, writing, teaching, service, and consulting. It also addresses the evolutions in narrative, rhetoric, and poetics that accompany this shift. We reject the understanding of texts and technologies as neutral objects that can be understood solely through distant readings and big data studies and opt instead for embodied engagement with texts and technology, understanding that texts and technologies shape lived experience and our scholarship. Several of the works included are fully born-digital—these works are summarized in the print volume and can be accessed in the online supplement—taking advantage of the platforms available to us for scholarly making, while others include augmentations and additional resources demonstrating the digital practices and thinking engaged within the text. The volume thus engages with questions and challenges of activist pedagogy, theoretical and methodological rethinking, institutional and administrative shifts, and applied, "maker"-driven work. These reflections are situated in practice—with scholars reflecting on their training and preparation for the work they are engaged in now, and scholars pointing towards the need for more engaged self-evaluation in the work they hope to do in the future.

While born from the Texts and Technology PhD, T&T, program at the University of Central Florida—soon entering its twentieth year—this volume aims at similar graduate degree programs at every institution. The contributors are faculty members, students, alumni, and visiting scholars who have participated in some ways with T&T. A broad range of contributors with different areas of expertise have converged through T&T and have brought their expertise with them to many other institutions. The program began with students who were mostly from the region around Orlando but has since expanded to include students from countries around the world. In the past few years, the program—which is well-balanced in terms of gender—has striven to end racial disparities in its faculty and student body with some success. Since its first days, the program has focused its research on intersectionality and oppression. Some of that research, focusing on race, is reflected here in work by Craig Saper and Barry Mauer. Identifying and addressing racial hierarchies will continue to be a focus of the program as it seeks to become more diverse.

The volume is divided into three sections: theorizing, teaching, and experimenting.

SECTION ONE: THEORIZING

A theory is an account of what things are, why they are the way they are, and how and why they work. A "thing" can be a physical thing, like a person or book, an activity, like reading or making, or an abstract concept, like the proletariat or being or love. Theory also overlaps with method, which is a description of process: how and why to do things in certain ways. The section looks at the "things" in the humanities and what we might do with them. Theory is no less important today than it was in the 1980s when it became a "thing" that people in the humanities did. We need theory to identify the ways in which our world is shaped, how it shapes us, what changes are taking place in it, and what is staying the same. In particular, we need grammatological theory that shows us our place and possibilities within the emerging electrate apparatus. Does education have an opportunity to shape society within electrate society as it did with the shift to print literacy in the Renaissance, or are we on the losing end of the battle with other forces such as commerce?

James Paul Gee, in "What Good Are the Humanities?," contemplates the humanities' value as we grapple with our future as a species—which seems to be very limited. Gee's title acknowledges that print-era humanities practices cannot prevail in a digital age and that more is needed. Gee posits a productive relationship between the humanities and activities outside of the academy. In particular, he finds poetry—and vernacular practices of reading it—to be a productive route. Poetry has value to ordinary people, but not when it is framed as an elite activity. Gee's late career turn towards vernacular poetry reading can be understood in terms of the libidinal turn: the focus on aesthetics and the polarities of attraction-repulsion that Kant first outlined in his *Critique of Judgment*. The age of digital media has upended the dominance of epistemology, ethics, and metaphysics in many institutions; the "culture wars" are largely fought on the field of aesthetic judgment. Without engagement with aesthetics and one's own libidinal investments, we are indeed unprepared to engage with the dominant institution of our age—entertainment, or, in particular, advertising. Advertising shares the libidinal machinery of poetry but subverts it for its own ends—commodification. Poetry provides the means to reclaim our libidinal energies from advertising.

Kirk St.Amant, in "Of Literacy, Community, Texts, and Technology," challenges common notions of literacy and examines the dynamics at work in connections between texts, technologies, and communities. He argues that literacy functions in relation to community expectations and to the uses of technologies to access and produce texts, highlighting variables individuals can use to map ideas of literacy in different communities. Such mapping can help foster literacy activities within and across communities, disciplines, and geographical areas over time. Through such an examination, this entry provides a framework for answering the all-important question of what aspects of texts, technologies, and community constitute functional literacy in our modern world.

The deregulation of the digital sphere has allowed much of it to become an ethical free-for-all where bullies act with impunity and ordinary people get hurt. Humanities researchers need help navigating digital spaces within an ethics of care. Cassandra Branham and Jennifer Wojton's chapter, "Ethical Considerations in Digital Culture Research," addresses the blind spots that many social media researchers have about working with human subjects. The authors particularly address studies involving members of marginalized groups, such as veterans and pop culture fans. They address numerous vital questions: how do we determine which online spaces are public or private? What counts as "publishing" online? Do users of the online space share the same understanding about privacy—or lack thereof—that content creators do? How do researchers distinguish between online authors and their data? What counts as "sensitive" information? Are researchers projecting stereotypes onto the group? Are participants able to correct misunderstandings in the researchers' work? What counts as labor in online groups and how do researchers avoid exploiting it? In all, the chapter provides valuable guidelines that go far beyond Institutional Review Board (IRB) guidelines in terms of mitigating potential harms to research subjects.

Increasingly, humanities scholars are confronting the aesthetic and affective realm as the ascendant, if not dominant, realm of judgment in the digital era. Carissa Baker's "Traversing Theme Park Stories: Towards an Expansion of Transmedial Narratology" rethinks the boundaries of "texts" to include environmental storytelling while demonstrating that narratological theory is far more flexible and useful than many critics had previously imagined. Baker argues that humanities research grows in relevance when it deals with current phenomena: "part of the assumption of a humanities demise may be a lack of understanding of significant questions and practices found in the area or the presence of contemporary, interdisciplinary approaches like new media studies or game studies." Theme parks are treated as marginal phenomena in much humanities scholarship but are central to lived experience for millions of people. Baker points out that theme park narratives exist in relation to other narratives in society:

> Narratives might be found in park marketing, company brands, employee culture, merchandise, and guest memories of experience that have been narrativized, but the main area of investigation is the set of narratives visitors actually travel to the parks for, their attractions (the term used for a variety of experiences including rides, shows, parades, films, walkthroughs, etc.). Parks also often have a backstory in addition to front stories and they act as a container for dozens of narratives.

Theme parks activate and build networks far beyond their physical locations. Transmedial theory recognizes that we can no longer confine ourselves to the traditional discrete "objects" of humanities study.

Continuing the discussion about the evolving meaning of "text," Erik Champion's "Not Quite Virtual: Technē between Text and World" addresses the developing field of virtual heritage—the preservation of virtual environments. Champion's work represents a key intervention in the history of the medium, which occurs when material that has been treated as ephemeral and disposable becomes archived and understood historically. Such moments—for example, when Henri Langlois began preserving films—are key to the development of a medium. Langlois's work allowed film scholars and makers to grasp currents and potentials in their medium that had gone hitherto unrecognized. Champion's work does the same. Compounding the difficulty of Champion's task is the proliferation of platforms for virtual projects, the rapid obsolescence of many of these platforms, as well as the fact that virtual worlds are dynamic and changing. How are scholars to compare and contrast virtual worlds if we are unable to access them through a common platform? Champion considers not only the benefits of virtual worlds but also their costs, such as the high cost of equipment, the erosion of privacy, and the environmental damage associated with burning fossil fuels to power servers and data centers. While Champion sees virtual worlds not as texts but as multimedia, he sees the humanities as encompassing both art and research about it, and more significantly, occupying the interstitial space between both. He cites Heidegger's notion of world-building as the link between Athens and Virtual Reality (VR), bringing into being the places for developing human potential. Most of all, he calls for the building of virtual worlds and augmented realities that require care and intention (e.g., techné), offer opportunities for people to create (e.g., painting and sculpting), show effects over time, and encourage critical thinking.

Nathan Snow's "The New Poetics of Computer Animation: Selective Augmentation and Animated Realism," available in our online supplement, considers one of the most powerful and profitable mediums that has appeared in the past century—computer-animated movies. Snow uses mirror neuron theory to discuss the way that computer-animated feature films create embodied experiences for audiences through the illusion of intention in unreal and normally inert objects that appear within computer-animated films. Mirror neuron theory posits that thoughts guide intentions and that audiences infer intentions—and thoughts—through character actions that they feel within themselves. Snow writes, "animation can, using the poetics of selective augmentation, present a world that is 'more real' than live action by using its unique unreal capabilities." Snow defines selective augmentation as occurring when animators "select certain materials or behaviors to highlight through formal techniques such as movement, textural detail, or color, thereby increasing their tangible credibility while simultaneously lessening their photoreality." The application of selective augmentation brings audiences to care more about certain things, such as how audiences came away from *Ratatouille* caring more about food. Such a powerful tool can shape audience experiences, creating new appreciation or dissatisfaction with reality. Whether we use this tool to move us towards a more just or unjust society remains an open question.

Section Two: Teaching

Teaching, like theory, is undergoing transition as teachers shift from print-based to digital ways of engaging with information and with students. What teaching practices are best suited to our digital age? What counts as "writing" in this environment? How are students becoming co-creators of knowledge? What kinds of new teaching spaces, real and virtual, are emerging? How are student identities engaged and developed in these new "classrooms"? How do we empower students to experiment in digital spaces and platforms? The chapters in this section respond with both practical and innovative guidance.

Jessica Kester and Jessica Lipsey's "Co-Constructing Authority in the Classroom Chora: Reflective Practices for Twenty-First Century Writing Teacher-Scholars" considers ways in which students' authority on digital writing, such as meme creation and social media use, can supplant the teachers' authority without leading to institutional breakdown. Everyday writing practices such as these often require craft knowledge that, as Carlo Ginsburg might say, is closer to intuition than to formal logic. First year writing programs, however, rarely institute disciplinary practices to empower students to co-create authority on these subjects or develop their intuitive writing skills. The authors cite Thomas Rickert's ambient rhetoric and Gregory Ulmer's chora as practical models for creating learning spaces in which co-construction of authority can occur. Such spaces are responsive. They give feedback—like a sound creates an echo—that increases the vital activity of reflection.

Dan Martin's piece "Metacognitive Experiences, Dialogic Pedagogies, and Designing Video Feedback" provides examples of multimodal feedback alongside an examination of how changing modalities can foster dialogic moments. Martin argues that rethinking the modality of feedback "can lead instructors to more metacognitive experiences about the quality of their pedagogy and feedback, which can further facilitate the development of what Martin Buber calls 'I–Thou' relationships between students and teachers that are inherently dialogic." Martin's work asks us to consciously reflect on how we build and maintain connections with students as part of learning, offering a particularly compelling call to action at a moment when social distancing and online education has transformed the platforms for building such connections.

Meghan Griffin's "Classical Education and Partnership Networks: A Model for Higher Education Innovation," focuses on how some educational institutions are collaborating with partners—such as family, local communities, and global entities—by uniting around an adaptable classical curriculum to prepare people to live good lives in the digital age. How do ideas and practices within education circulate throughout the culture? Ulmer refers to "the popcycle," which is the ensemble of discourses that shape human identity. Now that homeschooling and school choice are realities within the United States, classical education and partnership networks offer constructive approaches to engagement. Griffin explains classical partnership education "through an actor-network approach as a social pursuit of truth, goodness, and beauty across institution and organization types." This program seeks to impact students far beyond training them in professional skills; it aims for them to thrive in all areas and to increase "students' likeliness to engage in academic activities, develop academic plans, maintain healthy relationships, value civic engagement, and maintain a positive perspective of their collegiate experiences." The program offers classical education within Deleuze and Guattari's assemblages and rhizomatic networks, taking advantage of potentials that have increased with the proliferation of networked technologies.

Marci Mazzarotto's "Pedagogy of Play: Fluxus in the College Classroom" explores the history of the avant-garde's pedagogical activities and adapts them for use in the electrate humanities classroom. Mazzarotto links the tradition of play in avant-garde pedagogies with the experimental impulse in science by referring to Breton's first *Surrealist*

Manifesto, which drew upon Freud to justify Surrealist methodology. Fluxus artists and theorists, such as John Cage, took Surrealism further by institutionalizing the pedagogy of play in Mills College, The New School, and Chicago's Institute of Design. Mazzarotto emphasizes the role of discovery and chance in this work and presents three classroom applications: culture-jamming, mail-art, and performance.

In another digital piece, part of this volume's online supplement, Kenton Taylor Howard's "Life in the Megapocalypse" demonstrates an active approach to playful pedagogy. Howard's project showcases a moddable, transformable approach to queer representation in games, designed to be built upon with and by students. Drawing on Bo Ruberg's approach to queer game design and principles of educational games, Howard demonstrates an activist approach to educational design, suggesting that scholars seeking to benefit from digital, playful pedagogy must build systems alongside and with their students, creating moddable, shared spaces for creative work.

Section Three: Experimenting

In the experimenting collection, we put theory into action, considering how the unstable, changing, and playful spaces the humanities uneasily occupy are reshaping our work. Appropriately, many of these experiments cannot be contained on the page and exist in summary here with their full experience available online. The summaries of those works included in print provide a lasting entry point to their contributions as we note the longevity of the technologies and platforms powering innovative work is always subject to external forces.

The experimental works featured in this volume model what the humanities is called to become: born-digital, public-facing, multimodal, and alternative forms of scholarship. David Matteson puts this call into action in his Tracery-driven piece "The Cowboy/Gypsy Boot: The Wide Image as Method for Humanist Inquiry and Action," which is built upon Kate Compton's feminist library for procedural text generation. The work explores the value of unconventional modalities to challenge "wicked problems" (which are social or cultural problems that are resistant to resolution), engaging with Ulmer's work, and exploring the value of theory as method. Matteson confronts the forces of exploitation in the broader culture and within the LGBTQ+

community, using Ulmer's Mystory genre to explore how discourses of domination shaped his own process of identity formation.

Similarly, Laura Okkema's "The Deserters" offers a model for activist critical making. Built in Twine, an open-source tool for building interactive hypertexts, Okkema's work explores immigrant narratives through a personal archival exploration of her family's experience as refugees from East Germany. Incorporating both a narrative approach and the physical artifacts that embody memory, Okkema's piece challenges humanists to imagine new ways to share and "play" the past while demonstrating work at the intersection of "digital humanities discourses on activism and social justice, hypertext, electronic literature, critical making, and hacker culture."

Barry Mauer's "Citizen Curation," available in our online supplement, expands our understanding of "text" through a work that is half theory and half experimentation. Mauer explores the idea that anyone using off the shelf software, such as Comic Life, can produce curated exhibitions within comic "space." His work deals with public policy themes such as violence against LGBTQ+ and people of color. In February 2017, the Citizen Curator Project—responding to the Pulse Nightclub attack—invited community members, students, and artists to create a series of exhibitions in Central Florida focused on the theme "Eliminationism and Resilience." Mauer, who helped organize the project, contributed his work, "Pulse: A Consultation," which he discusses here in relation to the public sphere. Mauer agrees with Ulmer's view that the public sphere based upon literacy is collapsing, requiring us to invent an electrate public sphere. Whether such a project is possible is yet to be determined, but we will not know unless we try.

Craig Saper's "Good Times With the T&T Experiment: A Dyn-O-Mite Doctoral Program, Method, or School of Thought?" uses an experimental punning method that employs Ulmer's conductive logic to explore the dynamite resonances of "T&T" (shorthand for the Texts and Technology PhD program at UCF). This conductive method takes Saper through the 1970s show *Good Times* and discourses of race and oppression. Saper's work explores group identity, which is to be discovered and invented. Group identity is only partially under any group's control. The question of whether our work constitutes a program, method, or school of thought remains to be determined. Of course, these identities are not mutually exclusive, but they do bring with them different consequences; for instance, we refer to the Frankfurt School, the Birmingham School, and the Toronto School. The "school" designator implies that these were more than just programs but continue to occupy key positions within the history of ideas. If T&T is indeed a school of thought, what is it? Saper shows what a hybrid of disciplinary knowledge and mass media entertainment might offer. What follows in his chapter is a tour through the history of television, comparative literature, postmodernism, and studies of race and whiteness to locate a space for innovation in the humanities.

Stuart Moulthrop's interactive "The Hypertext Years?" both explores the history of "hypertext" as a lens for understanding cultural change through the construction of text and explores hypertextual futures through the work's form. He places a current platform powering accessible hypertext-making—Twine—in conversation with a history of literary and experimental hypertext, asking what emerges when we put these moments—and tools—in conversation. His provocation asks us to consider the unstable spaces that humanists currently occupy as intertwined with the hypertext's poetics, which, in turn, can provide mechanisms for challenging dominant narratives: "No doubt power and money will continue to favor kinetic dominance games, but as long as there is the software equivalent of cheap guitars, there will be people who pick them up and play otherwise."

We end with Gregory Ulmer's "The Cheshire Diagrams," which similarly asks us to embrace the unknown and the unstable. Ulmer's "Cheshire Diagrams" represent his recent efforts to reason beyond alphabetic literacy. Ulmer has contributed two pieces to our volume: the diagrams themselves—which are part of our online supplement—and a print chapter explaining and justifying this work. The print chapter leads us through the major concepts of his program, which he has built and elaborated over the past four decades, including heuretics, or the logic of invention; electracy, the apparatus or social machine after orality and literacy; conduction, the associative logic native to electracy; event, the position of thinking that replaces subject or object; and choragraphy, a figurative mapping of our being within a network of discourses. Choragraphy sets up a konsult, a dialogue oriented towards well-being within a scene of disaster—the Anthropocene—that employs avatar, also known as virtue. Ulmer invented genres—mystory and memorial—to realize this choragraphic dialogue by employing theopraxesis, which is "thinking, willing, imagining; knowing, doing, making." The Cheshire Diagrams is a rethinking of justice—

the first literate concept—in terms of the Cat & Mouse chase that runs through the history of modern comics and cartoons. If our literate concept of justice is replaced—or at least augmented—with the Cat & Mouse chase, what kind of a society can we build upon it? How should the educational apparatus prepare people to live ethically in such a society? These questions await our attention.

SECTION ONE: THEORIZING

1 What Good Are the Humanities?

James Paul Gee

This book is about the future of the humanities. We cannot be sure that there is much of a future left for the human species, given the effects of interacting complex systems we humans have set into disaster-prone over-drive. In this essay I have some observations, based on the personal experience of an old academic, of good the humanities might still serve and how this good could be as much out-of-school as in-school and certainly a cooperative project between the two.

My question in this essay is "What good are the humanities?" These days, this is a popular question as humanities departments in colleges and universities are in great decline and jobs for their doctoral students are close to non-existent (Hanson 2014; Massing 2019). Many people, from politicians to businesspeople to academics themselves, have begun to question the necessity of the humanities, especially since they do not seem to lead to "good jobs"—a leading concern these days. Of course, for most of the twentieth century, the humanities—like literature, art, and history—were thought to be foundational to an "examined life," and such a life was thought to be important for the full development of a human being.

In 1967, I took a summer course at Stanford University before I went off to college at the University of California at Santa Barbara. While I was in the course, there was a raging controversy in the country over the fact that Stanford wanted to change the Western Civilization course requirement to a World Civilization course. Some at Stanford were also beginning to champion non-Western literature as a worthy subject for "high literature" courses. All this caused great concern on the part of conservatives who argued that all Americans needed to be educated in the foundations of Western civilization and literature if we were to survive as a civilization. Indeed, they argued that Western civilization and Western literature had long been— and still were—major "civilizing" forces across the world.

Today, however, as Western civilization and literature requirements are declining everywhere, we hear not a peep from conservatives. They no longer care, it seems. By and large they appear now to view the humanities as an indulgence not worth public funding.

It is interesting to speculate about this change—how we went from viewing the humanities as a civilizing and unifying force to being largely irrelevant. Some have argued that when the humanities were viewed as a unifying force, capitalism was interested in mass markets, but now capitalism is centered on niche markets defined around different consumer-based identities and lifestyles (Bauman 1998). Today, many people care more about social sorting via clicking and consumption than social unity or the "elevation" of the masses.

There has always been a major problem with the claim that the humanities leads to "high culture" and are a "civilizing" force. The problem is that there is no evidence that the humanities necessarily humanize (Steiner 1967, 1971). Cultures like nineteenth- and early-twentieth-Century Austria and Germany were highpoints of the humanities, yet led to massive inhumanity even as German guards read Goethe and listened to Wagner in the camps. France and England were saturated with high culture and the humanities, and both led brutal empires that demeaned and killed many people. Surely some esteemed, elite-educated Western leaders have been, like Wilson and Churchill, highly problematic in terms of their recognition of "other people" as equally human and worthy. Of course, the humanities have always had other functions and can be an important resource in the search of a shared humanity with others across the globe.

Now that the humanities are gone as the propaganda arm of "high culture" or as a necessary "civilizing" force—and now that they are progressively deserted by colleges and universities as backwaters unable to raise money—it is a good time to ask if the humanities in any sense are "necessary" and foundationally important to humans. Conservatives, at least, lose interest in the humanities when it no longer serves as a foundation for hegemony.

A Bit of a Rant

Before I start my argument in earnest, I want to pause to engage in a bit of a "rant," one which will hopefully clarify my motives when I answer what good are the humanities. A key thing that led to the "death of the humanities" in my view was that they went to school as a requirement set in a canon and were used to introduce people to "elite culture."

Before the humanities went to school, people cared about them. Jonathan Rose's (2002) massive tome, *The Intellectual Life of the British Working Classes*, is full of stories from the eighteenth through the twentieth century of women, poor people, and nonwhite people who interpreted canonical literature as representing their own values and aspirations, not just those of the wealthy and powerful. For example, Mary Smith, born in 1822, was a shoemaker's daughter who stated: "For long years Englishwomen's souls were almost as sorely crippled and cramped by the devices of the school room, as the Chinese women's feet by their shoes," about reading Shakespeare, Dryden, and Goldsmith:

> These authors wrote from their hearts for humanity, and I could follow them fully and with delight, though but a child. They awakened my young nature, and I found for the first time that my pondering heart was akin to that of the whole human race. . . Carlyle's gospel of Work and exposure of Shams, and his universal onslaught on the nothings and appearances of society, gave strength and life to my vague but true enthusiasm (Rose 2001, 45).

Mary Smith interpreted what for us is "high literature," but what for her was "popular" literature, to say that even the daughter of a shoemaker was the equal, in intelligence and humanity, of any rich person.

Why did Mary Smith read canonical works as affirming her humanity and rights to equality in a hierarchical society? She identified *herself* with the characters and viewpoints in these books. She projected herself onto them. Though the hero was a male and a king in a Shakespeare play, Mary Smith did not distance herself from him, however much she might have wanted—and certainly deserved—female heroes. She saw herself as projected onto that powerful monarch.

Perhaps sometimes when Mary Smith read Shakespeare, she was a king and other times, a queen. Perhaps sometimes when she read Shakespeare, she was not a traditional monarch at all but a monarch shoemaker with the dignity and the human worth of a traditional monarch. Perhaps sometimes, she was all these and more. Remember, she was not just taking on the life of a virtual character in the book or play, but she was also projecting herself onto that character, creating something that both she and Shakespeare made—neither one of them alone.

Mary Smith read books that many of today's students find boring, but she read them with the excitement that today's students find in video games, because she read them much like those students sometimes play video games: actively, critically, and projectively. She projected herself onto the text so that a king or queen became her "avatar," also known as a new identity to think and feel with in the service of self-discovery, in the text.

In the end, Mary Smith—and many more like her—believed that canonical literature, far from representing the values of wealthy elites, undermined elites' values and exposed them for the hypocrites they were. The message Mary Smith got from such literature was that she was at least their equal and, in all likelihood, their better.

By no means did we ever need an official and definitive list of "Great Books." The canon is and was never a closed list. Any book is canonical—in the sense that it serves as a touchstone, not within an institution per se, but as a telling insight into the plight of humans—if it lends itself to the powerful projective work in which Mary Smith engaged and if it leads people to desire not more hierarchy but more opportunities for the display of human worth and the greater development of human capacities for all people. A work is canonical if it gives people, in Kenneth Burke's (1993, 19) phrase, new and better "equipment for living" in a harsh and unfair world.

In this sense, works like Ralph Ellison's *Invisible Man* and Gloria Naylor's *Mama Day* are fully canonical for me and many other people. There are many books written by women, nonwhite people, and poor people that never got on the "official" canon as a list due to the workings of racism and patriarchy but are most certainly, in my terms, canonical.

Traditional canonical works, like those of Homer, Shakespeare, Milton, and Dryden, function today quite differently than they did in

Mary Smith's day. Smith's society denied her any sort of schooling that gave her access to these books. In fact, her society felt it inappropriate for a shoemaker's daughter to be reading such books. She picked them up anyway in defiance and saw in them resonances with herself that just further proved her own intelligence and worth.

Schools, by and large, tamed literature. They made it into tests, multiple-choice answers, and standardized responses. Literature left everyday life and entered what Basil Bernstein (1996) called the regulatory discourse of schooling. Everyone now, finally, has access to the canon at a time when schools have rendered it toothless. Young people today have access to far more texts, images, and diverse media—of far more kinds—than even the wealthy of Mary's Smith time. Milton's *Paradise Lost* played a very different role in the textual ecology of Smith's world than it does for a young person today. For her, it was a precious book, hard won through a great deal of physical labor—to buy it, if she did not borrow it—and mental labor—to read it seriously. For a young person today, the book is cheap to buy, and the school tells them how to read it in the "right" way—or get a poor grade.

This is no plea for reading Milton, though I am sure many people still get a great deal out of traditional canonical literature when they read it of their own choosing, usually outside of school. There is plenty of evidence that people today still read and watch many things that serve some of the same purposes that canonical literature did for Mary Smith (Jenkins 2006b).

A Larger Question

End of rant. Now I want to start answering my question about the humanities' worth by putting the question inside a much larger question: "What is a human being?" Humans, of course, are animals of a certain sort. They are uniquely capable of large-scale collaboration with "strangers"—that is, people they do not know personally. A human can sit comfortably in a crowded restaurant surrounded by strangers. Other primates have an innate distrust for strangers and would never comfortably surround themselves with fellow primates they did not recognize personally (Slone-Wilson 2019; Tomasello 2019).

How did humans cross this great divide from small groups of mutually known individuals to large groups of unknown individuals in things like institutions, restaurants, and societies? Well, chimpanzees show the very beginnings of this process. Chimps roam in small groups of mutually known and related individuals, and they are often quite hostile to outsiders. However, sometimes several small bands range across the same large landscape and occasionally encounter each other. If resources are abundant enough, they can come to accept each other; as they do, they develop with each other a common variant of the "pant hoot" sound all chimps make. They develop what we might call a common dialect. This common pant hoot sound comes to signal that the several different groups are all, loosely, in the same "society." They can forage near each other and sometimes exchange females, though they never really collaborate much with each other more than that (Moffett 2018; Slone-Wilson 2019).

One thing that makes humans so capable of large group collaboration has been the development of a great many shared "signals" that we belong to the same "society" (Moffett 2018). These are signals that we associate with culture—like language, dress, gestures, bodily habitus, flags, food, and more. These signals can lead to unity, to a sense that, for example, "we are all Americans." In fact, it is such signals that allow Americans to recognize each other when they do not know each other—a foundation for large societies to exist.

However, shared signals of mutual belonging among people who do not know each other personally can, and often do, become divisive in two different ways. First, they most often become markers of "insider" and "outsider" and come to mean not just "us" but "us" against "them"—others who are who are less than us or people who may even be dangerous. Most societies across history achieved unity by treating their signals as signs of superiority to others who send different or "foreign" signals.

Second, signals of belonging to a society can get co-opted by subgroups to define who is "real" and who is not. Some groups in a society begin to see themselves as "in-groups" against "outsiders" inside their own society, as types of internal enemies. A good example is the polarized nature of the US today, where red and blue, rural and urban, and white and black vie to define who is the "real American" or the "authentic American" or "worthy," using sometimes common symbols interpreted differently (e.g., the flag). I do not mean to imply the poles are "equal." An extreme libertarian right-wing has, in many ways, co-opted the language and agenda of our politics and, in the act, pushed many ideas and policies out of the mainstream that even many "moderates" found essential to a modern humane state (MacLean 2017).

Finally, we can point out that while humans can, with some difficulty, move beyond loyalty to kith and kin and show feeling for and loyalty to a whole society, very few humans have such feelings for and loyalty to the whole of humanity. The whole of humanity is too abstract a concept to move most people emotionally. It seems that societies are the largest level most humans can feel that "belonging to" matters (Moffett 2018). Perhaps, most humans need some people to be defined as "other" and "less" in order to feel that they belong to something better and are, therefore, themselves better. Perhaps, it is even this sense of being "better" that fuels their loyalty to their own society.

Moving to an Answer

The humanities, as the marker of elite culture, often served to separate elites from people in need of being civilized; as we have seen, humans tend to take signals of belonging as something larger than themselves and their kin and also as signals of "us" versus "them" and "us" being "better" than "them."

We have mentioned that humans' ability to collaborate in large groups allows them to make impressive things, like bridges and bombs, which they sometimes use for good and sometimes for ill. One important thing that interacting humans give rise to are what I will call "inter-human artifacts."

The world is replete with inter-human artifacts. Stonehenge is one example. Stonehenge is the outcome of many persons, across time and space, interacting with each other and their environments at all different levels. It is a socio-historical interactive outcome. Stonehenge could have been different—or not existed at all—if even small parts of this system, as it evolved over time and space, had been different. Stonehenge is a contingent act—the outcome of complex processes of people, culture, environments, and history. Any complex system gives rise to outcomes that could have been quite different if we could run history again.

Stonehenge now sits there as a "thing." It is a thing which has achieved remarkable homeostasis over a long period of time. The practices that gave rise to Stonehenge are gone and so are the practices for which it was used. Indeed, we do not even fully understand these practices, but "it" is still there. It is a "gift" from the past, an offering from our fellow past humans that allows us to make meaning.

Since we know that Stonehenge is a thing that human interaction, in context, gave rise to, we present-day humans can look on it as a "gift," possibly a message, from the past. We can also ask what Stonehenge meant in the sense of "what was it used for and how was it used; what did people think and say about it?" This question, in the case of Stonehenge, is one that science can help us answer partially, though probably never fully. In this way, Stonehenge stands there with a partially discoverable meaning that we present humans did not create—a message from the dead.

What I have so far said is not meant to imply that as we study Stonehenge, we do not add meanings of our own. It is not to say either that it is easy or fully possible to distinguish between the two. It is to say that we can discover some meanings—how and why things were used or believed—that would not be available to us if Stonehenge was not standing there as a gift from the dead. It is also to say that Stonehenge can inspire people to make new meanings that would not have existed had Stonehenge not been there.

No other animals can and do receive so many meaningful gifts from their dead. No other animals do so much inspired by these gifts. In fact, humans spend an inordinate amount of time making meanings inspired by the dead. The way other animals are primarily inspired is via their genes or via alterations their ancestors have made to the environment—alterations that never led these animals to ask how and why they were made and for what uses. They do not ask this because they do not have language in our sense. Human language allows for the representation of things far in the past or future—and for fantasies—that no other animal communication system can. This fact gives us a clue that gifts from the dead take on a whole new meaning when creatures, like us, have language. These gifts become points of inquiry.

A termite can come across the mound of a long-dead species of termite and can, through its senses, come to know all sorts of things about it; however, the termite cannot inquire into what it means at a meta-level—in terms of grammar and a conscious appraisal of meaning as embedded in socially shared signifiers—to the past termites, nor can the termite be inspired to use the old mound as a tool for thinking about the present and future in different ways. These two things require language. It is because we humans have language that we can turn leftovers from the dead into artifacts via inquiry.

Not only is language required to treat leftovers as inter-human artifacts but language also allows humans to leave behind inter-human artifacts made of language itself.

An Interlude on Poetry and Me

When I was young, save for the books in my father's private room, our house had two books in it—*Mother Goose* and the Bible. My father had a third-grade education, but by the time my identical twin brother and I came around, he had taught himself to read, and he only read quite erudite Catholic theology books. He and his family were what people over the decades have called "white trash"—the earlier British term was "waste people." He came from many generations of American white poverty and left home at fifteen to earn a living when his father deserted the family.

My mother was a British citizen who came to the United States as a WW II bride and never became a US citizen. Here is an odd and interesting fact: When I was a child, our house had many images of the Queen of England on pottery and other things. That queen—as I sit here writing this in a coffee house in Cottonwood, Arizona, at the age of seventy-one—still sits on the British throne. With all the change I have seen in my life, Queen Elizabeth II may be the only real continuity left.

My mother was from the British working class—her father was a house painter—and had a high school education. I never saw her read as a child, though later in life she read novels occasionally. My father read his theology books in his room and occasionally discussed them with one of the many priests he knew from various orders.

My parents never read to us as children and, in fact, rarely discussed anything with us at any length. People in our social group back then simply did not do this with children. I often heard my father say, "Children should be seen and not heard."

All the families we knew through our Catholic school and the church—and we did not deal much at all with anyone who was not Catholic—were first-generation Italian-Americans whose ancestors had come from Southern Italy to pick fruit in the Santa Clara valley. These families—people with whom we spent a good deal of time, often visiting each other's homes by just dropping by—raised their children the way our parents raised us. None of them had much more education than my parents, and in the 1940s and 1950s, all of them, as well as my family, were trying to get into the middle-class or at least get their children there when they grew up.

I went to Catholic elementary school and then for six years to a Catholic seminary, a place I rarely left in those six years. I was exposed to next-to-no poetry or other sorts of literature in the seminary—and certainly none in elementary school—except in Greek and Latin—so it was all ancient stuff like Horace and Virgil.

When I left the seminary, I finished college at the University of California at Santa Barbara, majoring in philosophy, and went on to get a PhD in theoretical linguistics at Stanford, studying syntactic theory, semantics, modal logic, and the philosophy of language. By the time I took my first job as an academic at Hampshire College in Amherst, Massachusetts, I was the rare, educated American who had never really been taught literature in school.

Indeed, as I went off to my first job, there appeared to be no reason for me to have read literature since, at Hampshire, I taught courses on syntactic theory, such as Chomskian Generative Grammar. However, Hampshire was a very liberal liberal-arts college—then flourishing but now on the verge of going out of business. The students there were not required to take any courses at all. They graduated by doing projects and taking exams at various levels. They took courses only if they wanted to and could leave them at any time. There were no grades; instead, the students got written evaluations.

It was interesting, as a linguist, trying to sustain undergraduates' interests in a course like Government and Binding Theory in Generative Grammar when they could drop the course at any time. It was even hard to get them to want to start the classes. When I first arrived, I was stunned that there were forty students attending the first session of my class on Government and Binding. I was thrilled with such interest in a tough, technical subject. Alas, when they found out the course was not on S and M—or sadism and masochism, as they thought— but linguistics, thirty-eight left. The two that stayed finished the class and are today both full professors in good linguistics departments, having gone on from Hampshire to earn their PhDs in linguistics from Noam Chomsky at MIT.

The vast majority of students at Hampshire were interested in the humanities, and the School of the Humanities was by far the largest at Hampshire. Faced with few students in our courses, we linguists decided we needed to teach some sort of course on literature to entice the students away from the Humanities School and into our linguistics courses. None of us knew much about the humanities, though the others had read literature in school. Perhaps having been exposed to literature in school as a source of enforced interpretations and institutionally chosen texts is why none of them wanted to teach the course. In the end, I volunteered to teach a course on "stylistics" that would use linguistics to analyze poetry. I knew nothing about the area, though I had heard of it, and I had read exactly one poem written in English in my life.

At the time, I lived with a woman who spoke English, Italian, and Spanish and was extremely well read in the canonical literature of all three languages. I went home and asked her how I could very quickly get into poetry so I could teach the new class. She recommended I get *The Norton Anthology of Poetry* and just read through it. I did.

When I started the book, I thought to myself, "people say this stuff is important, valuable, and art; now, I will find out why it is so highly thought of." As I read the book, I was utterly stunned—just astonished. The poetry of people like John Donne, William Blake, Walt Whitman, Emily Dickinson, William Butler Yeats, Gerard Manly Hopkins, Robert Frost, William Carlos Williams, Adrienne Rich, Wallace Stephens, Marianne Moore, Anne Sexton, and many others all seemed transfixing but each in different ways.

When I moved on to read the novel *Moby Dick* for the first time, I found the book completely amazing. I saw it as Melville saw it—not as a story about a whale but as a whale of a story about everything. I came to adore C. S. Forester, Virginia Woolf, and then others, though Woolf will always be my favorite novelist—in part, I must admit, because of her ties to the Bloomsbury Group and its ties to philosophy.

So, what made a person utterly uneducated in poetry and literature be so moved by it? Later, when I started to teach the stylistics class, I found one reason that I was moved by the poetry was that I had not had it in school. School had not ruined it for me as, I found out later, it had for so many of the students who took my course—of course, not all literature teachers have ruined literature for their students. Another reason I think I was moved by poetry without schooling in it is this: as a non-middle-class person, raised apart from "the Tradition" and "high culture," I read these poems as marvelous linguistic expressions of the human heart, human dilemmas and longings, and human aspirations for meaning and worth. I read them as Mary Smith had read Shakespeare.

When I became an academic, I was, for the first time in my life, surrounded by people born into the middle, and more often, the upper-middle class. Many of them soon realized I was not "cultured," "couth," could not properly pronounce words I had seen only in writing but never heard in speech, and was ungrounded in literacy, education, and family of their sort. I did not eat, talk, or interact right, and I did not have the right values.

Reading poetry unschooled—stuff that I knew was supposed to be "High Culture" and not the sort of thing anyone I knew growing up would have read or discussed—I realized that I could understand, love, and use this poetry just as who I was, both as a human being and as one not born into the right class. I felt these authors were not speaking to the elite, the rich, and the highly educated but to people—people who had bodies and souls—to people as humans with the same loves and pains as each other, and to people as absolute individuals who could sing their own songs. I felt they were speaking to me.

When I came into my stylistics class to talk about poems that had amazed me, the students groaned when they heard the name of the poem. They had "had it" in high school and considered it a bore, irrelevant to their lives other than as a source of evaluation—which, at Hampshire, they could avoid just by leaving the class—but faced by my enthusiasm when I gushed over the verbal artistry of the poem and its powerful play with meanings, they sat transfixed. They saw the poem anew and wondered how anyone had made something so magical from something so boring and mundane. I make no claim I changed their lives—and I hate the movie *Dead Poets Society*. I only claim that humans often marvel when they see taken-for-granted things in new ways. The poetry spoke to them, as it did and still does when people read it and recite it, not as a school subject but as the essence of the magic contained in their language and their lives as that language applies to them.

Poetry and literature are—when not captured by schools, credentials, and literary high priests—examples of what I called in my stylistics class "semantic saturation." What I meant by this was that literary language, at its best, communicates meaning in its every aspect—in every sound, syllable, rhythm, morpheme, word, phrase, clause, sentence, and all the connections and juxtapositions of these in the literary work. Language structure, or form, and language content, or meaning, marry and intermingle, becoming one and the same or engaging in interesting dances of tension with each other. Giving credit to the ways in which poetry can enliven and call attention to language form does not mean that poetry is also and always a social, historical interaction among specific humans with their own specific autobiographies.

Some poets and novelists I got to know much later thought it was a horrible thing to "analyze" the language of poetry using linguistics as a tool. It was, they argued, bound to kill the poem and brutalize the students' sensitivities to poetry, but what I and my students discovered is that poetry is not like fake magic—the stuff of magic shows—where knowing how the trick is done ruins it. No, with good poetry—just as with good food—knowing how it is made allows you to cook and not just eat; to write and not just read; to savor the skill and art of others and try your own hand at it as well. Real magic is not the product of a trick.

Poetry is what we might call "slow language" in analogy to "slow cooking." Slow cooking is meant to get us to think about, reflect on, and work with every ingredient in a meal, making all of the ingredients into an ensemble where each ingredient matters in a particular way, where each ingredient interacts with every other one, and where the whole becomes not just more than the sum of its parts but a unique joy. Slow cooking makes something mundane magical and turns food into something both cultural and pan-human.

Just as good cooking helps people to transcend their brute reality as eaters and understand food as part of human culture, history, sociality, and the life of the mind and the body, so, too, do poetry and literature. At their best, poetry and literature can help people transcend their brute realty as speakers and understand language as part of human culture, history, sociality, and the life of the mind and body. I, myself, find that seeing poetry as a marriage of form, linguistic content, and socio-historical and socio-cultural relevance—and discovery—by no means detracts from seeing it as "literature" or "art."

The trouble is this: good poetry, literature, and music have, in a great many societies on earth—most probably all of them—come not to represent a thoughtful mediation on the nature of being human and sharing humanity with others or life with all living things, but instead has come to be a celebration or marker of "our" greatness as a specific group of people who are better than others or higher. A poem or a poet can become a fetish—not a verbal call to our shared humanity, but a sign of the elevation of a particular culture or group of "elites." Indeed, this happens all too easily.

EMILY DICKINSON

The value of poetry as a device for humane meaning-making does not reside in schools and universities or canons of good literature. It resides in an interaction between a human being as a "languaged" being and a poet who is hailing that person to more fully and carefully inhabit his or her language as a giver of meaning.

Emily Dickinson was a poet whose life shows the real point of poetry. She was a woman, a lesbian, and someone who questioned formal religion. She lived at a time in Amherst, Massachusetts—where Hampshire College is—in the nineteenth century when a person could be none of those three things and have a full life. Religion was everything, women were meant to be subordinate to men, and love outside of marriage—let alone with someone of the same sex—was a sin.

Emily Dickinson eventually simply went upstairs and rarely again came down from her room. She could not have a life out in the world, so she was determined to have one in her room. She wrote poetry—very little of which was ever published in her lifetime because it did not fit in with the fashion of the times.

Emily Dickinson wrote poetry that appears simple and amiable, but which is, in reality, minimalist art that strikes right to the heart of hypocrisy and cant, similar to William Blake's poetry. She wrote her poetry in the meter, or rhythm, of the Protestant Hymnal—often with religious references—to call us to focus on this life and the heart, not the next life and the soul.

Here is one of Emily Dickinson's poems, one of my favorites:

> ***My life closed twice before its close*** (96)
> Emily Dickinson, 1830–1886
>
> My life closed twice before its close—
> It yet remains to see

> If Immortality unveil
> A third event to me
>
> So huge, so hopeless to conceive
> As these that twice befell.
> Parting is all we know of heaven,
> And all we need of hell.

One way I read this poem is as a former devout Catholic who worried a good deal about heaven and hell. I can read Dickinson as addressing a Catholic world that subordinated this life to the next. I can read her as addressing, as well, a Protestant world—her world—that worried greatly about deeds and riches as signs that meant they were worthy of going to heaven and not to hell. These were people who lived in fear that, no matter what they did, they might not be "chosen."

I read Dickinson as engaged in the following actions: She wants to suggest that heaven and hell are here on earth and not in some afterlife. She wants readers to live their lives here and now, in the present world, and not in anticipation and dread of another after-life world.

I agree with these sentiments, though I know what it would be like to oppose them via my former devout Catholic identity. However, I could make this response to Dickinson: Why even use the words "heaven" and "hell"? For that matter, why write in the meter of the Protestant Hymnal? Why use religious language at all? Why not free ourselves from the whole thing, dismissing it as a matter of superstition?

Now, I could stop there, but if I search for an answer to my questions from the point of view of some identity I imagine Emily Dickinson as having written out of, I can have a good conversation with her from which I might learn something.

Something I have learned from Emily Dickinson's poem is that she is saying—see how I am now speaking for her—that there are truths in religious beliefs but not the truths most religious people see. We humans do have souls that, in some sense, transcend our bodies. Since religious people believe this, they imagine that when the body dies, the soul lives on and must therefore live on in some world. Some cultures might believe the soul lives on in this world as a "spirit" or "ghost," but Christians believe it lives on in an after-life, reaping its just rewards—or is just fortunate enough to have been chosen, for those who do not believe in "works."

Emily Dickinson, however, is suggesting that there is a part of each human that cannot die the way the body can. The body can be horribly traumatized only once and then dies and that is the end of pain, but there is a part of us humans—an emotional part—that can be horribly traumatized over and over again until the body dies. This part of us does not die when it is "killed." It lives on to "die" again until our body dies. If I stab your body hard enough, you die, but I can stab your soul repeatedly.

Given that Emily Dickinson believes this, she is also suggesting that if this soul part of us could not suffer such huge pain, it could not also enjoy such huge joy. There would be no big lows and no big highs. The highs—the loves gained—are all we are going to get of heaven, and so we better fully live them. The lows—the loves lost—are all we need of hell because without them, there could be no moments of transcendent joy, and so, we must not fear hell but allow for it.

This emotional part of humans is still mysterious to science. How do we humans exist as beings conscious of life and death, capable of foul deeds and wondrous altruism? How can anyone suffer the loss of a child and live on? How can anyone not feel the joy of real love as something to treasure fully and now?

Emily Dickinson's poem taught me that the better word for the part that dies many times before we die is not "emotion" but "soul." It also makes me see how deeply sad it is when any human being does not get an opportunity to risk and live life in full. Dickinson's poem is indeed a hymn worth singing, especially when we hear whispers of mortality in the dark of night and fear retribution for our weaknesses.

So, I am reading Emily Dickinson here as a former devout Catholic old enough to see death on the horizon. I hear her speaking to me as an outsider in her own time and place who sought sense in what others believed but rejected: their fears of life, bodies, love, and difference.

There are many other fruitful readings of Dickinson's poem. Though there are better and worse readings—since we must be faithful to who Emily Dickinson was as a person and to language itself as partially shared meanings—there is no one "right reading." There are as many as there are different readers making fair construals of who Emily Dickinson was—like all of us, she had multiple identities—and who she was writing as. Indeed, writing is great when it sets up multiple, good conversations.

By the way, while I have called Emily Dickinson by her full name in this text, I call her in my own mind just "Emily." This is because I feel her as a real person and a friend. She has helped keep me alive, and I have helped keep her alive.

A Poem as an Inter-Human Artifact

What Emily Dickinson's poem shows us, I think, is that as an inter-human artifact—a gift from the past—can be used in two ways. We can use inquiry to make of the poem something that allows us to think of ourselves as "better" and to judge others as "less." We can use it to create systems of ranking, testing, and control. That is, we can use the poem—or poetry in general—as part of the ever-present war of humans against humans as they contest over status, hierarchy, control, power, and the right to elevation or heaven. So, too, can Stonehenge be used for cultural or national chauvinism.

We can also use the poem as the basis of a personal inquiry in which we, often with the help of others, make meanings "for" and "with" Emily Dickinson—being fair to her and her context and her past—and for ourselves. Furthermore, we make these meanings in such a way that they apply very specifically and concretely to us and, at the same time, they apply equally and fairly to all humans in ways that elevate us all together universally. When we read this way, I will say we are creating a "specific universal." I use the term "specific universal" rather than the better-known term "concrete universal" because the latter term brings with it too many Hegelian tones—and Hegel has too much nation-statist baggage for my taste.

In treating an artifact as a specific universal, I see myself and my life in the artifact. At the same time, I see the artifact as about all humans as humans—as all equally worthy of life and flourishing, not as divided into better and worse. In the act, through specific understanding and universal understanding, I come to perceive my own life more deeply as one unique instantiation of diverse but still common human life and, at the same time, regenerate my link to all human life—indeed, all life on earth.

To choose to create specific universals rather than divisive signals is, I would argue, for many of us, a matter of survival in our highly inequal societies. It is in the realm of creating specific universals from inter-human artifacts that we humans finally rise above our miserable condition. It is here we should search for that most elusive force—human freedom. Of course, we will always have to make decisions about who we must separate ourselves from. We will always have to make choices between war—say, with white supremacists—and peace, but, perhaps, we can create specific universals that make even our white supremacists feel a wider sense of shared humanity.

Conclusion

So, now, let us answer my question, "What good are the humanities?" If we define the humanities as the desire and capacity to create specific universals out of inter-human artifacts, then I believe they are our last, best hope. They are, indeed, necessary and foundational to us as individuals, as humans, and as a part of all life. Thank goodness, they have now left school. They are once again free in the world, owned now by people like me and Mary Smith because the elites no longer want them. We will take them. We need them. The humanities are no longer "official." Now, they are personal and pan-human.

We most certainly should instantiate the view of the humanities I have argued for in our schools and other institutions. However, today, the humanities flourish out of school in interest-driven affinity spaces that are new sorts of informal organizations. To institutionalize the humanities in a new and non-elitist way would mean, as far as I am concerned, making rich connections among four things: schools and colleges, out of school learning and producing in affinity spaces, specific socially and culturally diverse groups of humans, and the shared nature of humans as humans. The humanities would be a force both for understanding the multitude of diverse experiences different humans and human groups have had and the essential elements that unite us all.

References

Bauman, Zygmunt. 1998. *Globalization: The Human Consequences.* Cambridge, UK: Polity Press.

Bernstein, Basil. 1996. *Pedagogy, Symbolic Control & Identity Theory.* London, UK: Taylor & Francis.

Hanson, Victor Davis. 2014. "The Death of the Humanities." *Defining Ideas: A Hoover Institution Journal.* www.hoover.org/research/death-humanities

MacLean, Nancy. 2017. *Democracy in Chains: The Deep History of the Radical Right's Stealth Plan for America*. New York, NY: Penguin.
Massing, Michael. 2019. "Are the Humanities History?" *New York Review of Books*. www.nybooks.com/daily/2019/04/02/are-the-humanities-history/
Moffett, Mark W. 2018. *The Human Swarm: How Our Societies Arise, Thrive, and Fall*. New York, NY: Basic Books.
Rose, Jonathan. 2002. *The Intellectual Life of the British Working Classes*. New Haven, CT: Yale University Press.
Slone-Wilson, David. 2019. *This View of Life: Completing the Darwinian Revolution*. New York, NY: Pantheon Books.
Steiner, George. 1971. *In Bluebeard's Castle: Some Notes Towards the Redefinition of Culture*. New Haven, CT: Yale University Press.
Steiner, George. 1967. *Language and Silence: Essays on Language, Literature, and the Inhuman*. New York, NY: Atheneum.
Tomasello, Michael. 2019. *Becoming Human: A Theory of Ontogeny*. Cambridge, MA: Harvard University Press.

2 Of Literacy, Community, Texts, and Technology: Rethinking Literacies from a Text and Technology Perspective

Kirk St.Amant

Literacy has become a central buzz word in modern education. Educators and non-educators alike increasingly view it as essential to everything from interacting via new media (e.g., digital literacy) to fostering scientific achievements (i.e., science literacy) (Gonchar and Engle 2020; Howell and Brossard 2021). This situation reflects a core element of literacy—what it is depends on the community defining it. As a result, establishing what literacy entails becomes a complex process that involves understanding the backgrounds and expectations of the communities using the term (Keefe and Copeland 2011). Fortunately, this relationship to community provides a context for examining the nuances of literacy.

Both scholarly and popular approaches to literacy encompass using texts and technologies to engage in discussions within communities. Groups determine what mechanism—or technology—their members should employ when creating texts for conveying ideas within the community (Gee 2015; St.Amant and Rice 2015). Both these texts—and the technologies used to produce them—are key to the survival of the community. They are the central mechanisms through which societies exchange ideas, discuss topics, and engage in the decision-making processes essential to a group's long- and short-term activities (Keefe and Copeland 2011; UNESCO Institute for Statistics 2008; Gee 2015).

Given the forces at work in today's interconnected, global society, a core question becomes "What constitutes literacy today?" An understanding of how communities use texts and technology is essential to addressing this question. Such understanding is also necessary to determine what constitutes effective literacy practices in modern society.

This chapter examines the dynamics of these connections between texts, technologies, and communities. The chapter identifies factors that affect what literacy is in relation to both community expectations and the technologies communities use to access and produce texts. The chapter also highlights variables individuals can employ to identify and connect—or map—perceptions of literacy in different communities. Such mapping helps foster literacy activities within and across communities. It can also apply across disciplines and areas over time. Through such an examination, this chapter presents a framework for understanding how factors of texts, technologies, and community constitute literacy in our modern world.

COMMUNITY, TEXTS, AND LITERACY

Literacy involves participation in community discussions (UNESCO Institute for Statistics 2008; Kliewer et al. 2004; Gee 2015). Yet, such participation is not random. Rather, literacy focuses on providing the members of a community with the tools needed to make meaningful contributions to a group. Such contributions are achieved through access to and participation in discussions involving issues of concern and importance to that community (Organization for Economic Co-operation and Development 2006; UNESCO Institute for Statistics 2008).

These community discussions take place through *texts*—mechanisms the community has selected for presenting information and discussing ideas. Members of the community have agreed that the use of these texts—versus other modes or methods—for conveying ideas represents an acceptable and a credible method of discussion within the community (Keefe and Copeland 2011; Postman 2005). Individuals able to create such texts are able to credibly participate in community discussions. Individuals who cannot generate such texts either cannot participate in community discussions, or their participation is considered less credible (Keefe and Copeland 2011; UNESCO Institute for Statistics 2008). In this way, literacy is central to interacting and participating in a society.

Texts are connected to *technologies*. Individuals need to use some tool to create the texts essential to participating in community discussions (Cambridge Assessment 2013; St. Amant and Rice 2015). Accordingly, one's opportunity to participate credibly in community exchanges reflects that person's ability to use the available technologies to produce the requisite texts (Postman 2005; McLuhan 2011). Specifically, individuals need to know how to produce the texts the community considers credible mechanisms for interaction (Keefe and Copeland 2011; Organization for Economic Co-operation and Development 2006; UNESCO Institute for Statistics 2008). This relationship between texts and technologies means engaging in community discussions involves individuals knowing what kinds of text to use and how to use the available technologies to create such texts. These interconnections of technologies and texts—as connected to community expectations—generally serve as the foundation of literacy.

Accordingly, *literate* individuals are persons able to participate in group discussions per their ability to create the texts a community considers a credible mechanism for sharing information. This situation assumes literate individuals also have access to the technologies needed to generate such texts and know how to use them to produce these texts. Without such knowledge, individuals cannot participate meaningfully in community discussions; as such, their voices or perspectives cannot become part of community interactions. These factors affect one's ability to be heard by and to contribute to a community, and they have the potential to prevent certain parties from engaging in community exchanges (UNESCO Institute for Statistics 2008). So central is this association of literacy with community participation that certain organizations view literacy as a human right essential to participating effectively in a society (UNESCO Institute for Statistics 2008; Lucksson 2006).

Dynamics of Text, Technology, and Literacy

Expectations of texts, technology, community participation, and literacy are not universal. Rather, such dynamics can differ from community to community as it is a construction of society (Keefe and Copeland 2011; Gee 2015). Literacy, moreover, involves how societies view certain technologies as mechanisms for creating the texts that allow for the meaningful exchange of ideas within the community (UNESCO Institute for Statistics 2008, Organization for Economic Co-Operation and Development 2006; Gee 2015). In essence, access to a technology that creates texts does not inherently mean one is literate. Rather, literacy encompasses the individual's ability to produce certain kinds of texts—those the community considers legitimate means for conveying ideas (Berkenkotter and Huckin 1995; Miller and Selzer 1985).

The community factor has important implications for how technologies—and their associated texts—are perceived by groups as representing "literate" actions and "legitimate" presentations of ideas. Thus, having access to certain technologies and being able to create particular texts (e.g., access to Twitter to produce the text of a tweet) does not make one literate. Rather, a society might dismiss such "non-conventional" texts and not include them in "meaningful" community exchanges where decisions are made (Funnell 2017; Mukherjee 2019). Consider, for example, how many "literate" authority figures in a society consider Twitter a threat to literacy and dismiss tweets—and those who make them—as superficial and non-credible (Barrow 2013). In essence, literacy is determined by one's abilities to *use an available technology* to *create texts* in ways that *meet a community's expectations* of "effective" uses of the technology to share ideas *with other members of the community*.

Aspects of Access in Literacy

These ideas of literacy are connected to the concept of *access*—the ability to participate in community discussions. Individuals who have access to a community are able to participate in the group discussions that could affect aspects of their lives. These processes are based upon the associations communities have for how texts and technologies facilitate such access (St.Amant and Rice 2015; Keefe and Copeland 2011; Postman 2005).

From this community-based perspective, we can posit that access-factors of literacy involve two interconnected concepts of texts and technologies—access to ideas and access to participation. Both are essential to communicating within a community. The two are also connected, each being a requisite for the other. These concepts, however, need to be understood as their own, independent entities. From there, individuals have the ability to examine how the two interconnect to create literacy dynamics in a community.

The first concept, *access to ideas*, determines whether individuals are able to review the discussions taking place in a community. A person's ability to do so is based on whether that individual can access the information presented in the primary form—or via the principal medium, format, or *text*—the community uses to share information and discuss ideas. So, if written texts are the format a community relies on to share information, literacy in that community involves the ability to read and understand information conveyed via those written texts. This ability to read allows individuals to access information and the related community conversation taking place through these texts.

This situation represents *primary access*—the ability for the individual to access information directly and in its original form or text. This access factor allows the individual to review and interpret texts according to that person's understanding of ideas and experiences in relation to a topic. This understanding is based upon the knowledge the individual has acquired and the individual's experiences as part of a particular community. In this way, such knowledge generally reflects the person's connection to and identity as part of a community. The result is a *primary literacy situation* as the individual can directly access information in the texts used by the community to exchange ideas. This situation differs from that of *secondary access*, in which one person cannot directly access the information conveyed in a text because that person lacks the ability to do so (e.g., the individual cannot read, so that person cannot directly access ideas in a written text).

In a *secondary literacy situation*, one individual must rely on another—a "literate" person—to access information. Such dependency limits where, when, and how—particularly if a fee for services is charged—an "illiterate" person is unable to access information and participate in discussions. Such dependency also limits the quality of information an illiterate individual can obtain because the literate intermediary decides how to convey the information contained in a text. For example, reading a written text word for word to an illiterate individual allows that person one kind of access to ideas. Reading a text silently and then summarizing the contents of the text for others who cannot read it represents a different kind of access in which ideas are filtered through the perspective of the person summarizing a text.

The ability to "read"—or to interact directly with the information in a text—is only part of the access dynamics of literacy. To truly participate in community discussions via texts, one also needs to create such texts. Only through the ability to create texts do persons have the opportunity to participate in, versus passively observe, community discussions. It is in such situations where the second access dynamic of literacy, access to participation, is key.

CREATIVITY, LITERACY, AND PARTICIPATION

Access to participation determines the active—versus passive—part of literacy. It is based on the idea that the literacy's objective is to allow an individual to participate credibly in community discussions. This engagement involves the individual being able to share that person's own ideas, opinions, and perspectives with members of their community in order to participate in processes like decision making. Doing so involves generating texts for conveying ideas—active participation—versus only consuming and reading texts created by others—passive observation.

To participate in community discussions, an individual must have access to the means by which members of the community present ideas. Such access is essential, for only through it can individuals share their perspectives via the mechanism the community uses for interactions (McLuhan 2011; Postman 2005). This kind of access represents the *productive aspect of literacy*—knowing how to produce information in the format the community uses to share ideas. Effective community participation requires an individual to produce texts in a form the community associates with *credible texts*—those texts the community perceives as meriting consideration and discussion. For example, if a community uses written texts for sharing information, then access to, and being able to participate in, this community discussion requires the ability to generate written texts.

The productive aspect of access to participation depends upon certain factors. To begin, one needs access to the *technology used to produce the texts* a community considers credible and worthy of inclusion in discussions. If a community considers physical, written documents as the credible texts for exchanges, then one must have access to the tools (e.g., pen and paper) needed to produce such texts. If a community instead considers blog postings the credible text for discussion, then individuals need to be able to access the computing technology—both hardware, like a keyboard and software, like a word processing program—needed to create such texts.

An individual must also be able to access the *venue in which such texts are shared* with the community. In the case of a digitally-based community, one must have access to the online environment or forum where these discussions take place. Such venues represent another kind of technology associated with texts. This time, however, the technology involves distributing and sharing texts (e.g., a distribution network) versus creating them (e.g., a printing press). If access to either technology—the tools for creating or venues for sharing texts in the community's preferred way—is restricted, the ability to engage in literacy practices and contribute to community discussions is limited.

Within such contexts, economic factors sometimes create barriers to the technologies individuals can access for producing texts. Until relatively recently, for example, the cost of purchasing the equipment needed to produce video-based texts, like film and television broadcasts, greatly limited who could use such technologies to share ideas. Similarly, the cost of constructing, owning, and operating broadcasting stations or movie theaters—and associated film distribution networks—create barriers to the venues individuals could use for sharing information. Thus, a range of variables might affect the access individuals have to participating in community discussions.

Access to technologies, however, is not enough. One must also have access to the knowledge needed to use those technologies to create and share texts. Just having a pen and paper, for example, does not inherently mean I can use that *material access*—access to needed tools for creating texts—to generate texts. I must also have related *usage access*—knowledge of how to use those tools to create texts—to employ them and craft the texts essential to participating in my community's discussions. Additionally, I need *distribution access*—the knowledge of and the ability to share my texts with the members of my community. This kind of access involves the following factors:

- Knowing which channels the community associates with the credible sharing of and consumption of information
- Having the ability to access and use the technologies associated with those channels
- Understanding how to use those technologies to effectively distribute one's ideas to members of a community

Without knowledge of these factors, an individual's abilities to be literate, according to community norms, and to engage in community interactions are limited.

The convergence of these access dynamics creates *literacy ecosystems*—the environments where communities create and consume information in order to engage in discussions and make decisions. Accordingly, literacy depends on one having all of these access abilities—both to review ideas and to participate in discussions—to be a literate person within the context of their community. What constitutes literacy in relation to access could vary from community to community. Such situations arise because the texts one needs to access, create, and distribute can change within a community and, over time, within and across communities. Therefore, what one needs to know—or to be able to do—in order to access texts and participate in community discussions via texts is not universal. One might need to know or be able to do something different dependent upon the group with which they interact (Keefe and Copeland 2011).

THE IMPORTANCE OF CRITICAL THINKING AND MEANING

Key to these forms of access—and to many aspects of literacy—is the idea of *meaning*. To be literate involves more than the mechanics behind an activity (e.g., the reading and writing processes). Literacy also involves the ability to think critically when engaging in that activity. Such critical thinking is central to drawing meaning from or contributing meaning to a group's discussion (Knoblauch 1990; Keefe and Copeland 2011). The ability to read (e.g., access) a text goes beyond knowing how to assemble letters into words, recognizing what a word is, and knowing the definition of a term. It also encompasses understanding the message a writer wishes to convey through those words or text—a process often called *decoding* (UNESCO Institute for Statistics 2005; Pepper 2017). Decoding, however, has the potential to be a complex activity. The intricacies of decoding often depend upon understanding and addressing the norms and of the community in which one uses texts to interact. Such situations reflect the concept of discourse communities—or the idea that community factors affect the ways community members engage in discourse.

In some situations, this decoding involves knowing when to interpret words and phrases literally to understand the meaning conveyed. In other cases, comprehending a text involves knowing when to intuit beyond literal meaning and deduce the message conveyed through a text. So, in a situation where I say, "Move over," am I using that text to request you literally, physically shift your position, or am I using it metaphorically to prepare you to be displaced from a social position? Determining which meaning is the correct one is a matter of thinking critically about the related text.

Such literal-metaphoric distinctions often reflect cultural convention or situational context; however, understanding such factors—and knowing when and how to apply them to decode or convey meaning in a text— is often a matter of community conventions (Kohl 2007; Ulijn and Strother 1995). Accordingly, to participate in a community's discussions one must 1) think critically about the message they wish to convey and 2) think critically about how the community will decode that message. Only after such reflection can one create texts the related community will both accept as part of the discussion and be able to decode (i.e., understand) as the author intends (Knoblauch 1990; Keefe and Copland 2011). Such situations arise because the critical component of literacy—knowing how to structure text to convey meaning—is central to decoding and understanding the message community members convey in the texts they create via different technologies (SMS Texting Dictionary n.d.). These group conventions for sharing meaning determine how communities use texts to share ideas and discuss concepts (Campbell 1998; Grundy 1998; St.Amant 2006). These factors of community convention for decoding texts become the elements one must critically consider in order to create texts a community will accept and understand per the community's conventions.

Essentially, effective participation in a group's discussions requires the construct of texts that reflect the community's expectations for conveying meaning in a given format. This process requires the individual to think critically in order to identify:

- The community with which one will convey ideas
- The meaning one wishes to share with that community
- The community's preferred mechanism of exchange (e.g., text)
- The approach the community uses to convey meaning in that medium or text

In some cases, achieving these objectives entails finding the most effective way of combining words into sentences, paragraphs, and pages to present one's thoughts (Williams and Bizup, 2013). In others, it might encompass the best method for describing a situation to prompt a group into action (Cialdini 2006). In still others, it might involve selecting the best medium or mode for sharing meaning with a group (Kostelnick and Hassett 2003; Rice and St.Amant 2018). In these and other situations, the individual's goal is to make a meaningful contribution to the community's discussion. Doing so involves critical reflection to identify the community's selected method of discussion, or text, to convey meaning in a way that reflects a writer's intentions and objectives and contributes meaningfully—per community expectations—to a community discussion (Jenkins 2009). Individuals who are able to do both are generally considered *literate* by the community with which they engage (Jenkins 2009).

This critical thinking element of literacy involves knowing how to think critically about 1) the meaning conveyed in what one is reading or when one is accessing information and 2) the meaning one wishes to convey when creating a text for others to read or from which others will access information. Both factors are central to understanding how texts gain the attention and consideration of a community. Both are also central to allowing individuals to participate credibly in community discussions. Such aspects of literacy are different from being able to read or write. (Reading and writing are both automatic processes that, once learned, individuals engage in reflexively.) These critical dynamics, however, are often as central to literacy as is the ability to generate the letters and words of texts.

This critical thinking component of literacy often underlies laments like "This person can't write!" The claim is not that the individual lacks the knowledge essential to using a pen to create letters on a page and combine those letters into words. Rather, a particular community views that individual as lacking the critical component of literacy—namely, how to combine those words to effectively convey meaning (Williams and Bizup 2013). Essentially, the lament that someone cannot write notes that the members of a community view the related person as lacking knowledge of how to convey ideas according to the community's norms and expectations for an effective written text. It is that critical thinking component of literacy—understanding and addressing the community's norms for conveying meaning via a text—the individual needs to learn. One could argue that this factor of critical thinking—focused on identifying, understanding, and addressing community norms—has historically been at the heart of much confusion and concern about literacy and fears of its decline (Dansieh 2011; Tomaszewski 2011).

These connections of community to discussion and to dynamics of access and meaning create a situation where definitions of literacy are not universal. Rather, they reflect the contexts and communities in which individuals access, produce, and distribute texts to engage with others (Keefe and Copeland 2011; UNESCO Institute for Statistics 2008; St.Amant and Rice 2015); as such, what constitutes literacy has the ability to vary over time and from community to community. Factors affecting this situation include what community the individual wishes to participate in, the medium of discussions available to that community, and the method of exchange the community decides to use.

Literacy, Foundational Knowledge, and Texts

The knowledge component of literacy frequently extends beyond the critical thinking and mechanical or procedural knowledge associated with accessing and creating texts. In many cases, this knowledge component also involves the base of information one draws from when producing texts. For texts to be perceived as meaningful by a community, those texts must often connect to certain information members of the community associate with the topics discussed at a given time. Failure to connect to such underlying knowledge often leads to the creation of texts community members consider non-meaningful. These failed connections can also result in the community judging a text's creator as "not literate" or "not literate in" an area. In this case, community members generally associate a lack of significant meaning with the premise on which an individual's ideas are founded.

This situation could occur when individuals create a text that shows they have no understanding of or background in a topic (Howell and Brossard 2021; McGurran 2021). Consider someone with no knowledge of finance trying to argue for certain monetary policies to a group of financial professionals. In this example, the community (e.g., audience) might consider the text's creator "illiterate" or "illiterate in the topic or finance" because that author lacks the foundational understanding needed to discuss the topic effectively within that community. As a result, the members of that community do not consider the text's creator as capable of meaningfully contributing to the community's discussion of that topic.

These disconnects in knowledge-based literacy also has the potential to occur when individuals know a topic too well or at a different level than members of the related community. Imagine, for example, a physicist using calculus to explain gravity to non-scientists who have no background in calculus. In this situation, the physicist authoring the text cannot—or cannot easily—convey ideas in ways members of the community can conceptualize, for the community lacks the level of foundational understanding (e.g., literacy in the area) needed to extract meaning from a text. Again, the author's ideas are rejected, for the community cannot determine how the text conveys ideas that contribute to the community's overall conversations.

In both cases, the individual has the mechanical or performative access needed to create texts in the medium the community uses to convey meaning. The difference, however, is in topical knowledge—the individual's knowledge of the topic is not at a level parallel to that of the community. For this reason, that person's texts are seen as lacking in meaning, for they cannot make effective, meaningful—or "literate"— contributions to a discussion. These factors reveal two interconnected components of literacy as related to texts and technologies:

1. *Performative or action component of literacy:* The ability to use a technology to perform an activity associated with accessing and producing a text (e.g., traditional "literacy" as being able to read and write or "computer literacy" as being able to use computers to produce a text, such as coding) (Cambridge Assessment 2013)

2. *Substantive or intellectual component of literacy:* Having the knowledge of a community-requisite topic or area to contribute meaningfully to community discussions (e.g., "literate in art" as having the knowledge essential to discussing art in a way a community considers meaningful) (Murphy Paul 2011)

Both components are connected to—if not defined by—texts and technologies. In the *performative*, literacy practices involve how individuals use technologies—from pencils to web editors—to access (e.g., read or interact with) or create (e.g., write or author), a text. In the *substantive*, literacy practices involve having and using certain knowledge of a topic to create a text an audience will consider worthy of consideration. Such literacy dynamics depend upon certain cognitive factors affecting how the brain processes information.

Cognition and Community Contexts of Literacy

The knowledge dynamics described in the prior two sections involve a different skills focusing more on cognitive versus mechanical or production processes. First, there is the knowledge of one's *audience*—how members of a community think and what they expect of texts (Ong 1982; Postman 2005; Gee 2015). The individual needs to know who the members of a community are and what method or mechanism they use for discussion (Grundy 1998; St.Amant 2006; Cambridge Assessment

2013). One also needs to know what topics the audience discusses—and know how audiences discuss those topics—via that medium (Driskill 1996; Campbell 1998; St.Amant 2006). Only by knowing, considering, and addressing these factors are individuals able to understand the meaning they access when reading texts produced by that community (Grundy 1998 and Gee 2015). Similarly, only by knowing and addressing such factors can individuals make contributions that the members of the community—the audience for which they produce texts—view as contributing meaning to, or being meaningful in, the discussion of a topic.

A second cognitive factor is that of *assessment*. In this case, the challenge is for the individuals accessing and reading texts to be able to assess if the information is worth consideration and if so, why or if not, why not. Individuals also need to consider how they feel about that information—and what others have said—and why (Campbell 1998; Grundy 1998). These cognitive and affective components of assessment—or critical thinking—are essential to choosing what information individuals draw from when crafting messages and if the related community considers such information meaningful or spurious (Driskill 1996; Campbell 1998; Grundy 1998). These factors also affect how individuals construct tests to argue for or against points made by other discussants. Finally, such cognitive factors influence how persons contribute to or build upon what other discussants have said in a way the community considers a meaningful contribution.

These cognitive expectations create a situation often referred to as "being literate in." In this case, the use of the preposition "in" with "literacy" indicates the author of a text has the foundational knowledge of a topic or area needed to participate meaningfully in community discussions of a topic in the selected medium of exchange. These literacy requirements hold true regardless of the medium used to engage in discussions. Accordingly, literacy is not a stable concept but has the potential to change as novel technologies are created, communities evolve, and new topics emerge. The better we understand such dynamics, the more effectively we can become and develop the ability to train others to be literate in using technologies to create texts considered meaningful by a community. The key involves understanding how factors of production and knowledge shape and are shaped by a community.

Factors of Genre

Effective communication within a community is not a matter of random presentations of information. It is instead based upon understanding the community members' experiences with using texts to convey ideas (Miller and Selzer 1985; Berkenkotter and Huckin 1995; Postman 2005; Gee 2015). The members of a community generally use technologies to create different texts, and each kind of text is associated with a different use and objective. These varying categories of texts are often called "genres," and community members use each genre to achieve a particular objective associated with community discourse (Miller and Selzer 1985; Berkenkotter and Huckin 1995; Grundy 1998).

The genre-related associations a community has for a text reflect the purpose for which members of that community use the related text (Miller and Selzer 1985; Berkenkotter and Huckin 1995; Grundy 1998). The members of a community use the genre of an editorial, for example, to posit opinions on topics of current interest to the related community. Likewise, many communities use the genre of an instruction manual to convey information about performing a process or addressing a problem when processes go awry (e.g., troubleshooting guides) (Ulijn and Strother 1995). In this way, a genre is a kind of text that others compose and read, and it is also a tool community members use to perform activities (e.g., the objective associated with the related genre).

Genres usually do not arise by chance. Rather, communities tend to shape them over time and do so in a way that reflects the discourse that occurs within a genre (Miller and Selzer 1985; Berkenkotter and Huckin 1995; Grundy 1998). This situation means genres are generally not universal; rather, they emerge and evolve within the context of the community (Miller and Selzer 1985; Berkenkotter and Huckin 1995; Grundy 1998). The genre of an instruction manual, for example, generally develops in response to a community's need for guidance in performing a particular process (Ulijn and Strother 1995).

The connection between genre and needs of the community can mean the genres of texts found in certain communities might not exist within others (Woolever 2001; Mikelonis 2001). Additionally, just because the same genre exists in two communities does not mean both communities associate that common genre with a similar purpose (Campbell 1998; Grundy 1998). To use the manual example, instructional materials created to facilitate unsupervised activities will likely have a different focus and objective than those meant to supplement actions done under the observation of a skilled practitioner. In fact, a community of individuals who perform activities under skilled supervision would likely not need to create or use instruction manuals to guide novices. This distinction is important in terms of the content and organization of texts individuals create via technologies (Ulijn and Strother 1995; Driskill 1996; Campbell 1998; St.Amant 2006).

These genre-related expectations can be seen in comments on the literacy levels of individuals. In cases when individuals bemoan "this person cannot write," that statement is often not challenging the ability of the individual to use a technology to generate a text. Rather, the issue is the text's creator failed to meet the genre expectations of the related community. That is, the writer might have assumed "I need to use genre X to achieve this purpose," but the related audience associates genre Y with this purpose. Such differences could lead the reader to think the writer has limited literacy because that writer lacked genre-related knowledge the community expected text vs. was lacking the ability to use technology to create a text (St.Amant 2006). Recent graduates, for example, might encounter this problem if their employers hold different expectations for writing—and for genres—than what they learned in classroom contexts.

Genre, Content, and Communities

For communities to effectively use genres, texts must contain the information community members associate with the related genre (Campbell 1998; Grundy 1998; St.Amant 2006); as such, individuals must meet the expectations a community associates with a particular genre's purpose. Doing so is essential for texts to be perceived as credible by participants in the related discussion (Miller and Selzer 1985; Berkenkotter and Huckin 1995). Failure to meet such expectations could prompt community members to consider a text non-credible and refute or ignore the ideas presented in it (Grundy 1998; St.Amant 2006). This situation means content—or the information found in a genre—is central to effectively using texts and technologies to engage with a community. Accordingly, individuals whose texts contain the content a community expects to encounter in a genre are more likely to be considered credible contributors who are able to engage effectively within the community's discussions (Miller and Selzer 1985; Berkenkotter and Huckin 1995; Grundy 1998).

Consider the following example: the members of my community associate the genre of a recipe with the purpose of accessing information on how to cook a particular dish. They would therefore expect texts presented as "recipes" to contain the content needed to achieve that objective—lists of ingredients, measurements of what to add, times for preparing and cooking, etc. Texts that meet these community content expectations would be considered credible, for they contain the information individuals expect to encounter in that genre to achieve the related objective (Miller and Selzer 1985). Texts that do not contain such information would not. Consider, for example, how a recipe that contains information on the qualities of certain foods—but no instruction on how to cook with them—might be perceived by many communities that use recipes. In such situations, the core content the audience associates with the genre of a recipe is missing, audiences cannot achieve the related purpose the associate with the genre, and as a result, the audience considers the text unusable and the text's creator as non-credible.

These content expectations also involve the order in which information appears within a genre. Information cannot be randomly presented within a genre. It must come in the sequence community members expect of that genre (Driskill 1996; Miller and Selzer 1985; Campbell 1998). These expectations influence—and are influenced by—the associations communities have for the relationship of genres to purposes (Miller and Selzer 1985; Berkenkotter and Huckin 1995; Driskill 1996; Campbell 1998). The members of a professional engineering community, for example, might expect content in instruction manuals to be organized as "purpose of process, tools used, actions to perform, troubleshooting." If, however, someone creates a manual that does not follow this order—say, processes to perform, actions to perform, troubleshooting, tools used—this non-standard ordering could cause confusion within the community (Miller and Selzer 1985; Driskill 1996; Woolever 2001). In this case, the community members might struggle to or be unable to "find" the information they need to perform a process via a genre because that information is not "where it should be." Even when communities are able to locate expected information, deviations in the expected organization of ideas could affect how individuals use the text to perform a process (Ulijn and Strother 1995). Creating credible texts in a genre thus involves knowing what content community members expect to encounter in a text and when in the text they expect to encounter it (Miller and Selzer 1985; Berkenkotter and Huckin 1995).

These genre factors have the potential to affect how a community perceives an individual's literacy. In such situations, concerns are not based on the author's ability to use technology to produce a text. Rather, they reflect that the content of the text—what it contains and how it is organized—does not mirror the expectations the audience associates with that genre (Campbell 1998; Grundy 1998; Woolever 2001). This situation is sometimes seen in higher educational contexts where faculty from different disciplines might associate different kinds and organizations of content within a particular genre (Hyland 2002). Therefore, the better individuals can identify a community's genre expectations, the more effectively they are able to use technologies to create texts that community considers worthy of discussion.

Genre-Technology Aspects

A number of factors also shape how a community expects individuals to use a technology to produce texts in a genre (Yunker 2003 and Esselink 2000). If, for example, readers in a community expect to encounter headings and sub-headings in a text, the author is expected to use a technology to create a text with those features. These practices could include the use of a pen to underline titles in a hand-written text or relying on software features to bold or italicize headings in electronic documents. In these situations, the limitations and abilities of a technology could affect community expectations of what genre-related factors the texts should include (Ong 1982; McLuhan 2011; Postman 2005).

A community's genre expectations also have the ability to shift as the mechanisms available for creating texts evolve, and such changes could be connected to new options for creating, organizing, and accessing texts. Instead of using a table of contents to locate information within a printed text, for example, individuals might expect technical features—such as hyperlinked menu bars—to achieve a similar objective within the once new technology of a website. These conventions, moreover, are not inherent to any text produced by a technology. Rather, the members of the community could adopt new genre expectations individuals are then expected to adhere to when using a technology to create certain texts (Pacey 1996, Postman 2005, and McLuhan 2011); in such ways, the evolution of literacy and technology are interconnected around the mechanisms available to create texts and influence genres.

Technology and the Evolution of Literacy

Community concepts of literacy are also connected to the scale or size of the group. The smaller and more intimate the group, often the lesser the need for a technology to share information across space and time (Ong 1982; Postman 2005; McLuhan 2011). If, for example, the community with which I interact is my family, the relatively small size of that group and the fact we often congregate in a common place at a common time (e.g., during family meals) means the presentation and exchange of information can usually be accomplished via oral exchanges. Here, the text used to exchange ideas is the spoken word, and the technology through which individuals produce such texts is spoken language. In such cases, literacy involves knowing how to orate ideas so the members of a family understand and are able to discuss when ideas are presented in that common space. As this small group situation has been central to human society for millennia, some scholars see it as the foundation for literacy in a society (Ong 1982; McLuhan 2011).

As groups grow, congregating all members in a common space at a common time for an oral exchange becomes difficult. As a result, the mechanism for community engagement has to change in order to accommodate such dynamics (Ong 1982; Postman 2005; McLuhan 2011). The result could be the development of a new technology, like writing, used to create a new kind of text, like written documents, that facilitate novel interactions. As this new community context differs in its uses of technologies and texts, ideas of literacy—per access to such discussions—evolve to address these new situations (Ong 1982; McLuhan 2011). In such instances, it is not enough that an individual be able to use language—a technology—to present oral arguments via spoken text. Rather, the new mechanism of interaction means individuals have to learn new approaches to access and present ideas via a new technology when creating the texts essential to effective discourse within the community (Ong 1982; Postman 2005; McLuhan 2011).

Final Thoughts on Texts, Technologies, and Literacy

Literacy involves using technologies to create texts and share meaning within a group. The ability to develop texts according to community standards marks one as "literate" in the communicated area and among members of the related group. In these ways, literacy is closely connected to audience expectations of what constitutes credible uses of a technology to create a text (Gee 2015). Being literate thus becomes a matter of *familiarity, form*, and *function*— knowing audience expectations, *familiarity*, well enough to address audience expectations to craft a text, *form*, and meet those expectations for what that text should do, *function*. The more we understand this familiarity-form-function relationship, the better we are able to research, understand, and address aspects of literacy in the modern world. Such an understanding of familiarity, form, and function can help us anticipate forces that could change literacy in terms of what it means and how to teach it.

This chapter represents an initial examination into the dynamics of literacy per the interconnection of texts, technologies, and communities. By comparing the technologies communities use to access and create texts, we gain a better understand the literacy expectations of different groups (St.Amant and Rice 2015). Mapping these factors according to community, access, cognition, genre, and technology allows us to gain a more complete picture of literacy across communities. Such knowledge allows us to familiarize ourselves with the expectations of both our own communities and others. We can then use this knowledge to better engage in greater literacy studies and literacy activities within and across different groups. The mapping of such aspects plays a central role in both conducting research in and enhancing understanding of the relationship between literacy and community. Such mapping also helps researchers and educators anticipate when and how changes in texts, technologies, and communities might affect the literacy practices of different groups.

REFERENCES

Barrow, Becky. 2013. "'Facebook and Twitter 'Harm Pupils Literacy:' Headmasters Claims Children are so Distracted by the Sites They Don't Bother to Read Books." *Daily Mail*, November 14, 2013. www.dailymail.co.uk/news/article-2507642/Facebook-Twitter-harm-pupils-literacy-claim-headmasters.html.

Berkenkotter, Carol, and Thomas N. Huckin. 1995. *Genre Knowledge in Disciplinary Communication: Cognition/Culture/Power*. Mahwah, NJ: Lawrence Erlbaum Associates.

Cambridge Assessment. 2013. "What is Literacy? An Investigation into Definitions of English as a Subject and the Relationship Between English, Literacy and 'Being Literate.'" *Cambridge Assessment*, January 2013. www.cambridgeassessment.org.uk/images/130433-what-is-literacy-an-investigation-into-definitions-of-english-as-a-subject-and-the-relationship-between-english-literacy-and-being-literate-.pdf.

Campbell, Charles P. 1998. "Rhetorical Ethos: A Bridge Between High-Context and Low-Context Cultures?" In *The Cultural Context in Business Communication*, edited by Susanne Niemeier, Charles P. Campbell, and Rene Dirven, 31–47. Philadelphia, PA: John Benjamins Publishing Company.

Cialdini, Robert B. 2006. *Influence: The Psychology of Persuasion*. Rev. e d. New York, NY: William Morrow.

Dansieh, Solomon Ali. 2011. "SMS Texting and Its Potential Impacts on Students' Written Communication Skills." *International Journal of English Linguistics* 1, no. 2 (2011): 222–29. doi: 10.5539/ijel.v1n2p222.

Driskill, Linda. 1996. "Collaborating Across National and Cultural Borders." In *International Dimensions of Technical Communication*, edited by Deborah C. Andrews, 23–44. Arlington, VA: Society for Technical Communication.

Esselink, Bert. 2000. *A Practical Guide to Localization*. Philadelphia, PA: John Benjamins Publishing Company.

Funnel, Jacob. 2017. "Is Social Media Really Killing Business Writing?" *emphasis*, May 25, 2017. www.writing-skills.com/is-social-media-ruining-writing.

Gee, James Paul. 2015. *Literacy and Education*. New York, NY: Routledge.

Gonchar, Michael, and Jeremey Engle. 2020. "Should Media Literacy Be a Required Course in School?" *New York Times*, October 26, 2020. www.nytimes.com/2020/10/26/learning/should-media-literacy-be-a-required-course-in-school.html.

Grundy, Peter. 1998. "Parallel Texts and Divergent Cultures in Hong Kong: Implications for Intercultural Communication." In *The Cultural Context in Business Communication*, edited by Susanne Niemeier, Charles P. Campbell, and Rene Dirven, 167–83. Philadelphia, PA: John Benjamins Publishing Company.

Howell, Emily L., and Dominique Brossard. 2021. "(Mis)informed About What? What it Means to be a Science-Literate Citizen in a Digital World." *Proceedings of the National Academy of Sciences* 118, no. 15 (2021): 1–8. doi.org/10.1073/pnas.1912436117.

Hyland, Ken. 2002. "Activity and Evaluation: Reporting Practices in Academic Writing." In *Academic Discourse*, edited by John Flowerdew, 115–30. London, UK: Routledge.

Jenkins, Henry. 2009. *Confronting the Challenges of Participatory Culture: Media Education for the 21st Century*. Cambridge, MA: The MIT Press.

Keefe, Elizabeth B., and Susan R. Copland. 2011. "What is Literacy? The Power of a Definition." *Research and Practice for Persons with Severe Disabilities* 36 (2011): 3–4, 92–99. doi.org/10.2511/027494811800824507.

Kliewer, Christophe, Linda May Fitzgerald, Jodi Meyer-Mork, Patresa Hartman, Pat English-Sand, and Donna Raschke. 2004. "Citizenship for All in the Literate Community: An Ethnography of Young Children With Significant Disabilities in Inclusive Early Childhood Settings." *Harvard Educational Review* 74, no. 4 (2004): 373–403. doi.org/10.17763/haer.74.4.p46171013714642x.

Knoblauch, C. H. 1990. "Literacy and the Politics of Education." In *The Right to Literacy*, edited by Andrea A. Lunsford, Helen Moglen, and James Slevin, 74–80. New York, NY: The Modern Language Association of America.

Kohl, John R. 2007. *The Global English Style Guide: Writing Clear, Translatable Documentation for a Global Market*. Cary, NC: SAS Institute Inc.

Kostelnick, Charles, and Michael Hassett. 2003. *Shaping Information: The Rhetoric of Visual Conventions*. Carbondale, IL: Southern Illinois University Press.

Lucksson, Ruth. 2006. "The Human Rights Basis for Personal Empowerment in Education." In *Listening to the Experts: Students with Disabilities Speak Out*, edited by Elizabeth B. Keefe, Veronica M. Moore, and Frances R. Duff, 11–20. Baltimore, MD: Paul H. Brookes.

McLuhan, Marshall. 2011 *The Gutenberg Galaxy*. Toronto, CA: University of Toronto Press.

McGurran, Brianna. 2021. "What is Financial Literacy and Why is it Important?" *experian*, June 8, 2021. www.experian.com/blogs/ask-experian/what-is-financial-literacy-and-why-is-it-important/.

Mikelonis, Victoria M. 2000. "Message Sent Versus Message Received: Implications for Designing Training Materials for Central and Eastern Europeans." In *Managing Global Communication in Science and Technology*, edited by Peter J. Hager and H. J. Scheiber, 203–31. New York, NY: John Wiley & Sons.

Miller, Carolyn R., and Jack Selzer. 1985. "Special Topics of Argument in Engineering Reports." In *Writing in Nonacademic Settings*, edited by Lee Odell and Dixie Goswami, 309–41. New York, NY: The Guilford Press.

Mukherjee, Shusree. 2019. "How is Text Messaging Affecting Teen Literacy?" *Citygoldmedia.com*, September 28, 2019. citygoldmedia.com/how-is-text-messaging-affecting-teen-literacy/.

Murphy Paul, Annie. 2011. "'Digital Literacy' Will Never Replace the Traditional Kind: We're Overestimating How Much Computers Will Teach Our Kids." *Time*, October 26, 2011. ideas.time.com/2011/10/26/why-digital-literacy-will-never-replace-the-traditional-kind/.

Ong, Walter J. 1982. *Orality and Literacy: The Technologizing of the Word*. New York, NY: Taylor & Francis.

Organization for Economic Co-operation and Development. 2006. *Assessing Scientific, Reading and Mathematical Literacy: A Framework for PISA 2006*. Paris, FR: OECD Publications.

Pacey, Arnold. 1996. *The Culture of Technology*. Cambridge, MA: The MIT Press.

Pepper, Mark D. 2017. "Popular Culture is Only Useful as a Text for Criticism." In *Bad Ideas about Writing*, edited by Cheryl E. Ball and Drew M. Low, 202–208. Morgantown, WV: West Virginia University Libraries Digital Publishing Institute.

Postman, Neil. 2005. *Amusing Ourselves to Death: Public Discourse in the Age of Show*. New York, NY: Penguin Books.

Rice, Rich, and Kirk St.Amant. 2018. *Thinking Globally, Composing Locally: Rethinking Online Writing in the Age of the Global Internet*. Logan, UT: Utah State University Press.

St.Amant, Kirk. 2006. "Globalizing Rhetoric: Using Rhetorical Concepts to Identify and Analyze Cultural Expectations Related to Genres." *Hermes Journal of Language and Communication Studies* 37 (2006): 47–66.

St.Amant, Kirk and Rich Rice. 2015. "Online Writing in Global Contexts: Rethinking the Nature of Connections and Communication in the Age of International Online Media." *Computers and Composition* 38, no. B (2015): v-x. doi.org/10.1016/S8755-4615(15)00104-8.

"SMS Texting Dictionary." n.d. *Mob1le*. www.mob1le.com/sms.html.

Tomaszewski, Jason. 2011 "Do Texting and 'Cyber Slang' Harm Students' Writing Skills?" *Education World*. www.educationworld.com/a_admin/arcives/texting_impacts_student-writing.shtml.

Ulijn, Jan M., and Judith B. Strother. 1995. *Communicating in Business and Technology: From Psycholinguistic Theory to International Practice*. Frankfurt, DE: Peter Lang.

UNESCO Institute for Statistics. 2005. *EFA Global Monitoring Report 2006: Education for All, Literacy for Life*. Paris, FR: UNESCO.

UNESCO Institute for Statistics. 2008. *International Literacy Statistics: A Review of Concepts, Methodologies, and Current Data*. Montreal, CA: Institute for Statistics.

Williams, Joseph M., and Joseph Bizup. 2013. *Style: Lessons in Clarity and Grace*. 11th ed. New York, NY: Pearson.

Woolever, Kristin R. 2001. "Doing Global Business in the Information Age: Rhetorical Contrasts in the Business and Technical Professions." In *Contrastive Rhetoric Revisited and Redefined*, edited by Clayann Gilliam Panetta (2001): 47–64. Mahwah, NJ: Lawrence Erlbaum Associates.

Yunker, John. 2003. *Beyond Borders: Web Globalization Strategies*. Indianapolis, IN: New Riders.

3 Ethical Considerations in Digital Culture Research

Cassandra Branham and Jennifer Wojton

Digital texts are often created without the same types of concerns for academic or aesthetic use as traditionally published works of writing, art, and research. The ways scholars think through these texts as cultural artifacts must shift to consider the burgeoning digital rhetorics that are sometimes imposed and created by the discourse communities in which these artifacts exist. These newer considerations based on digital, rather than traditional rhetorical and even ontological frameworks, often bring to the forefront unheard or under-represented voices. These considerations blaze a trail through the largely uncharted territory of digital culture.

Whereas many of the ethical concerns (e.g., anonymity, confidentiality, informed consent) present in non-digital writing research are still relevant in the digital domain, the context of the digital raises a number of ethical concerns that are not present when conducting research in non-digital environments. Some of these concerns include considerations of public versus private spaces, sensitive versus non-sensitive information, labor and exploitation, and authors versus human subjects (McKee and Porter 2008; Markham and Buchanan 2012).

Although the rich history of using qualitative research methods in cultural studies rests on an even longer history of qualitative research in fields such as anthropology and education, qualitative research methods must evolve as technological advances change the ways in which humans communicate and interact with one another and the world. This evolution must grapple with how to study the products of digital culture and even determine what counts as a valuable digital artifact to study for a particular purpose. Digital culture researchers also must be able to address the ethical concerns involved in research and ensure that research projects are designed and carried out in ways that are beneficial to the research population, particularly for under-represented groups. Though critical theories within cultural studies, such as feminist theory, privilege the lived experiences of people, a closer focus on the digital artifacts produced or consumed by under-represented groups is needed in order to create a deeper understanding of those communities and their often-unique ways of deploying themselves and their works online. The understanding gleaned can help create a knowledge base for researchers, empowering their subjects with critical information to aid in their own advocacy.

ETHICAL CONSIDERATIONS IN CONTEXT: CASE STUDIES

To discern which ethical considerations should be addressed, Sari Östman and Riikka Turtiainen (2016) argue that researchers need first to distinguish whether the digital culture research being planned is "with, on, or about the Internet." Scholars generally agree that ethical considerations for research that engages with online content need to be decided on a case-by-case basis (Östman and Turtiainen 2016; Shilton and Sayles 2016; Markham and Buchanan 2012). However, research projects that examine various facets of digital culture (e.g., social media communication or online fandoms) may not be intended to be replicable because they are related to a specific cultural time and place. As a result, these research projects may not provide detailed descriptions of methodological choices even though that would likely help to avoid the criticism of skeptical readers. When digital research projects do not provide detailed methodologies, it can be difficult to think through the ethical issues involved, such as privacy, ownership, and informed consent. Thus, this chapter provides real-world examples from the authors' research to illustrate both ethical considerations in digital culture research and practical strategies for planning ethical research. There are four prominent ethical considerations facing researchers in digital culture studies that we discuss in this chapter:

1. Public versus private spaces
2. Sensitive versus non-sensitive information
3. Labor and exploitation
4. Authors versus human subjects

Laying out ethical considerations for digital culture research helps to legitimize this area of study and provides a framework for scholars to use as a touchstone.

FAN STUDIES

One of Jennifer Wojton's research projects examines ways in which fan culture and mainstream entertainment media can shape and be shaped by each other through digital interactions and negotiations. Further, in conducting this project, she considered ways in which these interactions had the potential to foster community building and advocacy efforts beyond the limitations of the screen. The analysis focuses on the subject of asexuality as it is represented in the BBC's 2010–2017 television series, *Sherlock*. It traces multiple ways the traditional boundaries between fans and entertainment professionals have been breached as each group works to engage the other while pursuing their separate objectives, including social change, personal and professional acceptance or acclaim, and commercial profit.

VETERANS STUDIES

One of Sandy Branham's research projects examines the identity-presentation and narrative-building practices of military veterans in online social networking spaces like Facebook, Instagram, and Twitter. Although Branham is the daughter of a military veteran and a veterans studies researcher, her positionality on the outskirts of the military-affiliated population required her to continuously evaluate not only her own positionality but also the potential impact of her research for participants. Through a detailed, qualitative analysis of survey data, semi-structured interviews, and one extended case study of a student veteran's online social networks, she argues that stereotypical, exclusionary, and damaging tropes of the veteran, such as the veteran as war hero and the veteran as wounded warrior, can, in part, be resisted by the complex digital narratives crafted by veterans in social networking spaces. Additionally, Branham's research offers support for the argument that elements of one's social networking profiles, when viewed independently and decontextualized, can lead to invalid and unfair assumptions about the user's identity. Finally, Branham's project culminates in the identification of a number of digital literacy practices present in her participants' social networking use, as well as a set of pedagogical and programmatic recommendations for writing teachers and writing-program administrators interested in aiding student veterans in the process of transition and reintegration.

Clarifying or Refocusing Research Methodologies

Engaging in digital culture studies means focusing on a domain in which representations are mediated through images and the written or spoken word. Research methods that focus on writing, rhetoric, and representation can lead to practical strategies for studying something as seemingly ephemeral as digital culture. The tradition of using qualitative methods is well established in rhetoric and composition with a number of theorists, including Barton and Stygall 2002; Bazerman et al. 2010; Bishop 1999; Brown and Dobrin 2004; Heath, Street, and Mills 2008; Kirsch 1999; Kirsch and Sullivan 1992; McKee and Porter 2008; McKee and Porter 2009; Schell and Rawson 2010, discussing qualitative research methods from ethnographic or feminist perspectives. Similarly, researchers focusing on professional and technical communication—Blakeslee and Fleischer 2007; Conklin and Hayhoe 2010; Koerber and McMichael 2008; McKee and DeVoss 2007; Sullivan and Spilka 1992; Thacker and Dayton 2008—often examine the benefits of and ethical considerations involved with undertaking qualitative writing research. From a digital humanities perspective, interdisciplinary digital culture studies concentrates on the unique subject positions of groups or individuals living their lives within a dominant, hegemonic culture and does so by relying on qualitative research methods established in allied disciplines.

Most research in digital culture studies is heavily qualitative and, as such, is rooted in the basic tenets of qualitative research. Designing research methods to study digital culture, at first, may be perceived as necessarily antithetical to traditional methods that often position producers or experts and consumers or novices in codified relationships that do not reflect the kinds of interactions and interconnectedness that current digital culture facilitates. Scholar Shay David (2008) asserts, "Online knowledge communities are not microcosms of . . . larger social systems but new formations within and in continuity with them." The "negotiation" between "established knowledge systems" and new online knowledge communities results in those online communities being "social laboratories where community values, goals, and modes of interaction must be designed rather than received" (David 2008, 193). These "social laboratories" reflect the changing paradigm from online consumer culture to participatory culture in which much digital content via social media, websites, blogs, etc., are created and maintained by novices and not used for monetary gain (Jenkins 2006). The dwindling divide between those who have been traditionally considered "producers" of texts worthy of study (e.g., published authors) and those who have been traditionally considered "consumers" (e.g., readers and audiences) has led to unique ways for people acting and interacting online to assert their identities and to contribute to a broader understanding of online culture and community and the artifacts produced by them. Understanding how and why these knowledge communities "design" their digital spaces and structure interactions in ways that reflect their affiliations—and more broadly, their goals—contributes to a broader understanding of their culture and community and often, by extension, digital culture.

The traditional perspective on producers or experts and consumers or novices recognizes a clear distinction between the two groups, marked by differences in expertise, power, and privilege. However, these distinctions are often blurred in digital spaces, as is evident when examining various forms of online communication, such as interactions that occur in social networking spaces—particularly those that are perceived as private or semi-private—or interactions between fans and those who produce the objects of those fans' affection. For instance, fans of the BBC television series, *Sherlock*, and the producers of *Sherlock* (e.g., showrunners and celebrities) demonstrate how the digital space reframes the kind of relationship fans can have with the creators of the texts they love and the text itself. Fans become influencers—in the same way that there are social media influencers. A shift in perception regarding their ostensible power has been noted by researchers and echoed among fans. In our digital culture, fans revel in their ability to connect with showrunners and ultimately to influence the creation or direction of a show. According to Louisa Stein (2018, 401), "[F]ans 'spin' yarn out of the fibers of media culture, and that act of spinning . . . contributes to and shapes the very value of the media text, which becomes itself a product of fan work. Fan spinning (off) exists in conversation with industrial spinning (off), encapsulating the tensions inherent in fan/industrial relationships." For example, *Sherlock*'s showrunners, especially Stephen Moffat, are very much aware of the fan community's presence on social media like Tumblr and Twitter. Moffat makes use of this knowledge in unexpected ways that have resulted in fans having a direct influence on the show and, consequently, on the mainstream culture that consumes it. He knew, for example, that fans spent much of the two-year hiatus between the broadcast of season two and season three episodes theorizing how Sherlock survived a fall from a hospital roof. Moffat also became aware of fan fiction pairings not previously shown in the series. When Moffat wrote Sherlock's "return" episode—"The Empty Hearse"—to begin season three, he incorporated scenes that specifically referenced fans or responded to fan expectations regarding Sherlock's potential romantic relationships.

The kind of access that people have to celebrities and to authors in digital spaces changes the kind of relationships that they can have, and it affects the kind of cultural artifacts that are being produced. Mainstream media, which impacts everything from trends in television shows to fashion to food, has the potential to be influenced in concrete and meaningful ways when the producers of these trends or artifacts are connected to their consumers or fans online. This process demonstrates David's (2008) assertion that online communities are concomitant creators of cultural products that are delivered and negotiated outside of the digital realm. Some scholars argue that this relationship ultimately results in a kind of democratization that is not rooted in the traditional relationship between fans and showrunners, in which fan voices are, at worst, considered a nuisance and, at best, considered important only to capitalize on a revenue stream. In some cases, fans' perspectives and contributions seem to be valued on the basis of their own merit—though this point is constantly debated when researchers consider the positionality of fans also as consumers and generators of revenue for capitalistic endeavors. For example, fan access to the *Sherlock* cast and crew may be carefully controlled through an online Q and A in which questions are posed to cast members without the fans asking in person. This process indicates how showrunners Steven Moffat and Mark Gatiss reach out to heavily invested fans but, by the same token, may be creating the illusion that fans have access to these celebrities in ways that they do not because celebrity participation in fan activities is calculated and coordinated. It is certainly democratizing to see fan commentary replicated in mainstream media and elevated to a status in which their questions are deemed important enough to be answered by celebrities. However, despite a more unfettered contact being possible when fan-celebrity interactions are facilitated online, this type of activity is rarely utilized. Additionally, the democratization of the relationships between fans and showrunners or celebrities is further called into question when showrunners incorporate fan theories into a show. Though it may be exciting for fans to have this type of influence on the trajectory of a show, rarely, if ever, are fans able to monetize these ideas or otherwise receive specific credit for them. As a result, production companies and networks can be viewed as capitalizing on unpaid labor. This tension is one reason why providing a methodological framework for analyzing the practices of online writing and representation is critical to the evolution of methods appropriate for digital culture studies, especially when the framework results in the kind of "negotiations" necessary to create meaningful communication and representation in digital spaces.

In addition to focusing on the particulars of people's or groups' lived experiences online, qualitative research also focuses on the particulars of researchers. Although quantitative research is often impersonal—with researchers viewed as distinct and separated from the study and its results—qualitative research often focuses explicitly *on* researchers and encourages them to lay bare their own perceptions and understandings of the research problem, thus situating themselves within, rather than outside of, the context of the research (Rossman and Rallis 1998; Stake 2010; Sullivan and Porter 1997). This attention to the researchers' own positionality allows researchers to be self-reflexive when designing and enacting the research study. The continued self-reflexivity of qualitative research not only encourages researchers to understand and expose their own positionality—and the ways in which their background or context affects that positionality in their research study—but also encourages them to reflect on the research process while it is occurring. This acknowledgement of one's positionality and the recognition that "researcher values permeate inquiry" are also distinctly feminist approaches to research (Lather 1992). As a result of the "systematically reflexive" (Rossman and Rallis 1998) nature of both feminist and qualitative research methods, the research process becomes emergent and iterative.

Researchers should look to their specific disciplines to determine what is valuable to disclose about a researcher's subject position. For example, fan and media studies scholars Paul Booth, Karen Hellekson, Kristina Busse, Matthew Hills, and Henry Jenkins—to name just a few— disclose their personal investment in fan culture and attempt to make clear to readers of their academic works how they perceive that their subject position contributes to their methodology and scholarship as a whole. While some, like Hills, are fan-scholars—indicating that they are invested in a fan identity— others make clear that, although they utilize fan behavior, fandom is not their way of life. Many permutations can be considered, but all of them take into consideration researchers' subject positions in order to make clear how their experiences and values have shaped their study, rather than framing their methods and results as objective and removed from bias.

Ideally, qualitative research focuses on particular situations and particular research participants with the intent of improving participants' lives in some way. Gretchen B. Rossman and Sharon F. Rallis (1998, 5), qualitative methodologists and education policy reform researchers, identified the purpose of qualitative research as that which is designed "to learn about some aspect of the social world and to generate new understandings that can be used by that social world." Here, Rossman and Rallis point to the concern qualitative researchers have for their research participants. In essence, "empathy and advocacy are and should be part of the lifestyle of the researcher" (Stake 2010, 14), ideas that are also hallmarks of feminist research. Although there are a number of ways in which this can occur, Rossman and Rallis identified four general uses of qualitative research, described in Table 1: instrumental use, enlightenment use, symbolic use, and emancipatory use—all of which are designed to benefit research participants.

Table 1. Rossman and Rallis's (1998) Four General Uses of Qualitative Research

Instrumental Use	Findings are "intended [for] use by intended users" (Rossman and Rallis 1998, 12). "Knowledge is applied to specific problems [and] provides solutions or recommendations" (12).
Enlightenment Use	Findings "serve to enlighten the user" (13). Research contributes to accumulated knowledge, "enhances understanding [and] offers heuristic insight" (12), which, in turn, contributes "to a gradual reorientation of the user's thought and action" (13).

Symbolic Use	Findings are used to identify "patterns and create narratives that make sense of the world and its phenomena" (14). The research "process generates stories" that then become part of "cultural knowledge that offers new and often satisfying interpretations of familiar events" (14) and "crystallizes beliefs or values" (12).
Emancipatory Use	Findings are used by researchers and participants to "collaboratively produce knowledge to improve their work and their lives" (16). Research "becomes a source of empowerment both to the individual's immediate life and to change structures that dominate and oppress" (15–16).

When researchers are continually reflecting on their study and considering the tenets of "The General Uses of Qualitative Research" listed in Table 1, they are likely to be open to change, particularly when it becomes clear that changing the research design in some way could lead to increased benefits for research participants.

Remaining self-reflexive and focusing on the ramifications for research subjects and participants is of particular importance when researching a group to which one does not belong. For example, when researchers conduct a survey, their choices about how to deploy a survey, to whom, and by what means are critical. Being open to adjusting those parameters based on unanticipated feedback or resistance will likely help to finalize a methodology that reveals both practical and ethical considerations. In gathering participants for a 2015 survey on the digital literacy practices of student veterans, Branham followed the recommendation of a student veteran and posted the survey's link in several online communities for veterans. Although the majority of these posts received no attention, one post to a Facebook group elicited a negative reaction from one veteran. In response to the post requesting participants and sharing the link, one Facebook user commented, "We're not lab rats." Branham chose to respond by explaining that she was sensitive to his concerns, participation in the survey was voluntary, and her goal was to use the research to better do her job as a college writing instructor. The user responded again by telling Branham that "they"—presumably academic researchers—would never understand veterans, who were "a different breed."

Because the purpose of Branham's research is to help student veterans, not to create uncomfortable situations for them through the process of conducting research, she did and does not want to position herself as a researcher who fails to consider her population's best interest. She decided that posting requests for survey participants in online spaces in which she was not an active participant went against her stance as a researcher. After making this decision, Branham deleted all posts in the Facebook groups and other online communities for veterans. This decision illustrates two important aspects of qualitative research design—constant reflection is necessary because data collection can reveal blind-spots in one's method, and researchers must remain flexible enough to respond and amend methods in order to keep the best interests of one's participants central to the project as a whole.

Although placed in a different context, Stake (2010) identified the subjective and localized focus on the personal and the particular as one of the weaknesses of qualitative research. However, while qualitative researchers may decide to emphasize the particular while ignoring the whole, a significant amount of research into the particulars of any human situation is necessary to determine patterns and overall trends.

Many small studies, including those specific to digital culture studies that may focus on a limited number of online artifacts, are not generalizable across a broad population. However, small qualitative research studies can be aggregated and analyzed to allow researchers to come to general conclusions about a particular research question or set of related research questions. This approach was advocated by Haswell (2000) in his call for more replicable, aggregable, and data-supported, or RAD, scholarship in rhetoric and composition. In an effort to increase the presence and visibility of RAD scholarship in rhetoric and composition, Haswell noted that RAD scholarship need not rely on statistics and could include, for instance, a case study of one student when "the participant's background is defined, observation procedure and data analysis are specified, and participant's behavior is recorded to the point that someone else could conduct a comparable study to validate, qualify, and perhaps add to the first study" (2000, 201). Therefore, the challenge for qualitative researchers is to describe their study methodology and participant selection with enough detail to allow other researchers to replicate the study, leading to the possibility of generalizing findings.

However, as with any generalization, the risk of stereotyping is present. Stake (2010) argued that qualitative research contributes to stereotyping but also fights against it. By emphasizing a particular experience, dialogue, context, and multiple realities, researchers can lessen the chance of simplistic understanding; however, these researchers can also reduce the chance of improving generalizable knowledge (Stake 2010, 28).

In addition, for generalizable knowledge to accumulate, particularly in an inter-discipline like digital culture studies, researchers must understand the particulars that make up the whole. In order to resist stereotyping, researchers must understand the individual, the local, and the various contexts in which the topic of inquiry exists. Work in digital culture studies must be done in concert with other scholarly studies that should be clearly identified and explicated and should contribute to the development of knowledge. Further, and more important, we must consider whether the quality of life for individuals or groups who are the subjects of a study is likely to be improved through research resulting from an examination of the subject's presence/work in digital spaces. Attending to these considerations keeps qualitative research from losing sight of the subjects, rather than other researchers, as beneficiaries of the resultant research. A slight refocusing of the methodology of a qualitative research project can possibly lead to something as concrete as policy change or as important as more effective or efficient strategies for communication and connection with others online. For example, in the interest of developing a study that is focused on people and that values "different views" and "multiple meanings" (Stake 2010, 15), a relatively simple change that can immensely help researchers is encouraging participants in interviews or surveys to analyze their own interactions and the results of surveys and to report that analysis. Such self-reflection or respondent analyses may help researchers gain a deeper understanding of the culturally specific meaning being made through the information collected via interview or survey by respecting the value of constituents'—perhaps non-expert—knowledge. Researchers also may learn more about the meaning they are making through their own subject positions and perceived expertise—as Branham experienced during her research—which includes an extended case study of one student veteran's social media profiles and personas. After conducting a semi-structured interview with this participant, including a participant-led profile tour of his social networking profiles, Branham asked the participant to review her write-up of the case study. This reviewing process not only allowed the participant to elaborate on components of the case study that required additional context but also allowed the participant to identify and correct any misunderstandings that emerged during data analysis. Finally, this review process allowed Branham to indicate when the participant's views of his online interactions differed from her interpretations of the same interactions, furthering Branham's understanding of her positionality and the ways in which her stance as a researcher influenced her analysis.

When researchers develop a research plan that may especially involve minority or disenfranchised groups, they should resist common stereotypes associated with potential respondents. For example, many veterans do not identify with the two most common tropes associated with veterans—the hero and the wounded warrior. Despite these tropes being pervasive in popular culture and also, unfortunately, influencing non-veterans' understanding and treatment of veterans—both in society and online—researchers must be aware of and seek to avoid them. Thus, resisting these stereotypes and offering alternative understandings of veterans as a heterogeneous group must be primary concerns for qualitative researchers working with veterans and veteran-groups online.

Another common example of often misrepresented or misinterpreted online groups is fans, either within a specific fandom—such as that for an actor, television series, or character—or the much larger group of fans in general. Commonly publicized stereotypes of fans include assumptions about gender, age, and education, for example. According to Casey McCormack (2019, 273), "while digital media can be a transformative force for fans, it can also lead to the increasing commoditization and pathologization of fan attachment." Developing research plans that include data about fans' perceptions of themselves and the value of the texts that they produce in online communities may help eliminate the bias associated with common tropes or stereotypes.

While the ethical concerns relevant to qualitative research are applicable to digital culture research, a digital environment introduces a number of ethical concerns that are not present in non-digital research projects. Thus, as researchers continue to examine practices that occur in technologically-mediated spaces, it is important to understand how these digital spaces and tools create new ethical considerations for qualitative researchers.

Ethical Concerns in Digital Writing Research and Digital Culture Studies

While the history of qualitative research and associated research ethics is rich in writing studies, the scholarship that deals explicitly with digital research methodologies and ethics is more limited. Perhaps because so much rich scholarship in composition research and ethics associated with the production and analysis of prose has been prominent for decades, many scholars have not turned their attention specifically to ethics associated with online prose, even though the definition of "text" has been expanded as digital studies has expanded as a discipline. McKee and Porter (2008, 712) pointed out that "research that involves the Internet and other online spaces . . . is fundamentally composition research . . . because almost all communications that occur on the Web occur in writing." Although video and audio web communications have certainly increased since the time of McKee and Porter's publication, the definition of *writing* within writing studies has also expanded to include multimodal texts. Thus, McKee and Porter's argument still holds true—web-based communication is writing-based and, as such, should be of interest to scholars and researchers in communication or, specifically, writing disciplines.

McKee and Porter (2008, 712) defined digital writing research as that which "focuses on . . . computer-generated, computer-based, or computer-delivered documents; . . . computer-based text production; and . . . the interactions of people who use computerized technologies to communicate through digital means." Whereas many ethical concerns present in non-digital writing research are still relevant in the digital domain, the context of the digital raises a number of ethical concerns that are not present when conducting research in non-digital environments. The prominent ethical concerns unique to digital writing research are varied understandings of public versus private digital spaces, associated understandings of what counts as sensitive versus non-sensitive information, and understandings of authors and texts or data versus understandings of human subjects (McKee and Porter 2008, 731–37; Markham and Buchanan 2012, 6–8). In addition, to update ethical concerns initially stated by McKee and Porter (2008), researchers must understand what counts as "labor" in digital spaces to avoid exploitation.

Public Versus Private and Sensitive Versus Non-sensitive

Prior to the advent of the Internet and its widespread adoption, it was fairly simple to determine if a piece of writing was published or unpublished. Published work was considered available for public consumption, whereas unpublished work was the private property of the author. However, as writing studies researchers investigate the growing amount of writing happening on the Web, they must ask "Should the writing that happens in digital spaces be treated as public or private?" The answer to this question is "it depends."

According to a qualitative study conducted by Katie Shilton and Sheridan Sayles (2016), in which they interview multi- or inter-disciplinary researchers about the ethical challenges inherent in digital spaces, they come to a conclusion that matches the experience of the authors, as well. The Institutional Review Board's, or IRB, contribution to safeguarding ethical practices, particularly when artifacts are being collected online—through social media or websites—is severely limited. The majority of researchers interviewed in the study agreed that the IRB considers work published online to be a resource that does not involve human subjects and so liberally issues exemptions for digital culture research. Although some researchers cite this approach as an advantage, others wish that there was a deeper understanding for the kind of work that they do. Researchers of digital culture know that artifacts online are also artifacts that are tied up in people's lived experiences and identities online. The final and most valuable finding from this study confirms that the most helpful feedback on ethical research in online environments is peer review. This practice, too, has problems that Shilton and Sheridan (2016) discern; most prominently, peer review often happens after research is conducted and, consequently, is not very helpful in "mitigating harm." This conclusion leads to the recommendation that research plans be discussed with colleagues in order to ensure that ethical concerns are identified and dealt with in the planning stages of any research project.

As noted by McKee and Porter (2008), each platform for communication on the Web exists according to particular community standards of use and varying degrees of public access. Some platforms—particularly social networking technologies—also offer users some degree of control regarding whether their personal information is publicly searchable or available only to specified users. However, assessing the level of control that users of social media have over personal information and how that can inform a researcher's perception regarding the privacy of such information is complicated. In order to make this assessment, digital culture researchers' should consider a research subject's digital literacy. In other words, do participants realize that privacy settings are available and understand how to use them? Do they expect a degree of privacy that they have not availed themselves of because their digital literacy precludes this realization? Additionally, users of a particular platform, or tool within a platform, might have differing expectations of privacy than those stated by the creators of the platform.

Because of this widespread variation in understandings of privacy between platform and user, as well as the diverse types of writing that take place on the Web, McKee and Porter (2008) argued that digital writing researchers must consider—in addition to whether writing on the Web is public or private—whether the writing is dealing with topics of a sensitive nature. Thus, when determining whether IRB approval is needed to analyze writing on the Web, researchers must consider the expectations of privacy among users of the platform, expectations of privacy for the users whose writing is the subject of study, and the sensitivity of the writing topic. For example, while any information that a university professor posts on his or her publicly searchable academic blog would be considered public and non-sensitive information—and as a result, would not require informed consent for use—a post by a twenty-year-old university student in a discussion forum for individuals struggling with an eating disorder should be considered differently. Although the discussion forum might be publicly searchable, it is likely that, due to the sensitive nature of the topic and the fact that the forum is intended for use by people with eating disorders, users might consider their writing in this space to be private. In a situation like this, we argue that informed consent is necessary. Not only is it likely that this community of users have some expectations of privacy but the sensitivity of the topic requires that individuals be allowed to decide if they wish to participate in the research project.

One type of artifact used extensively in Wojton's work is fan fiction—paratextual stories and art that are created by fans and based on whichever source text interests them. Because these stories, archived online, are produced with the intent of reaching an audience, Wojton considers them public and semi-published because the site that she used, Archive of Our Own, is heavily moderated; as such, Wojton respects fair use stipulations and gives authors credit when referencing their work or using any directly quoted materials. Because of the nature of much fan fiction—often involving erotic pairings—the intended audience is not inclusive of the general public like a traditional work of fiction would be. The context of a fan work should not only be considered but discussed by researchers so that academic audiences understand the writer's purpose and targeted audience. Fan work is considered valuable for other fans' entertainment and sometimes for advocacy by those vested in what fan fiction has to offer. For example, fans may not only be entertained by stories involving favorite characters but may learn from their attitudes toward or discussions of their sexual orientation. Fan fiction writers may serve as allies of or advocates for readers looking for characters like themselves. Therefore, either having or developing a deep understanding of a fan-work's rhetorical purpose is necessary in order to create meaningful research methods. This understanding could be developed based on researchers' personal experiences as part of the subculture or their research into sources that provide adequate information about that subculture.

Branham's research, on the other hand, deals specifically with veterans communicating within social networking spaces with varying degrees of privacy about a range of sensitive topics. Her research revealed that, while some users have a nuanced understanding of privacy settings within social networking spaces, many users view social networking spaces as semi-private, regardless of their mastery of privacy settings. Additionally, users tended to perceive Facebook, for instance, as more private than Instagram or Twitter. Furthermore, some of Branham's participants discussed social networking communication that occurred within more restricted subsets of a larger social networking platform, such as communication within private or closed groups of Facebook. As a result of the diversity of texts being analyzed and discussed in her research, Branham considers her participants' texts to be both private and sensitive. Branham's participants, even those whose social networking profiles are public and fully searchable online, were required to provide informed consent and are identified in her work by pseudonyms to protect their identity. Similarly, when including screenshots of her participants' social networking posts as illustrative examples, Branham chose to redact images and other identifying features to ensure her participants' privacy.

Author Versus Person

McKee and Porter (2008, 733) argued that, although "some regard the Internet as a vast storehouse of available writings to be harvested freely by any and all researchers . . . not all postings to the Internet should be treated like books in a library." This quotation addresses the issue of how writing on the Internet is understood. Should writing that happens in digital spaces be treated as a text or data composed by an author, or is it part of the identity of an individual or, perhaps, multiple human subjects?

Again, the answer here is largely dependent upon the type of writing and the forum in which it is found. Some writing on the Web clearly operates according to print-based standards, such as writing published in online scholarly journals, magazines, or news outlets. Digital writing that falls into these categories is considered published and authored and can be used and cited accordingly. Although much of the writing on the Web does not fall into such clear-cut categories, all Web-based writing "of any sort in any venue, are pieces of writing in a tangible format—and, as such, they are copyrighted from the point of their distinction" (McKee and Porter 2008, 734). As a result, McKee and Porter (2008, 734) stated that in "most digital writing research, there is no such thing as a 'person.'" While Wojton's research of fan fiction supports this claim, Branham's research in social networking communication pushes against the assessment that "most" digital writing research is composed by an author rather than a human subject. Whereas authors intend for their writing to be publicly consumed, many people who write in the context of social media—with the notable exceptions of public figures—view their writing as interpersonal—and therefore private—communication rather than as a copyrighted text. Thus, instead of being understood as a text that is authored, the type of writing that happens in social networking spaces, in particular, should be read as communicative interactions.

Regardless of this distinction, McKee and Porter's (2008) assessment of digital writing, which emphasizes that fair use guidelines *always* apply, whereas informed consent *may be* necessary, is instructive. Again, researchers must assess whether the writing is or is expected to be private or public, whether the writing deals with a sensitive or non-sensitive topic, and whether the writing is considered published or semi-published. Although clear examples can be found in each of these categories, there will always be blurry spaces as well. In fact, even fair use guidelines are open for interpretation, as they are a set of principles designed to guide an individual in determining whether fair use applies in a particular situation or country. Thus, in addition to determining if the writing they wish to research is public or private, written by an author or representative of a person, digital writing researchers must also consider if and when fair use applies to their work.

Although Wojton analyzed works of fan fiction authored by fans for an audience of other fans and, in some cases, showrunners, Branham's data, consisting of communicative interactions within social networking spaces, does not have the same clear-cut authorial boundaries. Although individuals who communicate within social networking spaces are certainly composing posts for a particular audience, often using a combination of texts and visuals, Branham considers the communication that typically occurs within social networking spaces more similar to semi-private conversations that occur within a public space. With the exception of celebrities, social media influencers, or individuals posting with the intention of "going viral," the majority of social networking posts are not intended for consumption by the public at large. As such, these posts, Branham asserts, should be considered not as texts but as communicative interactions that represent part of the identity of the speaker.

Exploitation of Labor

Researchers also need to be mindful of the ethical implications of using various types of digital artifacts that can be easily gathered on the Web through websites, blogs, and social media. Misappropriating the labor of others in a way that authors could not have expected or sanctioned (e.g., using fan fiction texts or social networking profiles in a study) is inextricably connected to perceptions about and expectations for privacy. Researchers who gather artifacts online are never the intended audience and, as such, have to consider the extent to which they will benefit by using the labor of others without compensating them. This consideration of labor is why ethical qualitative research most often explicitly builds in ways in which subjects and their communities can benefit from the resulting research and considers ways to communicate meaningful results for the individuals and groups being studied. Participatory action research, for example, attempts to empower participants by actively involving them in the research process, with the goal of ensuring that "the research conducted by participants is oriented to making improvements in practices and their settings by the participants themselves" (Kemmis,

McTaggert, and Nixon 2014). In the case of collaborating with participants to design the study to allow the development of participant-identified benefits, researchers must be aware of their own positionality and take care not to make unilateral assumptions or decisions about what is beneficial or "good" for a particular group.

Ethical concerns regarding the use of digital artifacts are also complicated when considering that many researchers study digital culture among groups that may not practice and perform ethical behaviors themselves. However, regardless of the subject of research, it is still important to conduct research in ethical ways. For instance, if a researcher is studying the communicative interactions of an active online hate group, the goals and potential benefits for the researcher may clearly be at odds with the goals and potential benefits for the research participants. In situations such as these, researchers must be aware of this potential conflict and make assessments on a case-by-case basis.

A consideration of the benefits a study offers for research participants differs from traditional concerns about authorship or even about fair use. For example, Internet communities are often referred to as "gift economies." According to Bertha Chin (2014), in a "gift economy" the exchange for labor is often pleasure and recognition. In an attempt to reframe how fan contributions, in particular, are traditionally perceived as tertiary, Chin looks to the fans who create the content for their perception of the value of their fan-driven works. In an interview with a group of fans who spend both time and money to meticulously maintain a fan website and who reach a large audience of fellow fans, Chin reported that they feel they are contributing to fan culture in a significant way, and that is what is rewarding. This finding is significant because fans who operate in online communities are often vested in more than just the object of their affection; they are focused on community building and are likely to have a vested interest in research that has the potential to benefit their discourse community. Obviously, giving creators of content proper credit is necessary, but the issue becomes more complicated when researchers try to understand and communicate the proper context so that fans' work can be understood and appreciated in the way in which the authors intended it. Working in light of these considerations establishes a respect for the labor involved in producing and maintaining online content in a gift economy.

When researchers work with fan fiction, taking the time to explain and contextualize fan fiction narratives is critical to avoid taking them out of context and using them in a way in which the author did not intend. Many computer-mediated encounters Wojton examined in her research are dialectical, in which the participants engage in a discursive process regarding fundamentally different perceptions about their reality and navigate perceptions regarding their own identities and the subject positions of others. They grapple with ideas and contradictions that often stem from their lived experiences, despite the fact that these digital exchanges or encounters often occur in comments on fan fiction stories. At times, these interactions work to help participants and observers encounter and cope with alterity in many different forms. By engaging in a safe space for exploring complex issues regarding gender, sexuality, and sexual desire through an affiliation with a particular fandom via a particular text, fans often end up pairing an understanding of the rhetorical dimensions (e.g., culture, purpose, audience) of fan fiction with a practical, sometimes participatory, approach to the paratexts (e.g., comments sections). Consequently, the works of those discourse communities can be understood in the context of the author's lived experiences and the digital community setting. Researchers should mitigate the potential for fans being exploited, being misconstrued, or being made the object of a joke. Though much fan work is arguably of low quality, researchers should respect fan work by portraying the power relations involved in the work. For example, the digital fan community is responsible for determining which stories are deemed important and valuable. Stories or comments that strike a positive chord with readers are often rewarded with positive posts and organized according to the number of "likes" or "kudos." A high number of comments and "likes" or "kudos" can contribute to a text's popularity and consequently bolster the author's perceptions about his or her work. In this way, consumers of a story directly influence its popularity. Fan work, such as fan fiction, must be understood on its own terms if part of the goal of ethical research is to provide results and inferences that will be of value to its subjects. Establishing this contextual understanding of both the cultural and technological practices of communities online is the best way to mitigate the potential for groups or individuals to be misunderstood or even exploited.

Conclusion

Because of a myriad of individual ethical decisions that must be made when conducting digital writing research, scholars agree that ethical research design must be vetted on a case-by-case basis and with the support of institutional, organizational, and peer guidelines or feedback. In addition, McKee and Porter (2008)—as well as researchers engaging in participatory action research—advocate for researchers to consult with research participants during the design of the study. McKee and Porter (2008) also recommend, in accordance with the Conference on College Composition and Communication's, or CCCC, *Guidelines for the Ethical Conduct of Research in Composition Studies* (2003), that researchers consult existing research studies. However, in digital writing research, determining these multiple audiences can be more challenging (McKee and Porter 2008; Markham and Buchanan 2012, Shilton and Sayles 2016). In 2015, the CCCC *Guidelines for the Ethical Conduct of Research in Composition Studies* was revised to include a section on conducting studies involving digital or online media, which recommends that digital writing researchers "explicitly justify [their] research choices and [their] positioning as researchers when [they] plan, conduct, and publish [their] studies" so as to make clear the ways in which the researcher negotiates the topics of public versus private, author versus person, and informed consent. Thoughtfully designed qualitative research methods in digital culture studies recognize the value of explicit attention to context, situational details, and the researchers' positionality. Although the value of discipline-specific research methods is not in question, using the approaches and considering the framework provided by professionals who study ethical practices for writing and rhetoric are of value to digital culture researchers because of the text and image-based nature of communicative interactions.

References

Barton, Ellen L., and Gail Stygall. 2002. *Discourse Studies in Composition*. Cresskill, NJ: Hampton Press.

Bazerman, Charles, Robert Krut, Karen Lunsford, Susan McLedo, Suzie Null, Paul Rogers, and Amanda Stansell, eds. 2010. *Traditions of Writing Research*. New York, NY: Routledge.

Bishop, Wendy. 1999. *Ethnographic Writing Research: Writing It Down, Writing It Up, and Reading It*. Portsmouth, NH: Heinemann Publishing.

Blakeslee, Ann M., and Cathy Fleischer. 2007. *Becoming a Writing Researcher*. Mahwah, NJ: Lawrence Erlbaum Associates, Inc.

Brown, Stephen G., and Sidney I. Dobrin, eds. 2004. *Ethnography Unbound: From Theory Shock to Critical Praxis.* Albany, NY: State University of New York Press.

Chin, Bertha. 2014 "Sherlockology and Galactica.tv: Fan Sites as Gifts or Exploited Labor?" *Transformative Works and Cultures* 15. dx.doi.org/10.3983/twc.2014.0513.

Conference on College Composition and Communication. 2015. *CCCC Guidelines for the Ethical Conduct of Research in Composition Studies.* www.ncte.org/cccc/resources/positions/ethicalconduct.

Conklin, James, and George F. Hayhoe, eds. 2010. *Qualitative Research in Technical Communication.* New York, NY: Routledge.

David, Shay. 2008. "Toward Participatory Expertise." In *Structures of Participation in Digital Culture*, edited by Joe Karaganis, 176–99. New York, NY: Social Science Research Council.

Haswell, Richard. 2000. "Documenting Improvement in College Writing: A Longitudinal Approach." *Written Communication* 17, no. 3: 307–52. doi:10.1177/0741088300017003001.

Heath, Shirley Brice, Brian Street, and Molly Mills. 2008. *On Ethnography: Approaches to Language and Literacy Research.* New York, NY: Teachers College Press.

Jenkins, Henry. 2006. *Convergence Culture: Where Old and New Media Collide.* New York, NY: New York University Press.

Kemmis, Stephen, Robin McTaggart, and Rhonda Nixon. 2014. *The Action Research Planner: Doing Critical Participatory Action Research.* New York, NY: Springer.

Kirsch, Gesa E. 1999. *Ethical Dilemmas in Feminist Research: The Politics of Location, Interpretation, and Publication.* Albany, NY: State University of New York Press.

Kirsch, Gesa E., and Patricia A. Sullivan. 1992. *Methods and Methodology in Composition Research.* Carbondale, IL: Southern Illinois University Press.

Koerber, Amy, and Lonie McMichael. 2008. "Qualitative Sampling Methods: A Primer for Technical Communicators." *Journal of Business and Technical Communication* 22, no. 4. Thousand Oaks, CA: SAGE Publishing.

Lather, Patti. 1992. "Critical Frames in Educational Research: Feminist and Post-structural Perspectives." *Theory into Practice* 31, no. 2: 87–99. New York, NY: Taylor & Francis.

Markham, Annette, and Elizabeth Buchanan. 2012. "Ethical Decision-making and Internet Research." *Association of Internet Researchers.* aoir.org/reports/ethics2.pdf.

McCormick, Casey J. 2018. "Chapter 23 Active Fandom: Labor and Love in The Whedonverse." In *A Companion to Media Fandom and Fan Studies*, edited by Paul Booth, 369–84. Oxford, UK: John Wiley & Sons.

McKee, Heidi, and Danielle DeVoss, eds. 2007. *Digital Writing Research: Technologies, Methodologies, and Ethical Issues.* Cresskill, NJ: Hampton Press.

McKee, Heidi, and James E. Porter. 2008. "The Ethics of Digital Writing Research: A Rhetorical Approach." *College Composition and Communication* 59, no. 4: 711–49.

McKee, Heidi, and James E. Porter. 2009. *The Ethics of Internet Research: A Rhetorical Case-based Process.* New York, NY: Peter Lang.

Östman, Sari, and Riikka Turtiainen. 2016. "From Research Ethics to Researching Ethics in an Online Specific Context." *Media and Communication* 4, no. 4. doi: 10.17645/mac.v4i4.571.

Rossman, Gretchen B., and Sharon F. Rallis. 1998. *Learning in the Field: An Introduction to Qualitative Research.* Thousand Oaks, CA: SAGE Publishing.

Schell, Eileen, and K. J. Rawson. 2010. *Rhetorica in Motion: Feminist Rhetorical Methods and Methodologies.* Pittsburgh, PA: University of Pittsburgh Press.

Sherlock. 2014. Season 3, Episode 4, "The Empty Hearse." Directed by Jeremy Lovering. Written by Mark Gatiss. Aired January 1, 2014, on BBC.

Shilton, Katie, and Sheridan Sayles. 2016. "'We Aren't Always Going to Be on the Same Page about Ethics': Ethical Practices and Challenges in Research on Digital and Social Media." *IEEE Xplore*, March 10, 2016. doi: 10.1109/HICSS.2016.242.

Stake, Robert E. 2010. *Qualitative Research: Studying How Things Work.* New York, NY: The Guilford Press.

Stein, Louisa. 2018. "Chapter 25 Of Spinoffs and Spinning Off." In *A Companion to Media Fandom and Fan Studies,* edited by Paul Booth, 401–18. Oxford, UK: John Wiley & Sons.

Sullivan, Patricia, and James E. Porter. 1997. *Opening Spaces: Writing Technologies and Critical Research Practices.* Greenwich, CT: Ablex Publishing Corporation.

Sullivan, Patricia, and Rachel Spilka. 1992. "Qualitative Research in Technical Communication: Issues of Value, Identity, and Use." *Technical Communication* 39, no. 4: 592–606.

Thacker, Christopher, and David Dayton. 2008. "Using Web 2.0 to Conduct Qualitative Research." *Technical Communication,* vol. 55, no. 4: 383–91.

4 Traversing Theme Park Stories: Towards an Expansion of Transmedial Narratology

Carissa Baker

Visitors traverse a theme park attraction queue with expository signs about native wildlife. On the overhanging woven structure sits a map apparently symbolic of the rainforest, cut through by a winding river. Once loaded, guests sit in a stylized boat and meander down a waterway. Riders go through a series of scenes in a bioluminescent world, vaguely familiar to those who saw the *Avatar* (2009) movie. These scenes contain more immersive details, colors, and textures, augmented by projection technology. The sound begins with distant fauna, shifts to unseen creatures playing above or around the rider, and grows to a crescendo as the Na'vi people chant in the distance. The Na'vi and their direhorses walk towards something, and the boat follows the same path. The aural and physical experience culminates with an advanced audio-animatronic, the Shaman of Songs, loudly singing and playing drums. The vocals, in the fictional Na'vi language, are of connections and the Great Mother, Eywa; during this song, the shaman lights up fiber optic branches that connect to the deity. The attraction ends with small hints of the depth of Pandora's flora, along with the woodsprites floating away. Guests disembark and emerge in the Valley of Mo'ara, complete with glowing alien plants and waterfalls cascading off floating mountains. They arrive in a world at peace.

Na'vi River Journey, from Disney's Animal Kingdom's addition Pandora: The World of *Avatar* (2017), is a dark ride. This ride genre showcases scenes in an enclosed space, with guests in a ride-vehicle on a track or flume. The ride has no obvious narrator and no conflict. It does not follow Western dramatic structure, traditional linearity, or narrative conventions. Some fans have argued that this experience, unlike its sister attraction Flight of Passage—a ride that has explicit narrative and an obvious Hero's Journey—has no story and does not constitute storytelling. Former creative executive, Joe Rohde, refers to the purpose of the attraction as "just plain beauty," something that can be accomplished through non-narrative forms (Martens 2017). The attraction's soundtrack reads as poetry: "O beautiful forest/there are tears in the forest/woodsprites/we cry out, calling O Eywa" (Frommer 2017). A later verse reads, "By the People's will/The forest is singing," recalling the film's plot of the Na'vi revolting against outside oppressors. This allusion would perhaps signify narrative, and a few designers have aided by explaining their intentions. Production designer, Joe Cashman, refers to the "emotional tale[s]" of the vignettes riders see as they travel the river, including mystery, danger, whimsy, grandeur, celebration, and spirituality (Bishop 2017). Artist Stephan Martiniere (2018) likewise mentions the "emotional buildup" throughout the ride and the "journey" of the visitor.

Is there a story in this attraction? Is it a narrative? The answers are clear, if deploying an approach based on narrative theory. Na'vi River Journey has a setting, characters, and events in a chronology. It is *narrated* through design in the theme park medium's genre of *environmental storytelling*, wherein story events are represented with sets, figures, props, lighting, and sound. It has a bi-narrative structure with complex *focalization*—a duel perspective in which visitors witness an *in media res* storyworld and simultaneously go on a trip to experience the environment and attend the shaman's ceremony. In other words, Na'vi River Journey is a narrative even though it does not have a traditional plot. It is still a story, as Gérard Genette (1980) explains—something can remain story content even if it is "low in dramatic intensity or fullness of incident" (27). There has been a debate within design and fan communities about whether theme parks tell stories—with some conflating plot and story or narrative with explicit narration—and how they should tell stories—with some preferring environmental stories with no explicit narration while others wanting linear, explicitly narrated attractions with clear plots, and a handful wanting guests to interpret the scenes themselves instead of taking in a designer-imposed narrative. This debate could be simplified with the "systematic, thorough, and disinterested" approach to narrative analysis found in *narratology*, alternatively called *narrative theory* (Cobley 2005). Because of the pervasive use of narrative within the theme park, narrative theory is an obvious choice to deploy in theme park scholarship. In this chapter, I argue for the more widespread use of narratological principles in the study of theme parks and, reciprocally, for the inclusion of theme parks and attractions into the growing collection of narrative texts worthy of consideration within that approach. The application of narrative theory to theme parks can provide scholars with a better understanding of both the theme park medium and the diverse nature of narrative itself.

Narratology and Its Challenges

Narratology is a theory of narratives, often accompanied by the practice of narrative analysis. At its most basic level, narratology examines structures of narrative with results often "reached in a mechanical fashion," akin to structural linguistics (Prince 1982, 187). Key structural elements are identified in texts to "determine functions and relationships" (Jahn 2017) and perceive the text's *narrativity*, or its quality of being narrative. Scholars trace the roots of narratology to the classical distinction between *mimesis*—texts that imitate life or show stories such as plays—and *diegesis*—texts that narrate life or tell stories such as novels. Narratologists recognize elements of both within the same texts. There are common terms in the discipline, but the primary distinction would be between the two items that create narrative—story and discourse, or *fabula* and *sjuzet*. The story or fabula is the content or events, in chronological order, and the discourse or sjuzet is how these events are expressed, in any order. Genette (1980) adds to the distinction of story and narrative a third term, *narrating*, that indicates the performance of the narrative or the "producing action" of the narrative and the context of that production (27). Something must tell a story to be a narrative, according to Genette, but story and narrating are only understood through the "intermediary" of narrative (29). The narrative *instance* or situation is composed of the narrative voice or time and focuses on both the narrator and the audience. Other components frequently studied include *focalization*, the chronotope, and techniques related to discourse. Focalization is who perceives the information in a narrative—a layered understanding of point of view; the chronotope is a Bakhtinian term recognizing the planes of time and space; techniques related to discourse include the order of events illustrated, number of narrative perspectives, orientation of the narrator in relation to events, etc. Though narratology studies "form" over "substance" and avoids content interpretation (Chatman 1975, 299), examining structural components allows us to "understand, analyse, and evaluate narratives" (Bal 1997, 3).

Narratology—partly because of it being focused on storytelling, a ubiquitous human activity—has evolved over time, allowing current theories to shape it. Emerging from French structuralism and Russian formalism—added to by semiotics and altered as a "reaction" to post-structuralism—the approach has gone through "reorientation and diversification" over the years, often as a response to criticisms of the field (Fludernik 2005, 37). The primary debates surrounding the validity of the approach include its absence of context and its "text-centeredness" (Cobley 2005; Wolf 2003). The largest complaint about the approach is that the field is "guilty of repressing other concerns" or "futility in the face of social concerns" (Bal 1990, 720, 750) with its emphasis on language over what constructs language: culture. Monika Fludernik (2005) summarizes it as weighting language systems over the practices of people and excluding contextual attributes like history, ethics, or aesthetics. This is perhaps surprising considering that narrative itself is a "cultural attitude" and practice, making narratology itself a "perspective on culture" (Bal 1997, 222). "Postclassical narratology," however, has responded to the "cultural turn" in theoretical fields, accepting more ideas from cultural studies, psychoanalysis, feminism, race theory, Marxism, reader response criticism, and others (Chihaia 2012, 19). This introduction of new approaches represents an "ongoing rehumanization" of the field, also found in the sociocultural linguistics popularized by William Labov (Fludernik 2010, 925). Though not all scholars identify with its use, "contextualist narratology" interrogates the practice of merely looking at "the construction of the text itself" (Chatman 1980, 324). The field does often continue to use a "neutral" (Cobley 2005) way to analyze, though "text-grammars" and more quantifiable processes have "gone out of fashion" (Bal 1990, 728); however, the careful analysis of language patterns can conceivably reveal crucial attributes of cultural practice. For example, Mieke Bal (1990) finds through the recognition of gendering unknown narrators that, "ideology in language ... becomes visible through narratological analysis" (35). The "cultural embeddedness of narrative"

(Bal 1997) is an essential facet of understanding theme parks—cultural products created collaboratively and received communally—so this shift is beneficial (220).

The other primary focus of "narratological reconceptualization" (Wolf 2003) responds to the charge that narratology is "static," "reductive," and fails to "apprehend the richness of narrative in all its forms" (Cobley 2005). Multiple scholars argued the need to "diversify the corpus of narrative texts" (Gardner and Herman 2011, 4), though this modification of the field was not without tension (Gardner 2011, 53). Many current narratological works focus solely or primarily on literary fiction rather than non-verbal forms or other text-based non-literary work. The introduction of *transmedial narratology* underlies narrative theory being a functional approach for the study of theme parks.

The Transmedial Approach

Transmedial narratology, or "a framework for studying narrative across media" (Gardner and Herman 2011), changed the orientation of narratology in valuable ways that assist in theme parks' analysis (5). An important step was in recognizing a large range of narrative texts. Roland Barthes and others expanded the notion of what a text can be, and work in transmedial narratology has enhanced the definition of text even further. According to Bal (1997), a narrative text is "a text in which an agent relates ('tells') a story in a particular medium, such as language, imagery, sound, buildings, or a combination thereof" (5). Since "buildings" are incorporated in the definition, this leaves an opening for theme parks and their distinct narrative properties. Certain mediums combine elements and illustrate "the fluidity of available forms and how often they can be used in combination with new types of narrative form" (Ryan, Foote, and Azaryahu 2016, 206). Narratological analyses now include readings of film, television, comic books and graphic novels, music, painting, sculpture, dance, photography, digital texts, video games, oral stories, performance art, legal cases, museums, and cityscapes. Bal (1990), in fact, advocates for more inclusion of non-narrative texts in addition to narratives in other forms.

Transmedial narratologists have perceived that texts can combine multiple forms. Marie Laure-Ryan (2014) describes *multimodality* as "narrative forms combining a variety of semiotic channels." Comics and graphic novels combine visual and verbal arts, opera combines music and theater, and film is audiovisual. Relationships between media types can also be explored through notions of *intermediality*, media types connecting to one another; *remediation*, how old and new media shape each other; *convergence*, media systems coming together; and *transmedia* or *crossmedia storytelling*, stories distributed across media channels or adapted on various media channels. According to Kai Mikkonen (2011), comics are best understood by comprehending the "interplay" between visual and verbal elements (639). The concepts of multimodality and intermediality are integral to the study of theme parks, which may be an amalgam of the most media forms. One attraction may combine forms. For instance, Hong Kong Disneyland's Mystic Manor begins with ornate architecture; moves to a queue that contains music, written plaques, painting, and decorative arts like fans, headdresses, jewelry, etc.; and ends with a ride that comprises numerous artifacts, including sculpture, a synchronized musical soundtrack, dialogue, a short film, and the theme park features of motion on a track and environmental storytelling. Mystic Manor is a linear narrative with memorable characters, but it fuses multiple media genres to generate the narrative. Theme parks are a synthesis of media types and narrative texts.

One of the most significant contributions the transmedial approach allows is its emphasis on "medium-specific features" (Mikkonen 2011, 637). "Each medium has its own properties" according to Seymour Chatman (1980), and narratology, by examining medium-specific aspects, can help critics locate the "limitations" and "triumphs" of particular media (140). Transmedial narratology stresses how "particular media constrain as well as enable storytelling practices" (Kukkonen 2011, 34). Similarly, Jason Mittel (2007) notes that narrative theory is a tool for analyzing storytelling across media but cautions critics to stay aware when a "specific medium creates particular storytelling parameters, constraining some options while enabling others" (156). Along these lines, theme park attractions combine forms to the benefit of immersion but inhibit narrative depth through consistently brief duration. David Herman (2011) agrees that early narratology did not account for "medium-specificity" and defines transmedial narratology as a method that "explores how the constraints and affordances associated with particular media bear on the design and interpretation of stories" (159). Understanding medium features can thus assist in interpretation and evaluation of narratives. In transmedial narratology, Mikkonen (2011) maintains, "problems will arise if we assume that notions of narrative theory and mediation can be transferred from one medium to another without due modification" (651). Taking this idea further, he says narratologists can distinguish, through careful study, what is distinct about a narrative within a medium and what is universal to all narratives.

A conception of medium specificity helps us understand that narratives can be great in multiple mediums. In other words, evaluation of narratives cannot be based exclusively on the characteristics of quality narratives in a different medium. As Janet Murray (1998) avows, "[n]arrative beauty is independent of medium" (273); however, some may try to appraise a narrative based on the traits of a completely different medium. Ryan (2014) indicates that many think language has "narrative superiority over other semiotic media." Despite the fact that narratives are created because of "cultural, technological, and semiotic factors" (Ryan 2014) and that mediums develop in "different spatial and temporal conditions," language—especially within literary texts—tends to be privileged by critics (Sjöholm 2013, 18). Ryan's work mentions that non-linguistic narratives are seen as "parasitic on the narrativity of the original text." Some theme park texts easily illustrate this parasitism, such as a static scene from a fairy tale, whereas attractions with more original stories—not from intellectual properties—may present distinct manifestations of narrativity. The proliferation of scholarly works on media, as varied as comic books and video games, illustrates that alternate narrative schemes exist and should be interpreted and assessed with an appreciation of medium specificity. Henry Jenkins (2004) mentions that video games, for example, do not have "badly constructed stories"; they just "respond to alternative aesthetic principles" more than a literary narrative (124). Identifying the features of each medium's narrative would be the first step in effective evaluation.

Jared Gardner (2011) posits that it is rather surprising that a general narrative theory did not disappear since there are such "profound differences" between literary and cinematic narratives (53). The universality of narrative and its components are a primary reason for the approach's endurance. Chatman (1980) explains: "One of the most important observations to come out of narratology is that narrative itself is a deep structure quite independent of its medium" (121). One of the defining features of narrative texts is precisely "the translatability of a given narrative from one medium to another" (122). Thus, while it is important to find a "genre's specificity," locating distinctive qualities should not keep one from "recognizing relevant commonalities" (Jahn 2001, 674). Part of narratology is finding the "core concepts that could be translated across media and forms and that all narratives would have in common" (Cobley 2005). "The Little Mermaid" story has been narrated through literary text, painting, oral telling, cinema, theater performance, musical, ballet, video game, and theme park attraction; the discourse and affordances vary based on medium, but it is still recognizable as "The Little Mermaid" with its protagonist and story beats. Storyworld can also be considered "medium-free" and "applicable across media," so *Harry Potter's* Hogsmeade may be identifiable in print, film, video game, or theme park land (Thon, 2016, 71). Barthes (1977) asserts that "translatability of narrative is a result of the structure of its language" and that it is important to find which elements can or cannot be translated (121). Likewise, Gordon Pradl (1984) mentions that "certain underlying narrative structures remain constant" despite the "apparently endless diversity" of discourse. He finds this useful because it helps scholars understand children's development and principles of teaching and learning. Narratology, then, is a vital way to comprehend precisely what makes narrative universal and relate to human growth and understanding. H. Porter Abbott (2012) writes that story and discourse "mediate how we view the world" (154). If this is the case, and—through narratology—story and discourse are realized, narrative theory can be an endeavor in understanding central facets of our culture.

Theme Parks as Distinct Narrative Texts

Narrative is a "universal structure that transcends media" (Ryan 2002, 581). However, as Frank Rose asserts, "Every new medium has given rise to a new form of narrative" (2). The theme park, a medium that has grown in popularity and matured in design principles over the last sixty years, has its own narrative schema. The theme park possesses characteristics that make a unique narrative medium: their dimensionality, or prevalence of space as an organizing principle; scale, or their relationship to enormous expenditure and large space characteristic; communality, being an art form that is collaboratively created for millions of visitors; brevity, with narratives both short in duration and condensed in structure; a combinatory aspect, wherein many art forms are joined in one attraction; and a reiterative nature, where attractions are reproduced and updated continually but still considered the same narrative container.

This section will draw on two of these features, dimensionality and brevity, to demonstrate the potential of a narratological perspective.

One of the primary affordances of a theme park is its presence in physical space, allowing for dimensional, sensory experiences that can contribute to immersion. Most analyses of theme parks bring up spatiality or dimensionality. While there has certainly been application of narratology to a diversity of texts, I have yet to find a narratologist's analysis of parks or attractions. Nonetheless, scholars have referred to "dimensionality" or "dimensions of narrative space" (Baikadi and Cardona-Rivera 2012; Alexander 2010), "spatial thinking" (Bal 1997), and the "use of space" or a "spatial quality" (Kukkonen 2011). Jan-Noël Thon (2016) finds the creation of *storyworlds*, or "worlds evoked by stories," to be an important part of transmedial narratology—world-building is often a concept tied to space or the "spatial structure of the storyworld" (37, 47). Ryan (2014) considers stories to have constituents of four qualities—spatial, a world/setting with characters and objects; temporal, changes caused by events; mental, agents who react to the world; and formal, closure and meaning. It is possible to have story without an explicit setting. As Abbott (2012) contends, "I fell down," is still narrating a story event (20). In Ryan's view, however, it is a necessary component of the story being conveyed, whether explicit or not; in Abbott's example, he still fell down somewhere.

Spatiality may be a less common discussion in narratology, but it is present. Abbott (2012) concurs that there has been a "neglect of space in the study of narrative," recognizing the prevalence of verbal narrative and that "narrative space" or "narrative worlds" can be built with words (160). Abbott declares that audiences desire both time and space in narrative and confirms that "world-making" is now a "defining feature of narrative"—contentions that are plainly true in theme parks (165, 173). Susan Stanford Friedman (2005) brings up the lack of space, particularly, despite Mikhail Bakhtin's *chronotope* including both space and time: "Narrative theory, however, has largely continued its privileging of narrative time over narrative space" (192). She quotes Michel de Certeau's statement that "[e]very story is a travel story—a spatial practice," as indeed narratives are composed in/listened to in space but also possess space within (195). Friedman mentions a novel, Arundhati Roy's *The God of Small Things*, in which space is used not as a background but as a crucial element—as a "space that contains time" (203). Marie-Laure Ryan, Kenneth Foote, and Maoz Azaryahu (2016) wrote the first full book on the topic, connecting narrative and space while looking at everything from maps and video games to museums and cities—though theme parks are noticeably absent. Space can function as the "environment in which narrative is physically deployed" or the "medium in which narrative is realized" (Ryan, Foote, and Azaryahu, 2016, 1). Space as narrative packaging is literally present in theme parks, where spatial elements contain temporal ones. Dark rides, for example, are spatial containers with temporal narratives within. Ryan, Foote, and Azaryahu (2016) consider narrative geography, or layers of narrative space, narratives embedded in gameworlds and maps, locative narratives, and landscape narratives—all concepts that could be successfully applied to theme parks.

While theme park attractions can be visual and auditory, they will always have the component of space. This kind of spatial storytelling is meant to—as concept designer, Don Carson (2000), describes it—"tell a story through the experience of traveling through a real or imagined physical space." He continues, "the story is infused into physical space" and "designers can place story elements throughout their environments." This statement returns us to the concept of environmental storytelling—or stories told through aspects of the environment—which in theme parks can be sets, props, lighting, effects, sound, color, texture, etc. Jenkins (2004), in his article related to spatiality and environmental storytelling, refers to video game designers as "narrative architects," saying they "design worlds and sculpt spaces," something theme park designers do in practice (121). He finds that there are important ways environmental storytelling creates immersion, including by evoking "pre-existing narrative associations," staging narratives, "embed[ding] narrative information" in the space, and allowing for "emergent narratives" (123). The idea in his piece is that space should be a third feature studied in video games besides game and story. While a video game may exist without meaningful interaction with space, the storyworld may not matter much to the "gameplay experience" (Thon, 2016, 105), and stories can be told through primarily filmic techniques, like cut scenes. An absence of environment is simply not possible with theme park attractions. To experience an attraction, the visitor will move, walk, or ride. While, in some cases, stories are told through filmic or theater presentations, other attractions are narrated only by the environment.

Paul Graham Raven and Shirin Elahi (2015) examine the concept of scenarios and design in science fiction narratives and admit that it is hard for some to "make the imaginative leap and assume that design can tell stories" (53). They quote Bruce Sterling, who speaks of fiction as design rather than narrative because it "tells worlds rather than stories" (53). A similar criticism might be brought up with theme parks, and Deborah Philips (1999) argues that "stories are imposed upon the space . . . rather than intrinsic to it" (94). Many designers, on the other hand, would disagree, as they see all features of space as narrative devices, even lighting, signage, or ride vehicles. Design legend John Hench (2003) defined themed environments as "places designed so that every element contributes to telling a story" (1). He referred to making "space" into "story place" and mentioned that "[e]very aspect of the physical environment is a potential opportunity for storytelling" (69, 49). Jenkins (2010) states of Universal's Wizarding World of Harry Potter that "[t]he park is structured around places and not events," which—if referencing narratological principles—would signal a major alteration in narrative norms. In addition, Scott Lukas (2013) defines a "design story" as one that is "produced through forms of spatial design" (53). He breaks down variances between these and traditional narrative, illustrating that environmental storytelling or design stories are intrinsic to this medium and that "telling worlds" is indeed a way of telling stories.

What might be seen as a limitation in theme parks, narrative brevity, is similarly discerned through narratology. Narratologists look at "story time" and "discourse time"—also called "double time structuring"—to tag the duration of the original events versus the time it takes to communicate the story (Chatman 1980, 122). For instance, the events in a story might encompass years; whereas, the film might cover them in a couple of hours. A theme park attraction might cover them in a few minutes. Nearly all theme park rides are under twenty minutes, and many are under five. Within those minutes, a scene may be exceedingly brief. Sculptor Blaine Gibson notes that a designer is only given a "few seconds" to communicate meaning (Prosperi 2016, xiv). The theme park time crunch is necessitated by the high cost of creating experience in the physical world and by the precedent of succinctness in this kind of entertainment. There can be criticisms about this feature, including a lack of depth; a limitation on genre, with some genres harder to achieve; the difficulty of telling original stories, instead of more recognizable ones that can just be symbolized or alluded to; and the condensed nature of its plots. Parks rely on a kind of shorthand that includes utilizing familiar stories, symbols, metaphors, myths, and clichés, or reproducing only certain events within stories. An attraction may have a complete story or may be a "condensed version of a broader story," with designers hoping for existing narrative familiarity (John Wood cited in Naversen 2012).

Brevity impacts the construction of theme park narrative in other ways. Barthes (1977) mentions *cardinal functions*—or "nuclei"—in narratives that have direct impact on plot and *catalysers*—elements that are more descriptive and not necessary but transition between story events; the former cannot be removed without "altering the story" and the latter without "altering the discourse" (95). In the case of a theme park attraction, both types of elements may be removed. Entire story fundamentals—such as the villain's death—may be left out and catalysers may be removed, though setting is generally seen visibly, even if not discussed by a narrator. Barthes extends this idea to make a distinction between two classes of narrative based on whether they preference functions or indices—*functional* narratives accentuate action and *indicial* narratives preference description (93). These types of narrative are not consistent within theme parks, as an attraction can be primarily functional—like Disney's Splash Mountain, with key plot points in most every scene—or nearly totally indicial—like the original example of the Na'vi River Journey, communicating environment but no apparent plot. Indices are, however, still found in three dimensions between attractions by way of area development—the spaces between attractions within themed lands—or sometimes between scenes with environmental transitions.

Through application of narrative theory, other intricacies of theme park narratives can be discovered. Narratives might be found in park marketing, company brands, employee culture, merchandise, and guest memories of experience that have been narrativized, but the main area of investigation is the set of narratives visitors actually travel to the parks for—their *attractions*—which is the term used for a variety of experiences including rides, shows, parades, films, walkthroughs, etc. Parks also often have a backstory in addition to front stories, and they act as a container for dozens of narratives. It is easier to perform narrative analysis on specific attractions, and there are dozens of narrative types located in park attractions. There can be attractions with live narrators, animatronic narrators, or no explicit narration. Several are combinations like Magic Kingdom's Happily Ever After show, with narration, song lyrics, and stories depicted via projection mapped images—some of which make up a thematic narrative and others that contribute to montages. Attractions can have explicit storytelling through verbal or written means, like Universal's High in the Sky Seuss Trolley Train Ride, or implicit storytelling through environmental design, like Disney's Haunted Mansion, while others are solely interpretive, where the designer intends for riders to interpret the narrative on their own terms, like Efteling's Droomvlucht or Dreamflight, which is totally devoid of language or an intended implicit meaning. Mystic Manor introduces loveable characters in Lord Mystic and Albert the Monkey before the guest accompanies Albert through a clearly understood plot about a magic music box he should not have opened. Conversely, something like Mad Tea Party, a simple, flat ride, represents Disney's *Alice in Wonderland* film, providing no clear narrative, though it can stimulate memory with its stylized vehicles or the playing of the movie's music. Some designers would argue that even this experience will create a story—the one of enjoying that particular attraction with others—but, as noted, narratology is more easily deployed when considering purposely authored narratives.

A few attractions are very much based in the environmental storytelling genre often seen in theme parks, like Efteling's Spookslot, a kind of tone poem of the symphonic piece "Danse Macabre" created through environmental design and animatronics, or Disney's Swiss Family Treehouse that recalls the *Swiss Family Robinson* film or book with a walkthrough attraction—exemplifying the status of space in that narrative and of motion's ability to help a narrative unfold. Universal's Poseidon's Fury or PortAventura's Templo del Fuego (or Temple of Fire) are walkthrough shows, a kind of immersive theater generally seen in theme parks. Multiple attractions are other mediums entirely, as there are movies, though sometimes combined with motion and effects; video games, again often adding movement; stage shows; and even painting—such as Songcheng's Riverside Scene at Qingming Festival, a life-sized, animated digital display that transforms the famous painting from day to night. Other attractions are extensions of mediums, including the simulator, which combines film and motion or the occasional installation that combines a virtual reality system with a roller coaster. Scholarship and the medium's history indicate that theme parks are influenced by other forms, including theater and cinema, so it is no surprise that these forms might appear within the theme park. Nevertheless, narrative types derived from theme parks have also arisen, especially with the emphasis of motion or environmental storytelling, which have occasionally been translated into other mediums, such as video games or movies.

Some attractions, such as Efteling's Fairytale Forest, Sprookjesbos, or Europa-Park's Grimm's Enchanted Forest, Märchenwald, represent a mixture of narrative techniques. Within the same space, there are stories told through architecture, static dioramas, animated scenes, short films, effects, and mixtures of these together. Multiple hybrid attractions exist as well, including Disney's Sindbad's Storybook Voyage, a dark ride and musical; Disney's *Star Wars*: Rise of the Resistance, with both walking segments and multiple ride systems; Universal's Harry Potter and the Forbidden Journey, which combines environmental storytelling and cinema; or Fantawild's The White-Snake Maiden's Fury, which starts as a dark ride in a boat and ends as a special effects stage show on solid ground. More contemporary narrative techniques are evident in theme parks as well. While many theme parks produce adaptations of existing stories, including vast narratives like *Harry Potter* or *Star Wars*, a handful of companies—Disney, Efteling, Europa-Park, Fantawild, et al.—have started to create synergistic transmedia storytelling by way of basing novels, comic books, films, and video games on narratives that began within the theme park, such as Disney's Pirates of the Caribbean or Haunted Mansion. Similarly, Disney created an interesting application of large narrative with their Society of Explorers and Adventurers, or S.E.A., an interweaving and intermedial narrative that is distributed across parks, attractions, and time periods. Though they vary in approach, theme parks are filled with narratives and often ones that are non-narrative—an expository museum space at Epcot, for example—may still be a conceit related to "being in a different place." The queue for Disney's Expedition Everest—Legend of the Forbidden Mountain is designed to be a museum with expository plaques and displayed crafts, photographs, and books. By itself, it may not be narrative, but it fits within the overall narrative of the attraction—visitors to the Himalayas encounter a Yeti who is angry at environmental destruction—acting as the exposition, complete with a fictional curator and information that, while paired with the rest of the attraction, foreshadows the denouement.

One of the unique narrative features of theme parks is the fact that many attractions include two stories, one in which there may be characters and events that can be viewed by the visitor and the other in which the visitor is given a role in a story that is traversed, or performs actions that are separate from the perceived events. Ian Kay (2013) calls this the *bi-narrative structure* of theme parks, with an *observable story*, a third-person story where events and characters are witnessed, and an *expe-*

riential story, a second-person story where the guest is the protagonist. Splash Mountain, for instance, has an observable narrative about the trickster Br'er Rabbit, recalling Disney's film *Song of the South* and the original Uncle Remus tales. It also, however, is an experience for guests as they traverse waterways, go through peaceful and meandering spaces, and face thrilling drops and water sprays. In Universal's E.T. Adventure, E.T. must get home to save his planet, but the guest accompanies and helps him by biking him there, which E.T. personally thanks the guest for at the conclusion of the ride. At Six Flags Over Georgia's Monster Mansion, there is an observable monster picnic with multiple characters, but the theme song and dialogue explain that humans are invited to partake in the festivities. The narrative is about the guest's fun and frightening experiences. Hench (2003) described a kind of multifaceted structure when talking about Peter Pan's Flight, an opening-year ride at Disneyland (1955) and one of the most influential dark rides. He designates "three-dimensional staging," where the ride is a representation of the Disney film version of *Peter Pan*, a sensory experience for guests who will fly above London from the perspective of the characters, and a symbolic depiction of the human desire to fly, with the music about flying and the ride vehicle a flying ship that is actually suspended above the show scenes (39). Show writer Adam Berger's book *Every Guest Is a Hero* (2013) argues that nearly all Disney attractions are designed to represent some portion of the hero's journey: Joseph Campbell's concept of many stories having a similar structure of answering a call to adventure, facing challenges and revelations, and returning home after being transformed. Dozens of quotes from designers speak to the idea that the guest's experience is paramount in the theme park narrative.

Though multiple scholars and designers have spoken about earlier theme park attractions as passive, the additional narrative axis or focal point of the guest's experience has been a feature from the beginning. The 1901 Luna Park (Coney Island, New York) attraction A Trip to the Moon gave the guests passports to the moon and then proceeded to give them a ride experience and a post-show on the surface of the moon. The Disneyland attraction Snow White's Scary Adventures is frequently discussed as one in which the main character, Snow White, was initially not on the ride because the *guest* was actually Snow White, surrounded by frightening trees and pursued by the Evil Queen. Entire genres of attractions exist today to give guests significant roles in the story, including interactive dark rides, such as Walibi Belgium's Challenge of

Tutankhamon, where the rider's play-score determines when the story ends; interactive quests, like Disney's A Pirate's Adventure: Treasures of the Seven Seas, where the guest's actions influence the environment; and immersive theater, like Knott's Berry Farm's Ghost Town Alive!, where guest actions generate the daily story's path and visitors can cosplay and invent their own characters. Forms of theater include a participatory element, as well—interactive or immersive theater, happenings, epic theater, etc.—but there is still a lot of dramatic theater, while the experiential mode is the standard within theme parks.

The experiential story is even more pronounced now as theme parks have embraced interaction and immersion paradigms. Rohde explains that in Pandora: The World of *Avatar*, it is not about the "plotline of the film"; instead, "the story is about you" (Harpaz 2017). The characters from that film are not present, so the primary character is the guest. Creative executive, Scott Trowbridge, echoes this notion when he discusses *Star Wars*: Galaxy's Edge, saying "[w]e decided not to build a place you knew from the movies. We wanted to create a brand-new planet . . . that is rife with opportunities for you to discover your *Star Wars* story" (Leonard and Palmeri 2017). Though there are some characters from the franchise present in this land, it is the guest who plays a primary role in the unfolding of the narrative—something seen in the rides and the *Star Wars:* Datapad app. This allows visitors to complete actions like hack into systems for the Resistance. If earlier immersive spaces were about the guest visiting other worlds or other people's stories, the newer ones are about the guest's specific experiences and making their own stories. The perspective in narratives is often that of the narrator or a particular character, but in these newer cases, it is the audience itself, really allowing Genette's (1980) terming of the audience as "protagonist" to materialize. Instead of only viewing the stories of other characters, the guest is the main character in some narratives. As in hyperfiction or video games, external creators still construct the storyworlds and story beats, but today's guests have more influence within the narrative. Many attractions still contain a bi-narrative structure, but some recent attractions have particularly emphasized the experiential story of the guests, including the ride mentioned at the beginning of this chapter, Na'vi River Journey. That ride is intended to be *your* journey down the Na'vi river, where *you* will explore the landscape, experience emotions, and witness the shaman's song. Of course, it bears everywhere the mark of the designers who shaped the world, but the primary narrative perspective is that of the rider. Like other fixed narratives, though, it will be the same narrative, if not the same perspective, each time. If there is a primary affordance of theme park narratives, then, it is the primacy of the audience perspective in the enactment of narrative space.

BENEFITS OF NARRATOLOGICAL ANALYSIS

Considering the complexity in presentation and inconsistency in narrative types and techniques, in-depth study of theme parks and attractions is encouraged for transmedial narratologists. The multi-sensory and spatio-temporal character of theme parks ensures that inquiry will be complex and exercise the full capabilities of transmedial narratology. Thon (2016) states that the field can be expanded to "further illuminate the forms and functions of narrative representation across media," and the additional medium of theme parks would assist with that task (327). Similarly, the development of a "geographical narratology" would strongly benefit from close analysis of theme parks. Thon, Foote, and Azaryahu argue that "[t]he space of the storyworld has inspired the most extensive narratological activity, yet many of its domains remain unexplored or underexplored" (208). Spatial narrative is inextricable from theme parks, so it is a natural application of geographical transmedial narratology. The evolving field can also profit from a medium that represents where art is going—a convergence of disciplines and modes inching towards a synthesis of the arts. Theme parks consistently grapple with concepts of interactivity, immersion, transmedia, and convergence, so investigating them might lend insight into those topics, especially when compared with other mediums.

There are obvious ways in which narrative theory contributes to the study of theme parks. Through narratology, it is clear that theme parks are a narrative medium with identifiable affordances and limitations. The variety of narrative types and techniques is easier to locate when analyzing for structure. My research has found that designers, scholars, and fans do not always mean the same thing when they say "story," "storytelling," or "narrative." For instance, those who did not believe Na'vi River Journey was a story or storytelling probably meant it lacks the obvious plots or conflicts normally presented in Western dramatic structure. Narratology allows groups that interpret theme parks to establish consistent definitions for this terminology; as noted, there are debates about whether theme parks should tell stories, how they should tell stories, how much narrative should be emphasized, whether experiential orientations should be elevated above observational storytelling, and whether narrative should be explicit, implicit, or interpretive. A narratological approach can assist with clarifying these debates.

I have examined hundreds of attractions by searching for basic narrative features. The results proved that storytelling is pervasive in theme parks. Patterns emerged by analyzing the data, and more of these kinds of studies can help us identify prominent genres and narrative structures. They can solidify the theme park as a distinct medium, an emerging narrative form, and a meaningful endeavor. This method would also remove some of the value judgments associated with theme park texts, something scholars of comic books or video games have mentioned as well. If only determining the dominant narrative structures within parks, one may find there are no "great, or beautiful, or profound, or trivial narratives . . . there are only narratives" (Prince 1980, 50). Those structures demonstrate a theme park attraction's narrativity, and interpretation can spring from that. Interpretations can move beyond the most common ones seen in scholarship—primarily postmodern scrutiny, cultural studies, or Marxist readings—that tend to focus on ideology, and generally on Disney, and less on concrete narrative structures that form patterns throughout the global industry. Additionally, if there are differences within companies or world regions, these patterns can be discerned. While my research contributes to this work, theme parks have a sixty-plus year head start. There is fertile ground. Context should not be ignored, but narratological analysis can help with establishing a foundation that can then be read alongside the perspectives of the designers and the societal and company cultures that shaped those views. Codifying narrative practices and then combining them with an understanding of creative and social contexts will allow a deep understanding of this multi-layered art form. Discovery of medium features and narrative structures will likewise situate the art form into academic discourse, solidifying its existence as a medium worthy of scholarship.

There are reasons why narrative theory is a valuable approach for current media beyond theme parks. Gerald Prince (1990) finds that some scholars prefer to study story and some discourse, with another interesting area being the notion that the narrative universe is composed of "one or more worlds"—actual worlds, knowledge-worlds, moral-worlds, alternative worlds, etc. (273). Bal (1990) notes that ideology and societal practices may be made visible through structural analysis. She argues that narratology has relevance to multiple fields, that the approach has range and versatility, and that it can help a scholar position a text within history after detailed analysis. While she recognizes some of the areas where the field faltered, Bal (1990) makes a salient point that there should not be a denial of the "importance of the *questions*—rather than the answers—of narratology" (729). How are narratives structured in various mediums? Which structures are universal and which ones relate to specific media? How does structure shape perception? How are certain structures received by audiences? Though Prince (1980) reminds us that structural analysis cannot find the purpose of a narrative, which depends on context and audience interpretation, it can still identify structures common to all media forms and organize ideas in a way that can lead to locating purpose (63). There are numerous questions that narratology might elicit that can profoundly affect our understanding of texts. The application itself lends to classification and systematic readings, which can then be paired with other theories. The answers to the questions are thus of import; discovering patterns in narrative expressions and exposing narrative logic can help articulate how texts create meaning. Perhaps the most obvious reason narrative theory is valuable is that it theorizes and analyzes narrative—one of the most central aspects of being human. Throughout the course of my research, I have discovered hundreds of quotes about the importance of storytelling in culture. If narrative is one of the "commonest ways of applying an order and perspective to experience" (Onega and Landa 2014), and narratology applies order and perspective to narrative, it merits consideration (4).

A Google search for "death of the humanities" turns up dozens of articles, but part of the assumption of a humanities demise may be a lack of understanding of significant questions and practices found in the area or the presence of contemporary, interdisciplinary approaches like new media studies or game studies. The very real issues facing humanities disciplines may be exacerbated with stereotypes that archaic theories are deployed or that contemporary texts are not interrogated. Likewise, some forecasted the "death of narratology" as well, but the contextualist and transmedial branches of narrative theory suggest currency and validity (Fludernik 2005, 36). There have been reasonable criticisms of narrative theory, but as with the humanities, this field continues to evolve with a shifting comprehension of narrative texts. It is advantageous to investigate the texts of the era, and changes in society can, likewise, be traced through this examination. For instance, spatial texts can be recognized as a category of texts in addition to oral, literary, and digital forms, with the theme park an exemplar of the spatial form.

When the 2018 *Global Attractions Attendance Report* was released, it revealed that for the first time in a single year, more than a half billion guests visited sites owned by the top ten theme park companies (Rubin, 2019). Visitation is expected to increase after the pandemic and as the industry gets more competitive and expands within emerging markets. Though rarely discussed in the same articles as other art forms, one cannot doubt the intense popularity of this entertainment form—and this chapter only dealt with theme parks, not the other forms of themed entertainment. Hench (2003) found in theme park attractions "meaningful experiences" and believed it a form of entertainment that allows people to "transcend their everyday experience" (38, 9). This statement places the medium with other great created worlds that carry meaning and memory. The ways theme parks create meaning, and their reception or interpretation, can be vital to knowing where we have come from and where we are going. The study of theme parks can benefit from the application of narrative theory, and narratology can be enriched with the fascinating texts that are theme park attractions; the subject and praxis are mutually beneficial. Both are in some ways marginalized by a number of critics, and both find routes to update our conceptions of "text" in the humanities.

References

Abbott, H. Porter. 2012. *The Cambridge Introduction to Narrative.* Cambridge, UK: Cambridge University Press.

Alexander, Neal. 2010. *Ciaran Carson: Space, Place, Writing.* Liverpool, UK: Liverpool University Press.

Baikadi, Alok, and Rogelio Cardona-Rivera. 2012. "Towards Finding the Fundamental Unit of Narrative: A Proposal for the Narreme." *Workshop on Computational Models of Narrative*, 44–46. Raleigh, NC: North Carolina State University.

Bal, Mieke. 1990. "The Point of Narratology." *Poetics Today* 11, no. 4 (Winter): 727–53. Durham, NC: Duke University Press

Bal, Mieke. 1997. *Narratology.* Toronto, CA: University of Toronto Press.

Barthes, Roland. 1977. *Image Music Text.* Translated by Stephen Heath. London, UK: Fontana Press.

Berger, Adam. 2013. *Every Guest is a Hero: Disney's Theme Parks and the Magic of Mythic Storytelling.* 1st ed. Orlando, FL: BCA Press.

Bishop, Bryan. 2017. "Disney's Most Advanced Animatronic Ever is the Highlight of the Avatar River Ride." *The Verge*, May 29, 2017. www.theverge.com/2017/5/29/15702592/pandora-world-of-avatar-navi-river-journey-ride-review.

Carson, Don. 2000. "Environmental Storytelling: Creating Immersive 3D Worlds Using Lessons Learned from the Theme Park Industry." *Gamasutra*, March 1, 2000. www.gamasutra.com/view/feature/131594/environmental_storytelling_.php.

Chatman, Seymour. 1975. "Towards a Theory of Narrative." *New Literary History* 6 (2): 295–318. Baltimore, MD: The Johns Hopkins University Press.

Chatman, Seymour. 1980. "What Novels Can Do That Films Can't (And Vice Versa)." *Critical Inquiry* 7 (1): 121–40. Chicago, IL: The University of Chicago Press.

Chihaia, Matei. 2012. "Introduction to Narratology: Theory, Practice, and the Afterlife of Structuralism." *DIEGESIS: Interdisciplinary E-Journal for Narrative Research* 1 (1): 15–31. N.p.

Cobley, Paul. 2005. "Narratology." In *The Johns Hopkins Guide to Literary Theory & Criticism*, edited by Michael Groden, Martin Kreiswith, and Imre Szeman. Baltimore, MD: The Johns Hopkins University Press.

Fludernik, Monika. 2005. "Histories of Narrative Theory (II): From Structuralism to the Present." In *A Companion to Narrative Theory*, edited by James Phelan and Peter Rabinowitz, 36–59. Malden, MA: Blackwell Publishing.

Fludernik, Monika. 2010. "Narratology in the Twenty-First Century: The Cognitive Approach to Narrative." *PMLA* 125 (4): 924–30. Cambridge, UK: Cambridge University Press.

Friedman, Susan Stanford. 2005. "Spatial Poetics and Arundhati Roy's *The God of Small Things*." In *A Companion to Narrative Theory*, edited by James Phelan and Peter Rabinowitz, 192–205. Malden, MA: Blackwell Publishing.

Frommer, Paul. 2017. "Way Tiretuä—The Shaman's Song." *Na'viteri*, July 1, 2017. naviteri.org/2017/07/way-tiretua-the-shamans-song/.

Gardner, Jared. 2011. "Storylines." *SubStance* 40 (1): 53–69. Baltimore, MD: The Johns Hopkins University Press.

Gardner, Jared and David Herman. 2011. "Graphic Narratives and Narrative Theory: Introduction." *SubStance* 40 (1): 3–13. Baltimore, MD: The Johns Hopkins University Press.

Genette, Gérard. 1980. *Narrative Discourse: An Essay in Method*. Translated by Jane Lewin. Ithaca, NY: Cornell University Press.

Harpaz, Beth. 2017. "Disney Parks Offer Bold New Attractions." *Honolulu Star Advertiser*, April 21, 2017. www.staradvertiser.com/2017/04/21/travel/globe-trotting/disney-parks-offer-bold-new-attractions/.

Hench, John. 2003. *Designing Disney: Imagineering and the Art of the Show*. New York, NY: Disney Editions.

Herman, David. 2011. "Storyworld/Umwelt: Nonhuman Experiences in Graphic Narratives." *SubStance* 40 (1): 156–81. Baltimore, MD: The Johns Hopkins University Press.

Jahn, Manfred. 2001. "Narrative Voice and Agency in Drama: Aspects of Narratology in Drama." *New Literary History* 32 (3): 659–79. Baltimore, MD: The Johns Hopkins University Press.

Jahn, Manfred. 2017. *Narratology: A Guide to the Theory of Narrative.* Cologne, DE: University of Cologne.

Jenkins, Henry. 2004. "Game Design as Narrative Architecture." In *First Person: New Media as Story, Performance, and Game*, edited by Noah Wardrip-Fruin and Pat Harrigan, 118–29. Cambridge, MA: The MIT Press.

Jenkins, Henry. 2010. "The Night of a Thousand Wizards." *Confessions of an Aca-Fan*, July 21, 2010. henryjenkins.org/blog/2010/07/fear_and_loathing_in_hogworts.html.

Kay, Ian. 2013. "Bi-Narrative Structure." *Pure Imagineering: Theme Park Narratology*, September 17, 2013. pureimagineering.blogspot.com/2013/09/experiential-and-presentational-stories.html.

Kukkonen, Karin. 2011. "Comics as a Test Case for Transmedial Narratology." *SubStance* 40 (1): 34–52. Baltimore, MD: The Johns Hopkins University Press.

Leonard, Devin and Christopher Palmeri. 2017. "Disney's Intergalactic Theme Park Quest to Beat Harry Potter." *Bloomberg Businessweek*, April 19, 2017. www.bloomberg.com/news/features/2017-04-19/disney-s-intergalactic-theme-park-quest-to-beat-harry-potter.

Lukas, Scott. 2013. *The Immersive Worlds Handbook.* Waltham, MA: Focal Press.

Martens, Todd. 2017. "A Visit to Pandora—What We Learned." *Los Angeles Times*, May 2, 2017. www.latimes.com/entertainment/herocomplex/la-et-hc-disney-pandora-avatar-20170502-htmlstory.html.

Martiniere, Stephan. 2018. "The World of Avatar: Designing the Na-Vi River Journey Boat Ride." *Muddy Colors*, March 26, 2018. www.muddycolors.com/2018/03/the-disney-world-of-avatar-designing-the-na-vi-river-journey-boat-ride/.

Mikkonen, Kai. 2011. "Graphic Narratives as a Challenge to Transmedial Narratology: The Question of Focalization." *Amerikastudien/American Studies* 56 (4): 637–52. Heidelberg, DE: Universitätsverlag Winter Gmbh.

Mittell, Jason. 2007. "Film and Television Narrative." In *The Cambridge Companion to Narrative*, edited by David Herman, 156–71. Cambridge, UK: Cambridge University Press.

Murray, Janet. 1998. *Hamlet on the Holodeck: The Future of Narrative in Cyberspace.* New York, NY: Free Press.

Naversen, Nate. 2012. "Dark Ride Inventor John Wood." *Themed Attraction*, April 20, 2012. www.themedattraction.com/dark-ride-inventor-john-wood/.
Onega, Susana and Joel Angel Garcia Landa. 2014. *Narratology: An Introduction*. Abingdon, UK: Routledge.
Philips, Deborah. 1999. "Narrativised Spaces: The Functions of Story in the Theme Park." In *Leisure/Tourism Geographies: Practices and Geographical Knowledge*, edited by David Crouch, 92–108. Abingdon, UK: Routledge.
Pradl, Gordon. 1984. "Narratology: The Study of Story Structure." *ERIC Digest*. Urbana, IL: ERIC Digest.
Prince, Gerald. 1980. "Aspects of a Grammar of Narrative." *Poetics Today* 1, no. 3 (Spring): 49–63. Durham, NC: Duke University Press.
Prince, Gerald. 1982. "Narrative Analysis and Narratology." *New Literary History* 13, no. 2 (Winter): 179–88. Baltimore, MD: The Johns Hopkins University Press.
Prince, Gerald. 1990. "On Narrative Studies and Narrative Genres." *Poetics Today* 11, no. 2 (Summer): 271–82. Durham, NC: Duke University Press.
Prosperi, Louis. 2016. *The Imagineering Pyramid: Using Disney Theme Park Design Principles to Develop and Promote Your Creative Ideas*. Theme Park Press.
Raven, Paul Graham and Shirin Elahi. 2015. "The New Narrative: Applying Narratology to the Shaping of Future Outputs." *Futures* 74: 49–61. N.p.
Rose, Frank. 2012. *The Art of Immersion: How the Digital Generation is Remaking Hollywood, Madison Avenue, and the Way We Tell Stories*. New York, NY: W. W. Norton & Company.
Ryan, Marie-Laure. 2002. "Beyond Myth and Metaphor: Narrative in Digital Media." *Poetics Today* 23 (4): 581–609. Durham, NC: Duke University Press.
Ryan, Marie-Laure. 2014. "Narration in Various Media." *The Living Handbook of Narratology*, edited by Peter Hühn et al. www.lhn.uni-hamburg.de/node/53.html.
Ryan, Marie-Laure, Kenneth Foote, and Maoz Azaryahu. 2016. *Narrating Space/Spatializing Narrative: Where Narrative Theory and Geography Meet*. Columbus, OH: The Ohio State University Press.
Sjöholm, Cecilia. 2013. "Lessing's Laocoon: Aesthetics, Affects and Embodiment." *The Nordic Journal of Aesthetics* 46: 18–33. N.p.
Rubin, Judith, ed. 2019. *TEA/AECOM Theme Index and Museum Index: The Global Attractions Attendance Report 2018*. TEA/AECOM.
Thon, Jan-Noël. 2016. *Transmedial Narratology and Contemporary Media Culture*. Lincoln, NE: University of Nebraska Press.
Wolf, Werner. 2003. "Narrative and Narrativity: A Narratological Reconceptualization and Its Applicability to Visual Arts." *Word & Image* 19 (3): 180–97. N.p.

5 Not Quite Virtual: Technē between Text and World

Erik Champion

INTRODUCTION

My area is virtual heritage, which is not often mentioned in the same breath as text. Simply put, virtual heritage is the meeting of virtual reality and cultural heritage. In reality, most projects have been desktop-based, 3D, virtual environments, but more and more researchers have been exploring games and game-like environments, phone-based applications, augmented reality especially, and a growing but still surprisingly few have explored mixed reality (Bekele et al. 2018).

In line with the experimental intentions of this book, I have aimed for practical, conceptual, and critical experiments tied to infrastructure. In other words, I have aimed for modular and reconfigurable infrastructure-friendly projects—a scalable tinkering, if you will. An increasing part of my work also searches for metrics that return useful values of impact and engagement—for heritage is driven by a need to communicate why sites, artifacts, and value systems are significant and worth preserving, despite their toll on our attention and resources.

I suggest this field is a great example of why there is untapped potential for digital humanities research and education to investigate more thoroughly and imaginatively areas of visualization; collaboration; prototyping with pseudocode, if possible, and simple scripts; the development of team-based employable skills; the play between control and interaction; and the increasing importance of community engagement and impact via scholarly projects; but also increasing risks, such as erosion of personal control, expression, and privacy. A further issue, seldom discussed, is the environmental damage of sophisticated, high-performance hardware and ever-increasing internet bandwidths. Cloud computing servers and data centers are still often powered by fossil fuels (Deng et al. 2014).

3D Digital Humanities: Inside the Tent, but Nowhere Near the Marshmallows

Obviously, unlike some of the authors in this book, I do not research text-focused projects but virtual environments and related interaction technology—particularly, digital cultural heritage and more specifically, virtual heritage—issues. I see virtual heritage as a subset of humanities, not, primarily, as a subset of computing. Despite the increasing convenience of AR and VR devices—and even if we considered code as hidden but magical text—text experienced in virtual worlds is a problem; the brain has trouble solving navigation tasks spatially while reading text simultaneously. Virtual worlds also typically lack a rich and involving sense of embodiment or preservation techniques for both the content and the software, and they are still not integral components of scholarly impact and engagement (Jacobson et al. 2010).

Text can communicate a great range and variety of messages, adding to the richness of the digital landscape. So, there are indeed reasons for a lack of description of text-based components of virtual worlds. Meanwhile, text-based research and training in digital humanities has a long and prominent history. An obvious example is the development of The Text Encoding Initiative, TEI, seen by many as a crowning achievement, and it may well have led to the first conferences explicitly putting up the major tent poles of the digital humanities tent.

With any academic field, there is continual jostling over which discipline or sub-discipline is relevant and central or archaic and peripheral. In digital humanities, at least until the mid-2010s, I suggest the text-based disciplines have had a strong influence over determining what is or is not digital humanities and which fields have added most to its importance and potential.

In the chapter "The History of Humanities Computing," within *A Companion to Digital Humanities,* Susan Hockey has emphasized the importance of text-based digital humanities, based on the conferences she argues have been most prominent or important in digital humanities:

> Applications involving textual sources have taken center stage within the development of humanities computing as defined by its major publications and thus it is inevitable that this essay

> concentrates on this area. Nor is it the place here to attempt to define 'interdisciplinarity,' but by its very nature, humanities computing has had to embrace 'the two cultures,' to bring the rigor and systematic unambiguous procedural methodologies characteristic of the sciences to address problems within the humanities that had hitherto been most often treated in a serendipitous fashion. (2004, 3)

According to Hockey, digital humanities became interested in multimedia in the 1990s. She claimed, "an additional dimension was added to humanities electronic resources in the early 1990s, when it became possible to provide multimedia information in the form of images, audio, and video" (Hockey 2004, 15). I respectfully disagree. Multimedia was a part of digital humanities before the 1990s. For instance, 3D was a central ingredient in designing the Sydney Opera House around 1961. Croker noted the following:

> The analysis demanded a precise, computer-generated mathematical description of the geometrical form of the shells in order to undertake more precise calculations of stresses, forces, bending moments and deflections. The Sydney Opera House was one of the first buildings in the world to make use of computers in its construction process. (2017, 26)

Here, we enter an impasse: is humanities the scholarly research and development of the arts but not the arts itself? Or is digital humanities a field about creativity and innovation but not developed directly with creativity or innovation? Perhaps the humanities should ignore the awkward fact that music, arts, design, and architecture are often part of humanities faculties—the last three are certainly in schools in my faculty of humanities. Perhaps the humanities is only the discussion and analysis of these creative fields, or perhaps it is simply easiest to ignore their conferences and argue the emphasis on digital humanities has or will be text-based?

I do not agree that the humanities is only the discussion and analysis of creative fields. My first encounter with VR and humanities was 1990. My first attempt at digital humanities in 3D was in the late 1980s—I was coding simple games on a non-graphical pocket computer around 1982—developing memorials of classical art and art history in 3D multimedia and CAD packages during my architectural undergraduate degree. As part of my master's work, I used 3D CAD to develop stage blocking visualizations for theater around 1991 or 1992, and I was not one of the pioneers.

I know there were leading multimedia projects in the late 1980s, virtual and augmented reality in the 1960s, and panoramic multi-screen cinema prior to World War II. Unfortunately, digital humanities does not consider architecture or archaeology—or even music—as part of the humanities and typically forgets art history when it is convenient. For example, Edward Vanhoutte recounted how, in 1842, Italian mathematician, Luigi Federico Menabrea (1809–1896), published *Notions sur la machine analytique de Charles Babbage*, outlining the potential of the Analytical Engine. This was translated by Ada Lovelace, who, in 1843, penned an idea for how a computer could be used to create music (Vanhoutte 2013).

My main point is not a grumbling to-do with who invented what first (Dalbello 2011), but to point out that if scholars only look at one field but then extrapolate from that to speak to a huge, rambling area of investigation, not only are many fields likely to be overlooked but the challenges arising between fields and solutions possible through interdisciplinary collaboration are likely to be overlooked. Students who might relish these rich interstitial avenues for exploration and collaboration may never know about them.

And it is significant here that Hockey, herself, noted that Father Busa, the first recipient of the Busa award for "recognition of outstanding achievements in the application of information technology to humanistic research" in his 1998 acceptance speech (Hockey 2004, 4) "reflected on the potential of the World Wide Web to deliver multimedia scholarly material accompanied by sophisticated analysis tools (Busa 1999)."

Why would Father Busa see the potential of multimedia? The literature of the church was multimedia and multimodal (Manzolli 2016), illustration and calligraphy entwining with narrative. The church itself was a combination of art, sculpture, and architecture. Indeed, you could call some early church masterpieces, like Chartres Cathedral, also spatial narratives (Stec and Sweetser 2013; Meyers 1999). For many centuries, humanities reached out to people who could not read text directly.

As for Vanhoutte, he argued this:

> For the moment, we know that Digital Humanities tries to model the world around us through success and failure in order to arrive at a better understanding of what we know and don't

> know about humankind, their activities, [artifacts], and record. And this can maybe serve as a definition of the field. (2013, 147)

If digital humanities can be seen more as a project than as a field, then understanding current gaps, misunderstandings, or conflations may be of use in our application of technology. In this vein, I propose exploring how text and media can work together in more engaging and innovative ways in virtual worlds.

I have already published an open-access journal article on the broader topic, "Digital Humanities Is Text Heavy, Visualization Light, and Simulation Poor." (Champion 2016, 2). In that article, although I criticized formal digital humanities conferences and publications for accidental, or even inevitable, focus on text without other forms of media, I was really arguing for a closer relationship between text and media. I argued: that there is 'not always' a clear separation between written language and images; humanists and humanistic scholars do not always have to have high levels of literacy; non-text-based media can be part of digital humanities, for it is actually part of humanities, and visualization-incorporating media can provide suitable scholarly arguments.

The above article attempted to show the connection between written language and images and reveal to us that visualization literacy is a relatively unheralded but important civic concern—because we do not know how to critically read visualizations, we take on images and visualizations far more uncritically than we should. The article also revealed that visualization is part of the humanities, and visualization can be used as a scholarly argument rather just the presentation of something.

In 2022, this paper reads to me less as a criticism and more as a call for a better understanding of virtual worlds and their relationship to the digital humanities. An investigation into developing, teaching, and researching virtual worlds in digital humanities suggests we also need to examine or develop experimental methods and experiential exemplars because that is how we experiment with experience and recall the real world. My task here will be to convey to you why these experiential and experimental forays could be of importance to scholars in the digital humanities, but first we should consider whether the relative paucity of relevant digital humanities-derived theory supporting non-text-based projects may have affected their coverage and hampered their popularity.

Electric Text, Reading, and Digital Humanities

Perhaps the apparent low profile of non-text-based media in digital humanities is due to a lack of theory related to the unique aspects of digital media? There is, for example, Gregory Ulmer's theory of electracy. Ulmer (undated, 1989) explained it in the following way:

> What literacy is to the analytical mind, electracy is to the affective body: a prosthesis that enhances and augments a natural or organic human potential. Alphabetic writing is an artificial memory that supports long complex chains of reasoning impossible to sustain within the organic mind. Digital imaging similarly supports extensive complexes of mood atmospheres beyond organic capacity. Electrate logic proposes to design these atmospheres into affective group intelligence. Literacy and electracy in collaboration produce a civilizational left-brain right-brain integration. If literacy focused on universally valid methodologies of knowledge (sciences), electracy focuses on the individual state of mind within which knowing takes place (arts).

I understand Ulmer introduced *electracy* in *Teletheory* (1989), and although some seem to have valued this theory (Brunette and Wills 1993), I, like others, wonder if it relies on shaky scientific foundations. I have not found this theory as easy to apply as Ulmer apparently has. I would also agree with critics that it seems to take the medium or media for granted (Keenan 1995). That said, the way in which Ulmer leveraged his writing to encourage his students to develop, build, and prototype, I am in complete agreement with. One aspect of digital media so obvious that we often overlook it is how richly, expressively, and quickly a skilled student can prototype, mockup, and experiment with new, potential interfaces and interactive systems.

Another pedagogical theory I am more acquainted with—but even more wary of—is the concept of "digital natives," proposed by Marc Prensky. I agree with Jessica Frawley that "[i]t is too easy to stereotype students and assume that familiarity with one kind of technology meant mastery over many," and as a term, I also prefer digital fluency over digital literacy (Bartlett and Miller 2011; Miller and Bartlett 2012).

Technology is not neutral, but it is also not necessarily a tool or process; it is, rather, an art of making. Tabachnick noted (2004):

> Generally, the ancient Greek word "techne" is translated as "craft" or "art" but also "knowledge." Of these definitions, "knowledge" seems best. "Craft" places emphasis on the finished product of an artisan or craftsman where techne really implies the knowledge by which those products were created . . . Where episteme may be "knowledge for the sake of knowledge," techne is instrumental or oriented towards the deliberate production of something.

Here, I am retracing definitions that inspired philosopher Martin Heidegger—but not his ethical system. Heidegger wrote before the age of digital worlds, but his notion of world and the work of art bridge, for me, the gap between work and masterpiece and between text and world. Heidegger explained how new temples and new artistic masterpieces were portals between the past and the present. They captured the spirit of the past and the fading present, while invoking a sense of the new, beyond the freshness of the building itself. Heidegger stated (1975, 44–45) that "[t]owering up within itself, the work opens up a world and keeps it abidingly in force. . . . The *world worlds*, and is more fully in being than the tangible and perceptual realm in which we believe ourselves to be at home." Quite possibly, I am the only one who still sees this quotation as inspirational. For a team grant application to develop virtual reality models of early modernist world exhibition pavilions, I suggested we should rebuild virtually what was there, but also try to capture and evoke how fresh and new these world fair and architectural exhibition buildings would seem to the open-eyed and expectant public of that time. Not only did the others not seem to follow what I meant, I was also not sure how I could achieve the "shock of the new" in VR with the newness of what was the future to past audiences. For what was shocking and revolutionary then, most likely would appear as familiar and conventional to us today.

For instance, when we climb around the hill of Athens' Acropolis, catching glimpses of the temple, we are drawn to the very first clearing where we can view the temple above us. That clearing allows us to grab our breath, take in the angled relationships of the various buildings, finally understand the undulating path the ancient Greeks forced us to undertake, and enjoy our breaking out into the sun in front of the Acropolis as it sits bathed in the attention of the surrounding city below and far away. Unlike that clearing, these moments, these clearings, are few and far between. Most of our lives are mundane; we are seldom jolted into noticing what takes place around us and how it affects us profoundly. Akin to this typical state of forgetting, Heidegger (1977) defined a term, "standing-in-reserve," akin to a blunt and numbing instrumentality. This is a concept that also neatly describes our inattention to the outside world during our persistent use of digital devices and our mindless dependence on them.

Now I have moved from historical, even ancient, architecture to Heidegger's concern about modern technology. This seems far from the domain of text and text in the digital humanities. What links these two domains, architectural masterpieces and text? Not much, one could say, but deeper than the subject of text is the medium of reading—deep and involved reading. Great architecture compels us to experience it and the world anew, and great works of literature also compel us to immerse ourselves, imaginatively, even physically, into a world of suggestion. With reading appears a reaffirming sense of embodiment and expression. I do not get that connotation when I hear people talk about text in digital humanities. The experience of reading is lost, and text becomes what can be quantified and summarized for other mediums, word clouds, graphs, and scatterplots.

Architecture, archaeology, and geographic information systems, GIS, (Gillings 2002) have become so estranged as disciplines from the "traditional" humanities that the research questions and research potential of spatial environments are no longer clearly seen as humanities endeavors, and development in virtual reality and mixed reality is so technical and equipmental that it is too difficult for many humanities scholars to explore these immersive visualization fields for themselves. Perhaps some humanities scholars do not see many interesting questions that relate to humanities in virtual reality or in cultural heritage visualization.

I propose, in particular, that the terms "game," "virtual reality," and "virtual world" are concepts of direct interest to the humanities and that, indeed, humanities researchers have much to add to the exploration of these terms. I would especially like to point out that "place" is not the same as "world," and "world" is not the same as "game." In more clearly defining these terms, we may also see ways to help support local interaction *and* more global-scaled interaction—in other words, culturally and spatially immersive localization without completely severing connections to global data and networks.

What is particularly needed is more research on culturally sensitive and spatially intelligent writing interfaces; postural and body language tracking; culturally syntactical space; environmental affordances supporting the perception of culturally bounded space, while addressing insufficient 3D model infrastructure; a lack of research on shared collaboration in mixed reality and how context and content changes with group interaction; and new ways of evaluating and developing the student experience of humanities research in digitally immersive, spatial environments.

Case Studies: Conversing, Painting, and Moving in Virtual Environments

The nature and purpose of humanities is to question, assess, and adopt scientific discovery and technical invention to people and societies—to understand the role of "place" in history and culture. Hence, explorations of virtual worlds should also assess how they can pose and address humanities-related questions, not just provide simple laboratory-style tasks for a certain number of users—and the users in these user evaluations are often computer science undergraduate students, hardly representative of the general public.

For example, in 2003 and 2004, I programmed interaction in a virtual learning environment for a Japanese-English Language Learning class run by Ms. Sachiyo Sekiguchi—now at Meiji Gakuin University—at the University of Melbourne (Champion and Sekiguchi 2006). The virtual environment ran inside Adobe Atmosphere, an Internet Explorer-based 3D virtual world with a built-in chat window. The virtual Babel was a 3D virtual environment (Champion and Sekiguchi, 2006) designed for "enhancing second language (L2) learning in the modern classroom." I scripted methods for tracking conversations and key words between Japanese English-learning students and Australian Japanese-learning students.

My PhD project had also been developed in Adobe Atmosphere, and months before my PhD was submitted, Adobe Atmosphere was taken off the market after two years in beta and roughly six months in the wild as a commercial product. It was certainly not the only 3D world building and browsing tool to bite the bullet, but it included features for learning and teaching only sporadically improved upon by more recent software.

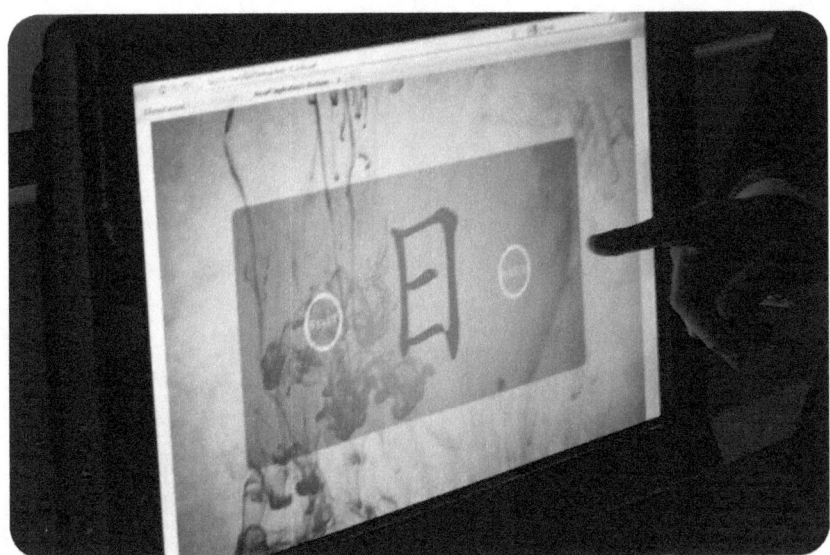

Figure 1. Taoism Touch Screen (Neil Wang, 2010–2011; Photo: Erik Champion).

In 2010 and 2011, I supervised a master's project (Figure 1) by Neil Wang on Chinese Taoism, using a finger touch-screen interface to teach participants about the four great arts of Chinese Taoism through drawing, writing, painting, and playing Go, empathetically (Wang and Champion 2011; 2012). The participant learnt about Taoism creatively and tacitly, through drawing in response to stimuli; viscerally, through finger-touch; and indirectly (e.g., not by points but by opacity of landscape paintings that appear according to the sensitive accuracy of the participant).

Virtual reality does not have to attempt to mirror reality. It could, for example, be designed to show past views or different interpretations in totally new ways (Figure 2). In 2018, I supervised a French intern, Agathe Limouzy. Agathe developed a game-like environment where two players had to learn how to coordinate a character. One player, watching a large digital monitor, wore a bandana with a Leap Motion controller monitoring her hands and relaying that information as they pointed, grasped, and so on to a character, whose legs were controlled by another player. That second player was in an HTC Vive virtual environment (an HTV VIVE is a virtual reality head mounted display). Variants of that game involved players controlling one hand and one leg each. It was fascinating watching these players learn how to work together, all the while immersed in different views of the same virtual environment.

Figure 2. Different VR equipment allows two players to control different parts of the same character (Agathe Limouzy, 2018; Photo: Erik Champion).

I believe that now, with masterpiece VR and Tilt brush (Figure 3), we have more advanced and immersively creative ways to spatially develop appreciation for different cultures. These VR-based painting interfaces can develop and export writing, 2D, and 3D digital artifacts with input from music or perhaps even from participant biofeedback. We can now potentially inscribe writing based on skill, concentration, or excitement into the digital bedrock of the virtual world. So, the interface is not the issue; I suspect the issue is marrying the potential of technology with the critical communication skills of the humanities—not only in a writing medium but also in a visual and aural medium.

Unfortunately, my chosen field is exemplified by increasingly sophisticated, unproven and expensive technology (Gillings 2002)—expensive to access, let alone preserve (Champion and Rahaman 2019)—with a decreasing emphasis on craft, art, personalization, and heritage values. Too many virtual heritage models and sites also lack scholarly appreciation or public engagement. Given these concerns, I am not convinced that we are entering an electrate age, or that, whatever age we are entering into, we are as equipped with the necessary critical and conceptual tools as we could be.

Figure 3. We can now paint and sculpt in virtual space, then export to 3D worlds (Photo: Erik Champion).

Virtual heritage projects could perhaps recapture historically-situated and contextually-appropriate inspirational senses of embodiment and expression, but I suggest they seldom do so. Virtual worlds seldom cajole us to question, and it has only recently occurred to me that they very seldom suggest how they are cared for or how to care for them. Early definitions of virtual worlds suggested they should be data-persistent—that you can revisit them days later, and they would still be there—but this negates a very important part of what it means to be a world. A world is not only a spatial expanse. It is not only a collection of roles and social values. It is also a material framework of cultural instructions to preserve values, objects, and intangibles because in the ever-changing, real world we are constantly in danger of forgetting how people view, value, and live in that world. One aspect of culture is that it continually attempts to hold onto the past, to build onto it as increasingly sophisticated and impressive foundations, but it is perpetually doomed by our distractions, forgetfulness, rivalries, and miscommunications and also by the decay, change, and regrowth of the natural world.

This is perhaps a very humanities-flavored view of what a virtual world means; in computer science, it is typically considered to be a synonym for a digital world—a persistent 3D representation of a space, possibly with interaction, and perhaps with a few buildings and some nice trees—but in the humanities, we often talk of the medieval world or the world of the Borgias, and we often talk of a world as larger than a single individual perspective. So how would we capture and communicate that in a virtual world? Literature achieves this by providing evocative and figurative language, inviting us to imagine, to add, to conjure from the faintest of clues.

I suggest virtual world designers should also consider how experiential realism, rather than photorealism, could provide richer and more engaging virtual worlds—and, by extension, richer and more engaging virtual heritage. Although you can use an internet search engine to find thousands of links to virtual worlds and digital humanities, I suspect very few of them explore this concept of world and why it could have great benefit to the digital humanities.

In practical terms, I am suggesting that virtual worlds should not be completely explorable and accessible. They should be semi-persistent, requiring the inhabitants to explicitly and expressively care for them and incorporating elements of interaction and personalization back into that virtual world. For example, in *The Question Concerning Technology* essays, Heidegger (1977) makes a distinction between technē and technology—the boundaries of the creative process and the care and intention involved of the artisan.

The creation of art is intrinsically linked with the care and intentions of the maker and the attempt to "bring something into appearance," which, in turn, Heidegger says is a type of freedom. Virtual worlds could also have "growing pains" or metaphors to convey the life, past life, and other unusual things derived from or otherwise associated with their creation and maintenance.

Preserving Virtual Worlds through Text

Implicit in this chapter has been a distinction between the cultural and the social. Cultural elements of places I suggest are embodied, material, and inscribed, reflecting values and beliefs that may outlast individuals. While social presence in virtual worlds may include shared, understood behaviors, speech, and interactions, social presence does not necessitate learning from artifacts or leaving messages and values that endure beyond one's own visitation.

This distinction means that my use and understanding of virtual worlds and cultural places in digital environments are not one-to-one translations of digital environments based on virtual, augmented, or mixed reality—conventional virtual environments or serious games. I still need to explore exactly how we capture the views, values, and actions of past users or present users, but I do not believe it is trivial, agreed upon, or already solved by tools in other fields of digital humanities. First, our related communities need to agree on definitions, aims, achievements, and challenges. Secondly, we need to provide working examples accessible to all, supported by shared evaluations and related data.

Given the lack of sustained and communicated research into the cultural aspects of virtual heritage, as communicated via digital humanities conferences and publications, I am wary of suggestions to apply text-based strategies to the preservation of virtual worlds. For example, Schreibman and Papadopoulos (2019) have suggested that virtual environments would be best preserved for and documented by Text Encoding Initiative, TEI, methods. There are so many fields, disciplines, and uses for 3D environments that not only am I convinced that we have yet to agree on standard concepts, terms, and methods but I am also not convinced current digital humanities methods for 2D content would fully capture the performative, immersive, and experiential features of virtual worlds. I reiterate that a virtual world, especially for cultural heritage purposes, is not merely a digital, 3D environment. These additional, complicated features must be explored and agreed on before we try to standardize them with tools and methods from a very different field.

Many of these projects are not just 3D models. They are also spaces, possibly even places. How do spaces differ from places? Places change you and are changed by you as you move through them and as you dwell. Dwelling, as an immersive experience, is also an aspect of archaeology and architecture but not of text because you can *dwell on* but not *dwell within* text.

However, the gap between artifact and text is not clear-cut. Text can be material and spatial—in the Mayan city of Palenque, distances to the glyphs helped stop sacred text being read by the general population—and medieval books were both Illustrative and graphic—monastic manuscripts were calligraphic works of art. Today's digital world is much more oriented towards a stressed but mobile population resulting in Head up Displays, HUDs, that generally favor less text but more graphic icons.

Yes, text is part of the world, for text conveys both artistic and expressive individuality, a particular movement, or spirit of the age or zeitgeist.

OTHER KEY CONTENTIOUS ISSUES

Perhaps we should concentrate on virtuality as distinct from virtual reality and abstracted, rather than as historically or culturally accurate or authentic. In my experience, creating completely non-realistic worlds is extremely challenging because of the lack of affordances and the time required to master the new rules and understand completely new conceptions of reality. While simple, artistic variants of virtuality may momentarily engage and inspire, cultural institutions such as museums are unlikely to offer more than ten or fifteen minutes for each participant to learn and engage in a virtual world as an exhibit.

Secondly, the opportunities to learn in virtual worlds are still not fully tapped, so to attack the Internet or virtual worlds is foolhardy. Consider the case of Professor Hubert Dreyfus, an academic philosopher more famous for his contributions to artificial intelligence. Turning his attention to the Internet, in the first edition of *On the Internet*, Dreyfus (2001) suggested internet-based environments and virtual learning environments could never replace traditional university classrooms. In the second edition (Dreyfus 2008), he admitted to a new fascination with virtual worlds thanks to Second Life. Other philosophers have also been too quick to criticize virtual worlds, thinking their sole aim is to re-create, as accurately and comprehensively as possible, the real world (Thompson 2016). One very large, new avenue of exploration is using the real world but not necessarily mirroring it. The potential creative opportunities in creating more accessible, creative, virtual worlds and mixed reality applications are now upon us. Game companies are now big enough to afford, support, and create films and other media. For example, Weta Workshop now has a spinoff studio in augmented reality, and the Steam game platform has collaboration options and a VR mode.

Conclusion and Potential Future Solutions

I have suggested that new forms of interactive and immersive embodiment may strengthen the impact and usefulness of text as a personal and highly artifactual medium. I also recommended considering text in terms of reading and applying it to 3D environments, raising the question as to how one reads place—through hermeneutics, perhaps. *Myst* (Cyan, Inc., 1993), for example, was a hermeneutic game engine. Like its sister activity, machinima, game modding offers another creative pathway—leveraging the interactive affordances of games to create new reflections on past accepted notions of genre, goal, and setting.

For education, I suggest we modify both marking and the design projects themselves to encourage more group-led creativity and group decision-making because genuinely collaborative design and reflection would also help the design of virtual worlds. Few great cities are created by just one person; I fail to see why this differs for virtual worlds. As Brett Bobley (St. Louis, 2014) declared in an interview:

> I've often said that digital humanities (or DH for short) is just an umbrella term—a term of convenience—that refers to a whole bunch of activities happening where the humanities interacts with technology. Perhaps one skill that most (but not all) scholars may find helpful is the ability to work collaboratively. The vast majority of the DH grants we make are to teams of people from different disciplines working together . . . we're seeing more Internet-based humanities resources, databases,

scholarly editions, and digital libraries that make incredible resources available for free.

My first point is that there is still space to reconsider text and text-based input in virtual environments, as well as the importance of sound and other multimodalities. With new technology—such as projection, portable AR and MR, physical computing, low-cost scanning and photogrammetry, 3D and 4D printing—text, the space-between text, and the wider activity of reading may all take on new creative and conceptual adventures. More accessible tools to paint and sculpt in virtual reality may be combined with biofeedback tracking and locative details to create unique, highly contextual and individualistic digital models and landscapes. Biofeedback, improved eye-tracking, and convenient ways to include sight of one's real-world hands into virtual environments will help increase the sense of scale, immersion, and virtual belonging, just as writing does.

Secondly, I suggest that we will move away from virtual reality towards more augmented reality, mixed reality, and augmented virtuality, encouraging us to re-invest in the real world rather than to hide from it in a hermetically sealed virtual reality. Here, TEI may indeed play a part, helping us separate 3D assets from the project so that new updates and new discoveries can be streamed at runtime into a live virtual heritage project.

Thirdly, VR worlds could be inscribe-able and semi-persistent, requiring visitors to learn to recognize cared for and uncared for places and artifacts and learn how to care, in turn, for aspects of these virtual worlds. Including dynamic elements to these virtual worlds could show effect over time of visitation, pollution, and erosion.

Fourthly, virtual worlds should afford and support questioning. The ability to add text in virtual worlds as indirect clues and support for quests is a time-honored method, but in general, virtual worlds do not incorporate text as clues—at least, not as often as games do. These hermeneutic aspects are not well described in the academic literature, but there is great significance here, not only in terms of how virtual worlds are read but also in how they are designed to be read. The question now widens. We are not talking about text per se but about reading. How can you or should you "read" a virtual world?

References

Bartlett, Jamie, and Carl Miller. 2011. *Truth, Lies and the Internet: A Report into Young People's Digital Fluency*. London, UK: Demos. www.demos.co.uk/files/Truth_-_web.pdf.

Bekele, Mafkereseb Kassahun, Roberto Pierdicca, Emanuele Frontoni, Eva Savina Malinverni, and James Gain. 2018. "A Survey of Augmented, Virtual, and Mixed Reality for Cultural Heritage." *Journal on Computing and Cultural Heritage (JOCCH)* 11 (2): 1–36. doi.org/10.1145/3145534.

Brunette, Peter, and David Wills. 1993. "Images Off: Ulmer's Teletheory." Review of *Teletheory: Grammatology in the Age of Video*, by Gregory Ulmer. *Diacritics* 23 (2): 36–46. Baltimore, MD: The Johns Hopkins University Press.

Champion, E., and S. Sekiguchi. 2006. "IEEE Xplore—Suggestions for New Features to Support Collaborative Learning in Virtual Worlds." *Third International Conference on Creating, Connecting and Collaborating through Computing* (C5): 127–134. DOI: 10.1109/C5.2005.25.

Champion, Erik Malcolm. 2016. "Digital Humanities is Text Heavy, Visualization Light, and Simulation Poor." *Digital Scholarship in the Humanities* 32 (1): i25–i32. doi.org/10.1093/llc/fqw053.

Champion, Erik, and Hafizur Rahaman. 2019. "3D Digital Heritage Models as Sustainable Scholarly Resources." *Sustainability* 11 (8): 1–8. www.mdpi.com/2071-1050/11/8/2425.

Croker, Alan. 2017. *RESPECTING THE VISION Sydney Opera House—a Conservation Management Plan*. Sydney, AU: Sydney Opera House. www.sydneyoperahouse.com/content/dam/pdfs/conservation-management-plan/soh_cmp_printable_1.pdf.

Dalbello, Marija. 2011. "A Genealogy of Digital Humanities." *Journal of Documentation* 67 (3): 480–506. doi.org/10.1108/00220411111124550.

Deng, W., F. Liu, H. Jin, B. Li, and D. Li. 2014. "Harnessing Renewable Energy in Cloud Datacenters: Opportunities and Challenges." *IEEE Network* 28 (1): 48–55. doi.org/10.1109/MNET.2014.6724106.

Dreyfus, Hubert L. 2001. *On the Internet*. 1st ed. London, UK, and New York, NY: Routledge.

Dreyfus, Hubert L. 2008. *On the Internet*. 2nd ed. London, UK, and New York, NY: Routledge.

Gillings, M. 2002. "Virtual Archaeologies and the Hyper-Real." In *Virtual Reality in Geography*, edited by P. Fisher and D. Unwin. London, UK, and New York, NY: Taylor & Francis.

Heidegger, Martin. 1975. *Poetry, Language, Thought*. Translated by Albert Hofstadter. New York, NY: Harper and Row.

Heidegger, Martin. 1977. *The Question Concerning Technology and Other Essays*. New York, NY: Harper & Row.

Hockey, Susan. 2004. "The History of Humanities Computing" In *A Companion to Digital Humanities*, edited by Susan Schreibman, Ray Siemens, and John Unsworth, 3–19. Oxford, UK: Blackwell.

Jacobson, Michael J., Beaumie Kim, Chunyan Miao, Zhiqi Shen, and Mark Chavez. 2010. "Design Perspectives for Learning in Virtual Worlds." *Designs for Learning Environments of the Future*, 111–41. Boston, MA: Springer.

Keenan, Thomas. 1995. "Teletheory: Have You Seen Your World Today?" *Art Journal* 54, no. 4 (Winter): 102. Los Angeles, CA: CAA.

Manzolli, Jônatas. 2016. "Multimodal Architecture of the Ode to Christus Hypercubus." *21st Generative Arts Conference*, 171–182.

Meyers, Victoria. 1999. "Space and the Perception of Time." *Journal of Architectural Education* 53 (2): 91–95. New York, NY: Taylor & Francis.

Miller, Carl, and Jamie Bartlett. 2012. "'Digital Fluency': Towards Young People's Critical Use of the Internet." *Journal of Information Literacy* 6 (2): 35–55. doi.org/10.11645/6.2.1714

St. Louis, Scott Richard. 2014. "Digital Humanities and Open Access: An Interview with Brett Bobley of the National Endowment for the Humanities." Accessed September 9, 2021. www.righttoresearch.org/blog/digital-humanities-and-open-access-an-interview-wi.shtml.

Stec, Kashmiri, and Eve Sweetser. 2013. "Borobudur and Chartres: Religious Spaces as Performative Real-Space Blends." *Sensuous cognition*, 265–91. N.p.

Tabachnick, David E. 2004. "Techne, Technology and Tragedy." In "Techné: Research in Philosophy and Technology" Special issue, SPT 7 (3). Accessed September 9, 2021. scholar.lib.vt.edu/ejournals/SPT/v7n3/tabachnick.html.

Thompson, Janna. 2018. "Why Virtual Reality Cannot Match the Real Thing." *The Conversation*. Accessed March 4, 2018. theconversation.com/why-virtual-reality-cannot-match-the-real-thing-92035.

Ulmer, Gregory. 1989. *Teletheory: Grammatology in the Age of Video*. New York, NY: Routledge.

Ulmer, Gregory. n.d. "Electracy and Pedagogy." Accessed September 9, 2021. users.clas.ufl.edu/glue/longman/pedagogy/electracy.html.

Vanhoutte, Edward. 2013. "The Gates of Hell: History and Definition of Digital Humanities Computing." In *Defining Digital Humanities*, edited by Melissa Terras, Julianne Nyhan, and Edward Vanhoutte, 119–56. Farnham, UK: Ashgate.

Wang, Li, and Erik Champion. 2011. "A Pilot Study of Four Cultural Touch-Screen Games." *Proceedings of the 12th Annual Conference of the New Zealand Chapter of the ACM Special Interest Group on Computer-Human Interaction*, 57–64. New York, NY: Association for Computing Machinery.

—. 2012. "Chinese Culture Approached Through Touch: Chinese Cultural Heritage Learnt Via Touch-Based Games." *18th International Conference on Virtual Systems and Multimedia (VSMM)*, 87–94. Milan, Italy. DOI: 10.1109/VSMM.2012.6365911.

6 The New Poetics of Computer Animation: Selective Augmentation and Animated Realism (Digital)

Nathan Snow

This chapter introduces the concept of selective augmentation for understanding computer-animated realism. Selective augmentation—a process in which animators select materials or behaviors to highlight through formal techniques such as movement, enhanced textural detail, or color, thereby increasing their tangible credibility while simultaneously lessening their photoreality—invites the spectator to "mentalize" heightened, caricatured depictions of textures and characters and, in so doing, addresses the current debate over animated realism as a concept. For example, can animation, a medium whose technology and practices often exclude it from the debates surrounding indexical reality, make a claim on any manner of realism? This chapter raises questions central to computer-generated animation poetics, namely in describing methods that 3D animated cartoons have used to both maintain abstraction from indexical reality while maintaining enough textural detail to encourage viewers, through the formal properties of the animation, to luxuriate in hyper-real depictions of fur, scales, and other textures. Abstracted yet detailed materials—while non-indexical—nevertheless grant audiences an opportunity to renew their appreciation for the everyday material spaces they inhabit. Because selective augmentation can offer viewers non-indexical—or non-anthropocentric—perspectives on reality in a way that feels tangibly real, animation provides a unique opportunity to both redeem the material world from obscurity and grant audiences a chance at experiencing the sublime in media.

View Nathan Snow's "The New Poetics of Computer Animation: Selective Augmentation and Animated Realism" online at https://bit.ly/reimagining-humanities or follow the QR code.

SECTION TWO: TEACHING

7 Co-Constructing Authority in the Classroom Chora

Jessica Kester and Jessica Lipsey

> *The students are helping to invent the future of writing. This attitude and relationship to learning has to be made explicit and encouraged, since students are unaccustomed to working in an experimental way.*
>
> —Gregory Ulmer, *Internet Invention*

More than ten years ago, the proliferation of self-sponsored writing in digital, social spaces prompted progressive writing studies scholars to rethink what counts as writing and what it means to teach and research twenty-first century writing. Kathleen Blake Yancey's 2009 report from the National Council of Teachers of English provides a concise summary of Web 2.0 effects and calls composition instructors to consensus: "It's time to support all forms of twenty-first century literacies, inside and outside school" (1).

Today, writing studies researchers frequently cite and explore Yancey's call empirically (Moore et al. 2016), theoretically (Vie 2008), and pedagogically (Mina 2017). Likewise, jointly authored disciplinary standards and statements like the "Framework for Success in Postsecondary Writing," the "WPA Outcomes Statement for First-Year Composition (3.0)," and "Professional Knowledge for the Teaching of Writing" reflect the impact of digital technologies and networked writing on literacy instruction. These texts form a corpus that eschews rigid writing rules for "habits of mind." Students' needs and their prior knowledge, especially in digital environments, are likewise affirmed as shapers of classroom practice. Respect for diverse writing styles, languages, and writers is also explicit in all three documents.

Fewer academic pieces address how students' participation in self-sponsored writing affects the theory and practice of authority in writing-rich classrooms. Of those that do, Charlotte Knox-Williams' (2017) essay about student-centered learning argues for a redistribution of power. Like us, she sees student authority in the classroom as necessary, but she neglects an important step between theory and practice—critical reflection by the instructor. Without reflection, progressive position statements and pedagogical innovations run the risk of becoming "academic branding"—spectacle lacking substance (Macedo 2018, 5). To address this under-theorized aspect of writing instruction in the twenty-first century, we will connect conversations in the digital humanities and writing studies that compel us to reconsider classroom authority—a move we call *co-constructing* authority. Then, we will justify and develop our position that co-constructing authority requires a theoretical move from place to space within the classroom chora. Finally, we will bring attention to our disciplinarily constructed subject positions through reflective activities. These reflective activities represent an essential, often neglected, step between the theory and practice of co-constructing authority with students.

Both the theoretical move we describe and the reflective practices we suggest are applicable for instructors in a variety of fields. Still, we acknowledge that the consequences of student-authority in practice vary from inconsequential to life-threatening and from empowering to unethical. We imagine ranges of co-constructing authority on a continuum where first-year writing, as a content area and an activity (Alder-Kassner and Wardle 2016), resides at one extreme, and an introductory chemistry course might realistically reside on the other. Within the broader scope of the digital humanities, a discipline that has—at its core—human-created texts and technology, it is unlikely that our argument for co-constructing authority as part of a twenty-first century writing pedagogy is moot. We anticipate and welcome a range of applications for co-constructing authority with students in classroom spaces.

Why Co-Construct Authority?

Like other disciplines and fields collected within the digital humanities, digital technologies shape writing studies. N. Katherine Hayles (2015) argues, "disciplinary traditions are in active interplay with the technologies even as the technologies are transforming the traditions" (28). The "interplay" Hayles discusses articulates directly with Yancey's call to affirm twenty-first century writing. Students now come to our writing classrooms with complicated, multimodal, social writing experiences collected from extracurricular literacy practices. Pew Research Center's most recent report (2019) regarding social media use in the United States confirms Instagram and Snapchat as increasingly popular among eighteen to twenty-nine year-olds, with sixty-seven percent and sixty-two percent of respondents, respectively, using these sites. Moreover, ninety percent of eighteen to twenty-four year-olds use YouTube and seventy-six percent still frequent Facebook (Perrin and Anderson 2019). These social media platforms, among other digital composing spaces, provide access and encourage hands-on learning. Students learn to write effective, purpose-driven prose to audiences composed of followers, friends, and members of online, special interest groups, for example. They also navigate genre conventions and collaborate with other people, applications, and algorithms to create meaningful multimodal text. Students' individual and collective experiential learning should de-center the writing instructor's authority. The instructor is not the only knowledgeable, practiced writer in the classroom.

Students' prior learning does not, however, make writing instructors obsolete. It is quite the opposite; students still need us. Co-constructing authority in a writing classroom means collectively examining experience—ours and our students'—to critique and transform what counts as writing, how it is assigned in classrooms, and how it is assessed. To accomplish this goal, students need help to convert tacit knowledge into explicit understanding, and to translate situational know-how into principles that can be transferred to other writing situations.

In working with graduate students in digital humanities labs, Janelle Jenstad and Joseph Takeda (2017) lay the foundation for our argument. They suggest that research assistants working on digital humanities projects should "become full collaborators, complementing and sometimes superseding the project leaders' expertise" (71) because "sometimes the person best qualified to make a judgment call is not necessarily the project director" (78). Specifying Takeda and Jenstad's "sometimes," requires a movement away from a model of authority built on a project manager's "overarching expertise" and toward a recognition of "domain expertise"— where a team member's knowledge of scripting and programming languages, for example, might supplant the project leader's (Jenstad and Takeda 2017, 77–78). In the writing classroom, we find Jenstad and Takeda's project-centered authority transgressions particularly applicable. From podcasting assignments to blogs and Twitter storms, instructors create newfangled writing projects, supposedly demonstrating a commitment to twenty-first century literacies (Saidy 2018). Yet, many instructors design assignments alone, along with the grading criteria, when students have more experience reading, listening to, and sometimes, writing these twenty-first century genres. Limor Shifman (2014) makes a convincing argument for devoting academic attention to memes because they represent effective, persuasive, empowering, enjoyable, and often subversive discourse. Now, consider who knows more about successful meme-making. Is it instructors or students? While students cannot always articulate what they know using our disciplinary language, many certainly know a good meme when they see one and can produce one to boot. The structure of tacit knowledge almost always amounts to knowing more than one can say (Polanyi 1966). Our argument for co-constructing authority is therefore based on the sophisticated, rhetorical moves students develop while practicing writing in networked spaces.

For example, Nancy Jo Sales (2017) investigates teen girls' experiences on social media. The girls Sales interviews articulate highly rhetorical writing processes. Specifically, they analyze their audience to plan what time of day to post to Instagram, with the goal of "trying to hit prime times for getting likes" (63). The captions accompanying their posts often exemplify the collaborative and social aspects of writing. For instance, Sales notes that the girls' captions were "a source of forethought, sometimes requiring groupthink, like a brainstorming session [. . .]—how to make them sound witty and clear" (63). Here we see evidence that these writers consider style and tone. One interviewee remarked, "I work so hard on my captions. Everyone has a group chat where they're like, 'Oh my God, help me with my captions'" (63). While the girls Sales interviews are not speaking the language of writing studies, clearly these writers have rhetorical writing processes. They write from a real sense of exigency and with purpose for complicated audiences. These audiences demand girls constantly create and recreate a complicated ethos—a persona appealing simultaneously to boys from a position of third-wave feminist sexuality and to girlfriends who readily become rhetors in the discourse via comments, likes, and emojis contributed to the digital text.

Digital humanities scholar Davis Baird (2004) argues that "'craft knowledge,' 'fingertip knowledge,' 'tacit knowledge,' and 'know-how' are useful concepts in that they remind us that there is more to knowing than saying" (18). Likewise, Harry Collins (2009) affirms hands-on exploration as a powerful, embodied form of knowing. Both scholars cite building and doing as appropriate and desirable for knowledge-making inside academic contexts like The University of Central Florida's Center for Humanities and Digital Research and maker-spaces like Ryerson University's Digital Media Experience Lab (Tucker et al. 2017, 205). We extend this line of reasoning to learning that exists beyond academic places, unsupervised by faculty, graduate students, or project directors. We extend contextual rhetorical effectiveness to the kind of learning that happens in the world and is affirmed or rejected based on impact.

We have argued that through their everyday digital writing practices, students gain tacit writing knowledge and skills relevant to the writing classroom. However, writing studies researcher, Ryan Shepherd (2018, 48), finds that none of the 132 freshman composition students he studies define writing in ways pointing beyond alphabetic text. This finding is important because we know students compose in multimodal mediums—Instagram and Snapchat being the most popular. Shepherd's (2018) survey data also confirms previous research (DePalma and Alexander 2015) that despite the presence of digital and multimodal out-of-school literacies, students do not often see their out-of-school writing as connected to in-school literacy practices.

Students need help moving from procedural literacies to critical literacies and, ultimately, to rhetorical literacies that allow them to return to their social spaces with new lenses and tools for composing in academic, public, and personal contexts (Selber 2004). Certainly, there is much we need to teach students, but there is also much they need to teach us.

To this point, the #transformDH movement specifically calls scholars to consider media-makers outside of academia relevant to digital humanities studies (Bailey et al. 2016). Because twenty-first century writing necessarily involves digital tools, cultures, and everyday literacy practices, we also extend this consideration to students' self-sponsored writing and the tacit knowledge produced through experimentation and practice. Students' writing knowledge and skills should, "productively destabilize the norms and standards" (Bailey et al. 2016, 71) associated with authority. The keyword here is "productively." Destabilization is not itself an endpoint but an opening—one that invites the kinds of collaborations and critical thinking that will ultimately advance academic disciplines, not dismantle them. The following paragraphs develop our position that co-constructing authority with students requires a theoretical move from place to space within the classroom chora—a concept we examine and visualize in the next section.

WHERE TO CO-CONSTRUCT AUTHORITY: THE CLASSROOM CHORA

If instructors understand and respect that students' prior composing experiences productively and powerfully decenter authority in the writing classroom, we must also reconsider the "where" of teaching and learning—the classroom itself. Instructors cannot effectively co-construct authority while simultaneously holding fast to the idea of classrooms as fixed places. Because students develop experiential writing knowledge in user-mediated spaces that intersects and diverges from academic writing conventions, we must move from *place* to *space* to productively conceptualize the twenty-first century classroom, or what we call the *classroom chora*. This move from fixed places to choral spaces extends the work of scholars like Thomas Rickert, Gregory Ulmer, and Yi-Fu Tuan who recognize "place" as a secure locus with stable boundaries and identities and "space" as a freedom platform, communally practiced.

Rickert's (2013) theory of ambient rhetoric is a valuable lens for imagining the classroom chora. Rickert, like Ulmer (2003) invests in deconstructing borders and revealing hidden rhetorical actors. The ambient environment is not just a static place where the rhetor autonomously composes; the ambient environment also responds. Rickert uses musical performance as a metaphor for ambient rhetoric. A musician playing their instrument in a certain environment produces a certain sound. The same musician with the same instrument in a different place produces a different sound. This move from place, the situated position, to space or chora recognizes the interplay between all influencers of musical sound—the text. The musician stands in a place, but the space, the chora, is the interplay of all the situated influences coming together. We see the writing classroom in the same way. It is a place where we meet students to do the work we do, but in that place, we also recognize the space—all the things around the students, both seen and unseen—facilitating interplay, networking, and knowledge production. Like Rickert and Ulmer, we use the rhetorical term "chora" to name the space. Like bell hooks (1994), we believe "the classroom remains the most radical space of possibility in the academy," (12) and the word "chora" is essential to productively co-constructing authority, as is reflection.

Though we rely heavily on Rickert and Ulmer for our definition of chora, tracing the idea back to Plato's *Timaeus* is helpful in conceptualizing the classroom as a choral space. Plato (2008) offers the term chora to theorize the potential of becoming. Plato's (2008) chora is the third "kind of nature" (113) in a three-part creation story of the cosmos—"what is," "what is created," and chora "the *in which* and *from which* of all generation" (113). The chora is the *condition* under which things come into being, and what comes into being is influenced by the chora (Sallis 1993). A vital characteristic of chora for Plato and his contemporaries is that the chora is more than an empty receptacle and more than what is visible.

Because the chora is neither directly discernable or tangible, Ulmer (1994) suggests working with chora via "extended analogies" (67) to reveal the choral space and preserve the ambiguous nature of the term. For example, Ulmer (2003) compares chora to the vibrating screens his father used to separate "raw aggregate from his quarry . . . into four sizes of rock and sand" (107). In this analogy, the chora stores, retrieves, and organizes the material within the workspace; it is invoked as a mediating space for invention that holds together "diverse quantities of information" (Ulmer 2003, 68). For Ulmer (1994), "everything having to do with new media may be rethought within the perspective of the chora" (69). The chora as new media—or really, new media as chora—is full of inventive potential. Ulmer's chora not only reveals the active nature of the media on the composing process but also the unexamined parts of ourselves that influence rhetorical choices, and, as our reflective exercises will later probe, how we enact authority in writing classrooms.

Rickert (2013) uses "ambience" as an extended analogy of the chora to "illuminat[e]" (43) how technologies and new media influence rhetorical choices. Rickert's chora "opens an ambient perspective" (56) that divests authority from the subject and object position of the rhetor to the ambient environment around the rhetor. Chora, as a rhetorical term, offers a way to consider the unseen actors that affect rhetorical considerations. Further, Rickert argues that technology and new media are more than tools or mediums; technology, the Internet, and "ubiquitous computing" (285) are always present and act as more than passive transmitters. Despite Rickert's call to consider communication technologies as part of ambient rhetoric, students and instructors sometimes look through technologies, and the chora, instead of at them. As a result, the influences and opportunities of choral spaces, and the technologies within, go unnoticed. Attuning to rhetorical ambience can orient instructors to see opportunities in the choral space.

Both Ulmer and Rickert theorize from these important points—there are unseen actors in the chora and the chora disrupts our understanding of the visible. What we take from Ulmer and Rickert's work with chora is a perspective. It is a way to see the classroom differently. By donning the choral lens in the classroom space, we recognize writing experiences and authority beyond the classroom as relevant to writing instruction and practice.

In engaging a choral perspective, we cannot *not* rethink the classroom space and our positions in it. Are instructors experts? Absolutely. We have a responsibility to use our expertise to facilitate the best possible learning environment. The beauty in seeing the classroom as boundless and expansive is that it gives us a new way to consider authority. Yes, the structure suggests that the teacher is the authority figure in the room, but if we concede that students know things, we can change the situated place of knowledge transmission to an expansive space of knowledge production. Knox-Williams (2017) calls a classroom with shared authority "a single system that connects separate agents in an interplay of forces" and "a site of dynamic and non-linear interactions" (237–238). Knox-Williams makes the move that we want to make—she deconstructs the classroom. She unmaps the classroom territory to allow reassessment of teaching and learning, with the express goal of situating students at the system center.

Geographer Yi-Fu Tuan (1977) writes, "place is security, space is freedom: we are attached to one and long for the other" (3). For Tuan, when space becomes familiar, it becomes a place. As instructors, we often create the classroom as a place by associating only the landmarks, or tools, that we deem appropriate given our disciplinary subject positions. Students, in turn, recognize the classroom in our image. To recognize what students bring to the classroom, we need to disrupt our versions of the classroom place and embrace the choral space and all the knowledge our students bring about writing. We can co-construct a place within this space, but not without students' input.

The design of the classroom place complicates understanding the classroom as a space for negotiating authority. While novel learning environment exist on some campuses, the state colleges in which we teach and the universities in which we were educated contained classrooms with heavy desks in rows, facing an instructor's lectern. While many instructors do good work by moving desks, creating circles, and disrupting place, this effort is not enough. In fact, altering the physical environment might lull us into thinking we have shifted authority, when what we really must disrupt is ourselves. Without examining our own ways of thinking and being, we are apt to enact our disciplinary authority and ignore the tacit writing knowledge students bring to the classroom chora. As a complex, dynamic, and, at times, chaotic expanse of individual and shared knowledge, values, and experiences, as well as corporate and academic platforms, we imagine our classroom chora as pictured in Figure 1.

Figure 1. Conceptualization of Classroom Chora

Here, the classroom place remains physically fixed with rows of desks facing the instructor's lectern, but the classroom chora is filled with intersecting and diverging sources of writing expertise that, we argue, instructors' and their students should attend to by co-constructing authority. Our depiction also makes explicit the proprietary, profit-driven communication and information platforms that mediate self-sponsored writing in networked, public spaces. Far from neutral tools, composing technologies influence how students compose and how their discourse is then distributed. In our classroom chora, we want to look *at* composing spaces and the writing experiences and knowledge they engender, not through them. We hope to avoid technology myths that position technologies and their interfaces as neutral. Therefore, our choral space purposefully and intentionally visualizes the mix of academic interfaces and the networked, social writing spaces that exist within the classroom chora. This image can be a glimpse into Rickert's ambient rhetoric and Ulmer's choral space. It is filled with possibility for teaching writing in the twenty-first century.

Beyond accepting our argument for co-constructing authority with students in classroom spaces, and beyond embracing the classroom as a choral space, we must also examine ourselves and what we bring to the classroom chora. As writing instructors, we are the intermediaries between theory and practice, though the relationship between the former and latter is recursive, not linear. The following section includes a rationale for reflection and a list of suggested reflective activities for instructors—a necessary element in discussions of twenty-first century pedagogy and co-constructing authority with students in the classroom chora.

How to Co-Construct Authority: Reflection

Our academic backgrounds, cultures, and experiences unconsciously shape how we apply theory, make curriculum, and interact with our students, unless we take time to investigate our ideologies. Barry Mauer (2017) proposes that critical, poetic examination of our "sense-making apparatus, our social order, and our understanding of past experiences" (58) may help expose "blind spots" (61) in reasoning. Once exposed, there is an opportunity for transformation or adjustment. While Mauer's (2017) practices are aimed at students, any attempt to co-construct authority in classroom spaces is diminished without concentrated, critical reflection about our "sense-making machinery" (59). We, therefore, apply student-centered reflective strategies to ourselves.

Ulmer's mystery pedagogy and Mauer's classroom practices offer inspiration for the reflective activities in the following section. These activities focus on just one element of the "popcycle," Ulmer's term for the combined institutions—family, community or history, entertainment, and discipline—that shape identity. We focus here on discipline. We feel justified in excluding the other identity constructors because anyone teaching at the college level has spent a concentrated amount of time within a discipline and has enacted various parts of that discipline's ideology in order to be appropriately degreed, credentialed, interviewed, and placed within an academic department or school. Through years of schooling, disciplinary conventions ratified a particular worldview—an ideology that shapes what instructors do in the classroom. Because our disciplines instructed us in different places and times than we are currently teaching students, we recognize a need to make visible our default disciplinary ideology, not the ideology we wear as a brand (e.g., twenty-first century writing pedagogue or co-constructor of authority). Our embedded ideology and related pedagogical practices may belie the disciplinary changes ushered in by the expansion of students' digital, networked, and social writing. Thus, we must take time to reflect.

Many academic fields recognize reflection and metacognition as vital components of the student learning process. It is no different for faculty. Reflection, for faculty, can initiate "instructional and curricular change" (Flash 2016, 231). When we take time to consider how our disciplinary upbringing affects the classroom chora, or even what our disciplinary upbringing looks like, we create opportunities for growth. Through reflection-in-action, Yancey posits that "by analyzing our own thinking patterns, by considering the ways these patterns align with or diverge from our intentions, we can adjust and refine the ways we think and work" (as cited in Flash 2016, 229). When we reflect on our assumptions, beliefs, and practices, we can begin the journey toward what Pamela Flash calls "a dismantling of entrenched and unproductive pedagogical thinking" (231).

The reflective practices we outline are not a formula for co-constructing authority in the classroom chora. Instead, we offer a point of departure—meaningful, reflective exercises to encourage self-examination. Ulmer contends that investigating our subject position is a productive place to start because it is coloring what we do. Our default values drive our pedagogy even if we've told ourselves we've put Yancey's call and the digital humanities' maker-movement into practice. Critical reflection is necessary for true collaboration and transformation.

References

Alder-Kassner, Linda, and Elizabeth Wardle. 2016. *Naming What We Know: Threshold Concepts of Writing Studies.* Boulder, CO: University Press of Colorado.

Bailey, Moya, Anne Cong-Huyen,, Alexis Lothian, and Amanda Phillips. 2016. "Reflections on a movement: #transformDH, Growing Up." In *Debates in the Digital Humanities 2016*, edited by Matthew K. Gold and Lauren F. Klein, 71–79. Minneapolis, MN: Regents of the University of Minnesota.

Baird, Davis. 2004. *Thing Knowledge: A Philosophy of Scientific Instruments*. Berkley, CA: University of California Press.

Collins, Harry. 2009. *Tacit and Explicit Knowledge*. Chicago, IL: University of Chicago Press.

Committee on Teaching, Learning, and Assessing Writing in Digital Environments. 2004. "CCCCs Position Statement on on Teaching, Learning, and Assessing Writing in Digital Environments." *Conference on College Composition and Communication*. Accessed June 27, 2019. cccc.ncte.org/cccc/resources/positions/digitalenvironments.

Council of Writing Program Administrators. 2014. "WPA Outcomes Statement for First-Year Composition (3.0), Approved July 17, 2014." Council of Writing Program Administrators. Accessed June 27, 2019. wpacouncil.org/positions/outcomes.html.

Council of Writing Program Administrators, National Council of Teachers of English, and National Writing Project. 2011. *Framework for Success in Postsecondary Writing*. Accessed June 27, 2019. wpacouncil.org/framework.

DePalma, Michael-John and Kara Poe Alexander. 2015. "A Bag Full of Snakes: Negotiating the Challenges of Multimodal Composition." *Computers and Composition* 37: 182–200. N.p.

Flash, Pamela. 2016. "From Appraised to Revised: Faculty in the Disciplines Change What They Never Knew They Knew." In *A Rhetoric of Reflection*, edited by Kathleen Blake Yancey, 227–49. Logan, UT: Utah State University Press.

George, Diana. 2002. "From Analysis to Design: Visual Communication in the Teaching of Writing." *College Comoposition and Communication* 54 (1): 11–39. Champaign, IL: National Council of Teachers of English.

hooks, bell. 1994. *Teaching to Transgress: Education as the Practice of Freedom*. New York, NY: Routledge.

Jenstad, Janelle and Joseph Takeda. 2017. "Making the RA Matter: Pedagogy, Interface, and Practices." In *Making Things and Drawing Boundaries: Experiments in the Digital Humanities*, edited by J. Sayers, 71–85. Minneapolis, MN: University of Minnesota Press.

Jones, Natasha N., Moore R. Kristen, and Rebecca Walton. 2016. "Disrupting the Past to Disrupt the Future: An Antenarrative of Technical Communication." *Technical Communication Quarterly* 25, (4): 211–29. New York, NY: Taylor & Francis.

Klein, Julie Thompson. 2015. *Interdisciplining Digital Humanities: Boundary Work in an Emerging Field*. Ann Arbor, MI: University of Michigan Press.

Knox-Williams, Charlotte. 2017. "Between the Devil and the Deep Blue Sea: Power, Control, and Authority in the Classroom." In *Putting Theory into Practice in the Contemporary Classroom: Theory Lessons*, edited by Becky

McLaughlin, 226–240. Newcastle upon Tyne, UK: Cambridge Scholars Publishing.

Macedo, Donaldo. 2018. "Introduction to the 50th Anniversary Edition." In *Pedagogy of the Oppressed*, by Paulo Freire, translated by Myrabergman Ramos, 1–33. New York, NY: Bloomsbury Academic.

Mauer, Barry. 2017. "Curating the Mystory: Ideology and Invention in the Theory Classroom," In *Putting Theory into Practice in the Contemporary Classroom: Theory Lessons*, edited by Becky McLaughlin, 56–76. Newcastle upon Tyne, UK: Cambridge Scholars Publishing.

Mina, Lilian W. 2017. "Social Media in the FYC Class: The New Digital Divide." In *Social Writing/Social Media: Publics, Presentations, and Pedagogies*, edited by Douglas Walls and Stephanie Vie, 263–82. Fort Collins, CO: The WAC Clearinghouse.

Moore, Jessie L., Paula Rosinski, Tim Peeples,, Stacey Pigg, Martine Courant Rife, Beth Brunk-Chavez, Dundee Lackey, Suzanne Kesler Rumsey, Robyn Tasaka, Paul Curran, et al. 2016. "Revisualizing Composition: How First-Year Writers Use Composing Technologies." *Computers and Composition*, 39: 1–13. N.p.

Perrin, Andrew, and Monica Anderson. 2019. "Share of US adults using social media, including Facebook, is mostly unchanged since 2018." Washington, DC: Pew Research Center. Acessed June 27, 2019. www.pewresearch.org/fact-tank/2019/04/10/share-of-u-s-adults-using-social-media-including-facebook-is-mostly-unchanged-since-2018/.

Plato. 2008. *Timaeus*. Translated by Gregory Andrew and Robin Waterfield. Oxford, UK: Oxford University Press.

Polanyi, Michael. 1966. *The Tacit Dimension*. New York, NY: Doubleday.

Rickert, Thomas. 2013. *Ambient Rhetoric: The Attunements of Rhetorical Being*. Pittsburgh, PA: University of Pittsburgh Press.

Saidy, Christina. 2018. "Beyond Words on the Page: Using Multimodal Composing to Aid in the Transition to First-Year Writing." *Teaching English in the Two-Year College* 45 (3): 255–73. Champaign, IL: National Council of Teachers of English.

Sales, Nancy Jo. 2016. *American Girls: Social Media and the Secret Lives of Teenagers*. New York, NY: Alfred A. Knopf.

Sallis, John. 1993. *Chorology: On Beginning in Plato's Timaeus*. Bloomington, IN: Indiana University Press.

Selber, Stuart A. 2014. *Multiliteracies for a Digital Age*. Carbondale, IL: Southern Illinois Press UP.

Shepherd, Ryan P. 2018. "Digital Writing, Multimodality, and Learning Transfer: Crafting Connections between Composition and Online Composing." *Computers and Composition* 48: 103–14. N.p.

Shifman, Limor. 2014. *Memes in Digital Culture*. Cambridge, MA: The MIT Press.

Ulmer, Gregory. 1994. *Heuretics: The Logic of Invention*. Baltimore, MD: The John Hopkins University Press.

Ulmer, Gregory. 2003. *Internet Invention: From Literacy to Electracy*. New York, NY: Pearson Education, Inc.

Vie, Stephanie. 2008. "Digital Divide 2.0: 'Generation M' and Online Social Networking Sites in the Composition Classroom." *Computers and Composition*, 25 (1): 9–23. N.p.

Yancey, Kathleen Blake. 2009. *Writing in the 21st Century: A Report from the National Council of Teachers of English*. Champaign, IL: National Council of Teachers of English.

8 Metacognitive Experiences, Dialogic Pedagogies, and Designing Video Feedback

Dan Martin

INTRODUCTION

Multimodal forms of feedback like video feedback, VF, have become increasingly popular tools for evaluating and commenting on student writing in higher education, but there is very little research on VF that examines how instructors design and implement VF and how that design process impacts their teaching. To fill that gap, this chapter investigates how three professors from three different disciplines used VF for the first time to respond to a student writing assignment. The findings for this study demonstrate that making VF can facilitate reflective self-dialogue that provides instructors with a metacognitive experience. With these findings, I argue that VF helps instructors to reflect on the advantages and limitations of their feedback and to facilitate dialogic teaching strategies for their students. Reflecting on teaching habits and practices as a means to improve teaching and learning is characteristic of dialogic pedagogies. Altering pedagogical approaches to accommodate student learning can also instantiate "I-Thou" relationships between students and teachers (Buber 1965, 170). Martin Buber argues that I-Thou relationships between students and teachers are the epitome of dialogic pedagogies because they value student learning and place the student at the center of their learning. Reshaping teaching approaches to enhance student learning sends a direct message to students that their learning is privileged and valued. I-Thou relationships are also capable of dismantling the authoritative discourses that Mikhail Bakhtin insists constrain teaching and learning and objectify students because they place students at the center of teaching and learning (1994).

There is a dearth of research on how instructors make VF and how their processes for making VF impact their feedback and teaching. James Lamb (2018) identified what makes multimodal feedback more or less effective for students, but his research did not examine how teachers made multimodal forms of feedback or the effects the making process had on their teaching (49). Breanna Campbell and Ann Feldman (2017) argue that using multimodal feedback to respond to writing "enhances decoding" and "build[s] relationships" with students (5), but they did not explore how the instructor designed multimodal feedback or describe what that design process looked like. Cynthia Selfe (2009) highlights the values of learning through sound, image, and text in her work on multimodal writing, and she emphasizes that teachers should use "semiotic dimensionality" as a frame for expanding how they design and implement multimodal forms into their pedagogy (618); however, Selfe does not directly examine how instructors build semiotic dimensionality into their curriculums or how incorporating sound, image, and text can lead to a more comprehensive purview of an instructor's feedback process. None of the research on feedback has examined how making VF can promote reflective self-dialogue that can facilitate metacognitive experiences characteristic of dialogic pedagogies.

I-Thou, Authoritative Discourses, and Dialogic Pedagogies

Dialogic pedagogies are built on metacognition and dialogue between students and teachers, students and themselves, and students and their classmates. Irene Ward (1994) maintains that there are five key principles in developing a dialogic pedagogy—dialogue with yourself, your teacher, your institutions, your friends or classmates, and a dialogue in writing with these and multiple other voices to increase the overall understanding of the issues (171). Inner dialogue leads to deep learning, and Peter Neville Rule (2015) reiterates that idea when he discloses that "dialogue is pivotal to teaching and learning, both in the sense that teachers and learners engage in dialogue with each other (external dialogue) and within themselves (internal dialogue)" (144). John Flavell confirms that using VF for the first time facilitates self-reflection and internal dialogue that can lead someone "to establish new goals and to revise or abandon old ones" (906). According to Flavell, one of the first experts and researchers on metacognition, "[m]etacognitive experiences are any conscious cognitive or affective experiences that accompany and pertain to any intellectual enterprise" (906). His research reveals that "metacognitive experiences are especially likely to occur in situations that stimulate a lot of careful, highly conscious thinking," and this is especially true "in novel roles or situations, where every major step you take requires planning beforehand and evaluation afterwards." Furthermore, these metacognitive experiences "can affect your metacognitive knowledge base by adding to it, deleting from it, or revising it" (908). Metacognitive experiences can provide writing instructors an opportunity to improve their feedback habits, to position their students as a "Thou," and to dissolve I-It relationships with their students. For Martin Buber, the I-Thou relationship is the foundation of a dialogic pedagogy, and the I-It relationship is anti-dialogical.

In the I-It relationship the "I" position is authoritative and the teacher or institution typically occupies that position. The "It" position is a placeholder for the object. The I-It relationship separates the I, or subject, and It, or object, positions instead of connecting them like the I-Thou relationship. Martin Buber (1965) theorized I-Thou to be the product of a "natural combination" and the I-It as the product of a "natural separation" (23). Taylor W. Stevenson (1963) extrapolates on Buber's theory and emphasizes that the I-It relationship is "characterized by objectification, categorization, and utilization" while the I-Thou relationship is "characterized by betweenness, presentness, and uniqueness" (193). The I-It and I-Thou form a dichotomy that can complicate the development of dialogic pedagogies. The "I" in an I-It position sees and treats the student as a passive receptacle who is incapable of adequately contributing to his or her own learning (Freire 1968). Vincent Adkins (1999) explains that teachers foster I-It relationships when they treat students as containers to be filled with information and act as spectators in their students' learning, instead of active participants. He declared that "the student in the I-It dialectic . . . is regarded as a vessel, an object to be filled with information and not experiences" (178). Institutional discourses tend to position students as objects to be filled with knowledge to maintain power over them. Institutions, like universities, use authoritative discourses (Bakhtin 1984, 457) to construct I-It relationships for faculty and students that uphold and perpetuate banking concepts (Freire 2005) of education that hinder teaching and learning and demand subordination from students.

Authoritative discourses separate students and educators into I, Thou, and It subject positions, privilege I-It relationships, extend the institution's authority, and intimidate students. Bakhtin's theory helps explain how the authoritative discourses students encounter in higher education systemically objectify them and exert and maintain an overtly disproportionate amount of power over them. Bahktin contends that authoritative discourses rely on being "privileged" and "distanced" (1984, 457) to obfuscate institutional objectification, and they carve out complex boundaries that force students and educators into subject, I or Thou, and object, It, positions that are hard to cross or escape. The distant and unclear boundaries of an authoritative discourse are a form of usurpation and gatekeeping that complicate how the individuals trapped within oppressive boundaries locate the boundary and escape or dismantle it. The privileging of an authoritative discourse requires a continued obedience from students that further impairs their ability to locate and combat the discourses that control and limit how they learn.

Bakhtin (1994) professes that an authoritative discourse in higher education demands a hegemonic loyalty from students because loyalty "is indissolubly fused" with the authoritative discourse's ability to privilege "political power, an institution, [or] a person" (79). Larson and Phillips (2005) further explain how authoritative discourses in higher education are anti-dialogical and anti I-Thou. In their examination of how a preservice teacher, Claire, managed a variety of authoritative discourses in higher education, Larson and Phillips break down how authoritative discourses promote dominance, power, and control over student learning and send mixed messages about learning that intimidate students and situate them in the "It" subject position. They explain how authoritative discourses "played upon her subjectivities and her emerging identity as a teacher of literacy. This is perhaps most illustrated in an analysis of the e-mails and transcripts from Claire. Such an analysis reveals dramatic shifts in her thinking and articulation of reading instruction as influenced by discourses of power" (13). The authoritative discourses Claire encountered in her courses hindered her ability to identify as a teacher and became a barrier that interfered with her learning. One method to combat these types of discourses is to design and promote pedagogies that ask instructors to reflect on their feedback and teaching processes.

Making VF requires transduction and remediation when moving written comments from print to video, initiating a reflection process for educators. Turning written comments into video comments requires instructors to transduce their feedback content and to remediate print conventions for making feedback into making VF feedback. Moving written feedback into VF can disrupt an instructor's feedback norms and initiate some level of self-reflection. Salmon, Rossman, and Dipinto (2012) argue that teachers "develop automatic teaching routines," and that this "automaticity can inhibit teachers' awareness and critical analysis of teaching and learning" (70). Automated feedback can occur when teachers rely on the same forms, modes, and mediums to deliver teaching lessons and feedback year after year, course after course. This automaticity can make teachers unreflective of the pedagogical effectiveness of their feedback. Making VF can aid an instructor's disruption of automated feedback. Creating VF requires teachers to think about their comments through new modes. Speaking their comments aloud and watching themselves speak and gesture in the video can lead instructors to metacognitive experiences that facilitate deeper pedagogical reflection about the effectiveness of their feedback.

Methods

I conducted three case studies with three professors from three different disciplines—a historian, a psychologist, and a nanoscientist. The subject of each case study was the instructor of record for the course, and the subjects' names have been changed to protect their privacy. I examined how each professor created and implemented VF as a teaching tool for the first time, and I interviewed each professor at the beginning, middle, and end of the course, for a total of nine interviews. The first interview attempted to discern how the professors were currently using feedback in their courses before this study began. I wanted to get a sense of how the subjects understood the feedback process for themselves and for their students before they began the study so that I had more opportunities to see if using VF reshaped their understanding of feedback and teaching. The second and third interviews were given after each subject in the study implemented VF on one assignment at least one time. During these interviews, I asked each subject about the advantages and disadvantages of implementing VF and how using VF was impacting their teaching and feedback. In the next section, I explore the findings of those interviews and how making VF initiated self-reflection and self-dialogue, leading to metacognitive experiences and dialogic pedagogies.

META-REFLECTION AND ROGER THE HISTORIAN

Roger, an associate professor of history, disclosed that creating and delivering VF made him more conscious of the quality of his feedback and its effectiveness for his students. Designing VF prompted Roger to consider how he provided students with feedback and how useful that feedback was, much more than he had considered it when giving written feedback. For example, Roger realized that he was making the same comments over and over in his VF, and he began to question how effective those similar comments were for his students. He admitted, "My first concern was I felt like I was saying the same thing every time. So, after a while, I started thinking, 'am I helping them?' because what I'm saying is all very similar" (R. Doe 2018b). He also became more cognizant of the variability of his tone of voice and how his students might interpret or misinterpret it. He became highly critical of his appearance in the videos, too. Roger said, "I also paused with the language I use because I thought I was coming across as being too technical, and yet I wasn't sure how to say it any differently. I didn't want to get too casual, too comfortable, and I'm not really sure why" (R. Doe 2018b). Eleonora Papaleontiou-Louca argues that using multimedia to construct knowledge can facilitate metacognitive activity because multimedia allows someone to add "new representations," with sound, image, and text, to create knowledge (2008, 13). Video, as a medium, gave Roger the affordance to hear and see his feedback with alternative representations and to evaluate the holistic effectiveness of his feedback from new angles and perspectives. His new set of representations for the feedback process became most evident in the final interview.

In the third and final interview, Roger reiterated his concern with his tone of voice and body language and the effect it might have on his students' ability to utilize his feedback. His continual expression of these concerns demonstrates a slight shift in his perception of his feedback and pedagogy. For example, he noted some of the differences in how he thinks about feedback when he gives his students written comments versus VF:

> Maybe because I'm not familiar with the video, but also cause I'm watching myself and hearing myself that I need to be more explicit in what I'm trying to say. I need to be more detailed or more precise in the language I'm using. Where you're right. When we're doing written comments, we're so used to doing it, and then it starts with blah, blah, blah, and then it's done. (2018c)

Making a video allowed Roger to watch himself over and over and contemplate the quality of his feedback, how he appeared to his students when he delivered it, and how that feedback sounded, and since he was inexperienced and somewhat cognitively uncomfortable with making VF when he began the study, he appeared to be even more aware, hypercritical, and over-reflective of his feedback. Flavell's (1979) work on metacognition again highlights how "metacognitive experiences are especially likely to occur in situations that stimulate a lot of careful, highly conscious thinking" or "in novel roles or situations, where every major step you take requires planning beforehand and evaluation afterwards" (908). Creating VF for the first time is a new cognitive situation that can stimulate conscious thinking about the feedback and lead to metacognitive experiences for educators.

King, McGugan, and Bunyan (2008) also found that instructors became increasingly more aware of their feedback in their study on audio feedback. One teacher in the study is quoted about her experience creating audio feedback, and she revealed, "I was thinking this person will be listening to this . . . so I will say, 'this is quite good' or 'this needs some work.' Not just the tone of voice but the actual words I was using" (155). The act of creating an audio file and speaking aloud initiated a critical awareness of the feedback content for the instructor that may not have occurred in similar ways when she used written comments. Moving the location of the feedback can alter how teachers see, hear, and think about their feedback. Delagrange (2011) explained that "[c]hanging the location of information . . . changes the way we think about the information, not just conceptually, but visually, aurally, and kinesthetically" (88). Moving feedback into a new medium reshapes how instructors see, hear, and understand the value of their feedback. Changing the mode of the feedback gives the educator a larger purview of their feedback process to critically examine because it initiates reflective dialogue that can help refocus teacher attention on student learning, position the student as a Thou instead of an It, and facilitate pedagogical adjustments and improvements that benefit students.

Once Roger began designing VF, he immediately noticed that his assignments needed to connect to his feedback more succinctly, and formative feedback is dependent on the quality of his assignments and how those assignments are introduced and sequenced into a course. He also realized that he needed to articulate the goals of the assignment more clearly so students understood the learning goals for the assignment and were able to have as much time as possible to complete the assignment. Roger stated, "One of the things I thought is, maybe I needed to introduce the assignment a little bit better than I did, a little more clearly. Maybe I needed to situate what we were learning in a different way" (2018b). Roger admits that these types of introspective moments about his feedback and teaching are rare when he provides written comments:

> I'll write comments on a paper and then I'll put it aside and that's probably it. Here [with VF] I was making comments, or I was making a crib sheet. I'm recording it and watching it again. If there's something in there I don't like, and I only did this like twice, I'd rerecord it. So I was being more thoughtful. (2018b)

Roger may have become more thoughtful with his feedback because he did not want to have to rerecord another video, prompting him to think about the quality of his VF more thoroughly so that he did not waste his time. He became more tactical with his feedback approaches, which is a sign of metacognitive knowledge. Papaleontiou-Louca (2018, 13) explains that "[m]etacognitive knowledge . . . can lead somebody to select, evaluate, revise and abandon cognitive tasks, goals, and strategies" that may not be effective. This metacognitive process continued for Roger as he made more and more videos and started to perceive his feedback content in ways that had previously gone unnoticed. He added:

> In fact, when you watch them [VF], you'll probably see a couple of times where I'm almost pausing, as if I want to get into something else and I don't because I'm conscious of what I'm perceiving, as I don't want to do this too long. I don't want to take too long with this because I don't want—well, first, my time—but also I don't want a student to stop watching it because I'm being too verbose. (2018b)

Roger's increased attention to his audience translated into him taking additional time to consider how his students were hearing and viewing his feedback. He decided that it was important to contemplate how his students might use his comments and how they might receive and digest them, moving his attention towards developing a student-centered focus on feedback and away from authoritative discourses for feedback design that promote I–It relationships with students.

Watching his VF gave Roger an opportunity to consider how accessible or inaccessible his comments were and if his language was too verbose; making VF forced him to consider the value of his comments more than he had done before. Roger said, "I wrote [the feedback] down. Then, when I'm getting ready to video it, I thought, 'OK, were those the accurate things?' I'm almost thinking about the grading or the feedback more than I would have if I had just written it" (2018c). Since he had no experience using VF, he had no idea how his students would react to his video comments, and he became more critical of those comments. Roger was worried whether the students would "get [his] point" on the video, saying, "I guess I'm ultra-conscious, sensitive, to them understanding that [more] than I ever would be from a written comment" (2018b). It is unclear what exactly made Roger "ultra-conscious" of his feedback quality while making VF, but using a new medium to design and deliver feedback made Roger more deliberate with his evaluation and assessment of his feedback. Roger revealed:

> Most of us, when we write comments, we may read it through before going [on], but a lot of us we wrote them and then it goes. With the videos I was watching every video. So I'm like I shouldn't say that. I shouldn't say that. But then I'm like why am I saying that? Why did I write the assignment that way? So it makes you really focus more on it. (2018c)

After watching his VF and reflecting, Roger suggested that he missed several opportunities to generate more effective comments on broader, global concerns, rather than on grammatical and mechanical issues. Seeing himself on video gave Roger a new space to analyze and assess the limitations and advantages of his comments. He mentioned, "I'd say things like, 'you have some readability errors from punctuation and capitalization.' Very basic stuff that I'm not too concerned about, but I was saying that, and the fact that I was saying that meant that some of the bigger issues I didn't have to address" (2018b). Because he spent too much time on grammatical and mechanical errors that, in reality, he was not overly concerned with addressing, Roger had little room to address global issues in his students' writing in the VF that he would have preferred to address. He did not intend to devote so much attention to evaluating grammar in lieu of more productive global and local comments, but watching himself in the videos allowed him to see this limitation in his feedback and to initiate changes.

When Roger agreed to participate in this study, he initially saw the project as a means to become more self-aware of his pedagogy. He told me that our initial discussion of the project during the first interview and some of the brief training I gave him on using the video recorder for the VF were, in and of themselves, metacognitive experiences for him that changed how he saw his teaching right away. Roger contended that VF "gave me a whole different way [of] looking at what I'm assigning, how I'm grading it, and what I'm trying to get out of it with the students" (2018c). He further expounded upon how designing and delivering VF facilitated several metacognitive experiences for him. He stressed:

> Even though it took three and a half hours, afterwards I was like, 'wow.' [Making VF] forced me to focus on the class more in ways I wouldn't have done before, and, so, afterwards that energizes me. It might mean I have more work I need to reprint up, but it's refreshing material that if I wouldn't have done that, I would not have been thinking about refreshing material that way, if that makes sense. (2018b)

Notice that Roger mentioned that he would not have considered refreshing his course material had he not made VF. Learning how to use a new medium to deliver feedback made Roger want to revise his course materials because he noticed something in his feedback and teaching that he had not been able to previously see. This result suggests that, at the very least, instructors can use VF as a tool to assess and evaluate their feedback and teaching and to determine if their feedback is capable of facilitating dialogic pedagogies and I-Thou relationships.

Cheryl Rosaen maintains that video, as a teaching tool, has a capacity to "provide opportunities to promote observation and reflection through repeated viewings" (2015, 6). Teachers can watch and review their VF multiple times and develop critical habits for reflection that can lead to developing better feedback. Reflecting on pedagogical behaviors and feedback patterns that lead instructors to redesigning their teaching materials is dialogic. Teaching tools and approaches that increase self-reflection and lead to improved pedagogies are, by definition, dialogic and capable of providing a jolt to stale pedagogies. Crook et al. studied VF and revealed that many of the subjects in the "study found that the use of video had prompted them to think how to use the feedback opportunity more wisely and to think more broadly about feedback processes" (2012, 394). However, the staff continued to rely on written feedback because they were most comfortable with that delivery mode, and they had the most experience thinking and generating feedback with that mode. This outcome suggests that learning to use new mediums for feedback takes time and that many instructors will revert back to using the forms of feedback they know well or feel most comfortable using. McCarthy (2015) asserted that using alternative mediums for feedback requires instructors and students to manage different evaluation criteria, which may be difficult to grapple with when doing it for the first time; however, it is this grappling process that can lead to more metacognitive experiences. Designing VF can challenge how educators see, hear, and think about their feedback during the making process.

METACOGNITIVE EXPERIENCES AND WILLIAM THE PSYCHOLOGIST

William, an associate professor in psychology, also experienced metacognitive experiences when making VF. Like Roger, he too began to self-dialogue and self-reflect about his feedback process while making VF. William conveyed that he became increasingly aware of what his feedback meant while he was recording it. He disclosed, "I've got to say something for each [student writing assignment]. What am I going to say? So, I figure out something to say, and I check it off. I've got to talk about it, so I have to have more to say than just a sentence. And, so, probably I'm spending more time thinking about it" (W. Doe 2018c). Designing feedback with a new medium prompted William to contemplate whether his comments were relevant, which is not something he said he had done before with his written feedback. When further describing how he designed the content of his VF, William specified that he did not want to make a video to simply thank a student for completing the assignment or to tell a student that he or she did a great job. For him, there was little value in making a video to notify students that they did well on an assignment or activity or to provide them with a series of summative comments that they would be unable to use on the next assignment or use to revise their previous work. William indicated that he had never considered interrogating his written feedback in this way and that using VF gave him more space to critically consider the weight and value of his comments. His internal dialogue about his pedagogy and feedback approaches led to an increased concern for student learning and instantiated a metacognitive experience, which helps to reposition his students as an "I" rather than an "It."

During the interviews, William continued contemplating how well he articulated his feedback in the videos and wanted to discuss whether he should rerecord the videos if he found them problematic or unclear. He was afraid his students would not be able to follow or use them. He (2018a) asked me, "When I videotaped it and I didn't say it exactly the way I think, is it worth it having to redo the whole video or just let it go?" His consistent reflection on his presence in the video, on how well he sounded and appeared to his students, is a definitive step away from the authoritative discourses in higher education that tend to undervalue and ignore pedagogical reflection in favor of teacher-centered classrooms. Watching his VF made William hyperaware of his paralinguistic activity, initiating reflective self-dialogue that triggered a thorough examination of the effectiveness of his feedback. His self-awareness further explains why William continued to exhibit concern about his eye-contact in the VF. After watching himself in the videos, he grew increasingly apprehensive and distressed about his lack of eye-contact at times, and the impact it might have on his students. The newness of this experience made him more metacognitive about how his students might read his eye-contact.

Papaleontiou-Louca asserts that metacognitive experiences "may be more apt to occur when the cognitive situation is something between completely novel and completely familiar" (2003, 14). The novelty of using VF for the first time facilitated more introspection about presence and eye-contact for William. Having to learn how to use a new medium made him more critical of what he was doing, which is why William struggled to figure out a way to maintain better eye contact with the camera when recording the videos. He recounted, "I'm looking down here and the camera is on me, so that doesn't look good. I want to look in the camera and speak to them, so then I have to hold it up there. So, I taped each one. I was taping each [student paper] to the monitor beside the camera" (2018a). His concern with eye contact further demonstrates his concern for students, and the numerous attempts to improve their feedback experience helps to potentially establish and solidify I-Thou relationships between him and his students that can disrupt and erode authoritative pedagogies.

William also evinced signs of meta-awareness when contemplating the background frames of the videos and how those backgrounds might influence his students' perception of him and his feedback. He said, "The first thing I do is I line up and say, 'Okay. What's the view?' Sometimes I say they don't want that view. So, yeah, that's the first thing that I do. And once I do it for the first then I forget about it. But, yes, I do. Each set, I line up and look at the background" (2018b). Making videos intensified William's audience awareness; he continually considered how to improve his students' experiences with his VF. He elaborated on the video background frames and how he kept negotiating those frames, saying, "once in a while I brought the camera home and did it at home, and then I wanted to try to keep it a very neutral background and not show off too much of my apartment and stuff like that" (2018b). Watching himself on video made him anxious about his appearance and how his students might read or misread that appearance, which led to more overt apprehensions about his feedback process and quality.

METACOGNITIVE EXPERIENCES AND JOE THE NANOSCIENTIST

Joe, an assistant professor of nanoscience, also had metacognitive experiences that reshaped how he perceived his feedback. He explained:

> It was kind of weird watching myself. I was watching myself and it's hard to use body language, and I think that's something I want to try to do a little bit more 'cause I was sitting there talking, and I missed the kind of moving around and using my arms and hands to be more expressive. (J. Doe 2018b)

Joe watched himself give feedback on the videos and noticed that he was underutilizing the affordances video provided him, needing to take advantage of body language to communicate more effectively with his students. He also exhibited some frustration with how his assignments connected to his feedback. His first significant metacognitive experience occurred when he realized that the assignment and the VF were not synthesizing like he intended. Joe noted larger problems with his assignment structure after discovering that his VF was somewhat disconnected from the assignment and its learning outcomes. He felt that his videos were getting too long and that his feedback was losing its overall value. He declared:

> the first time [making VF] I had a lot of do-overs. One of the videos was like four minutes, I think, or over two minutes, which I think is getting long. I would get stuck in my thoughts, or things like that. Or I wouldn't like what I was doing. And, so, for this time, I made the assignment itself a little bit shorter, so I had to spend less time reviewing what they wrote. (2018c)

Joe noticed areas in his feedback that failed to connect with the assignment and learning outcomes.

Joe claimed to have difficulty providing VF on the assignment he used for this study because it was too complicated. It required students to complete several difficult tasks at once, making it harder for Joe to structure and organize his feedback in the video. He told me he adjusted the assignment so that he could provide more succinct feedback to his students. Making and watching the videos made Joe aware of a disconnect between the assignment and his ability to provide feedback on that assignment, and this disconnect forced him to alter the assignment so that his feedback became more useful for his students. He decided to use what he defined as "less topics" in the assignment because "in the first assignment I had like three or four questions. So, I limited it to two questions for the second assignment because the nature of the discussion is very open-ended. I do need to take some time and think about what they presented" (2018c). Joe noticed that the assignment he was using did not allow him enough space to provide comprehensive formative feedback and that he needed to make and implement a series of smaller assignments that allowed him more time to read the student work, think about that work, and then develop formative feedback. Joe needed additional time to design his feedback and to think about what he wanted to say to his students. He insisted that he needed to manage the workload required to generate formative feedback more effectively if he wanted to spend an adequate amount of time contemplating and developing comprehensive feedback. Using a new medium to create feedback gave Joe a chance to identify where and how his assignment failed to set up formative feedback. After making VF, Joe realized that his assignment required students to complete too many learning tasks. His students would be unable to manage the amount of feedback required for the assignment, which led to his organization problems designing the VF. Grappling with a new medium was a metacognitive experience for Joe that made him more conscious of the value of his feedback and how his assignment was connected to his feedback.

CONCLUSION

This chapter argued that designing VF facilitated metacognitive experiences for educators through self-dialogue and self-reflection and that metacognition can lead to pedagogical improvements that can undermine authoritative discourses in higher education. Implementing VF provided opportunities for professors to reflect on their teaching and to develop more dialogic approaches for teaching that reposition students as a "Thou." Transformative approaches to teaching, like dialogic pedagogies, ask instructors to experiment with semiotic materials and to build and deliver multimodal learning experiences that open new spaces for students and teachers to connect with each other. Anna Smith and Katrina Kennett (2017) insist that teachers have to redefine teaching so that it highlights how multimodal teaching tools like VF can promote dialogic learning experiences. James Paul Gee (2004) argues that transformative pedagogies rely on the use of every mode and medium to teach, and he professes that teaching requires an understanding of how learners need sounds, images, words, and modal combinations to learn. Gunther Kress and Jeff Bezemer (2008) also indicate that multimodal resources create unique "potentials for learning" (235) for students and teachers, and that "producers as well as users of learning resources—visual artists, editors, writers, teachers, and students—are regarded as meaning-makers or sign-makers" (236). Incorporating VF in teaching and communicating with students can initiate more metacognitive experiences for instructors about the quality of their pedagogy and feedback, which can further facilitate the development of I-Thou relationships between students and teachers, subverting authoritative discourses that impede or obstruct teaching and learning.

REFERENCES

Adkins, Vincent. 1999. "Buber and the Dialectic of Teaching." *The Journal of Educational Thought (JET) / Revue De La Pensée Educative* 33 (2): 178. Calgary, CA: Werklund School of Education, University of Calgary.

Bakhtin, M. M. 1981. *The Dialogic Imagination*. Translated by C. Emerson and Michael Holquist, edited by Michael Holquist. Austin, TX: University of Texas Press.

———. 1994. *The Bakhtin Reader: Selected Writing of Bakhtin, Medvedev, and Voloshinov*. Edited by Pam Morris. New York, NY: E. Arnold.

———. 1999. *Problems of Dostoevsky's Poetics*. Translated and edited by C. Emerson. Minneapolis, MN: University of Minnesota Press.

Bezemer, Jeff and Gunther Kress. 2008. "Writing in Multimodal Texts: A Social Semiotic Account of Designs for Learning." *Written Communication* 25: 166–95. Thousand Oaks, CA: SAGE Publishing.

Borup, Jered, Richard E. West, Rebecca A. Thomas, and Charles R. Graham. 2014. "Examining the Impact of Video Feedback on Instructor Social Presence in Blended Courses." *International Review of Research in Open and Distance Learning* 15 (3): 232–256. doi.org/10.19173/irrodl.v15i3.1821.

Bitzer, Lloyd. 1968. "The Rhetorical Situation." *Philosophy and Rhetoric* 1 (1): 1–14. University Park, PA: Penn State University Press.

Boud, David, and Elizabeth Molloy, eds. 2013. *Feedback in Higher and Professional Education: Understanding It and Doing It Well*. New York, NY: Routledge.

Brophy, Jere. 2008. *Motivating Students to Learn*. 2nd ed. Mahwah, NJ: Lawrence Erlbaum Associates, Inc.

Buber, Martin. 1965. *I and Thou*. New York, NY: Charles Scribner's Sons.

Campbell, Breanna, and Ann Feldmann. 2017. "The Power of Multimodal Feedback," *Journal of Curriculum, Teaching, Learning and Leadership in Education* 2: 1–6. Omaha, NB: College of Education, University of Nebraska at Omaha.

Crook, Anne, Alice Mauchline, Stephen Maw, Clare Lawson, Robyn Drinkwater, Karsten Lundqvist, Paul Orsmond, Stephen Gomez, and Julian Park. 2012. "The Use of Video Technology for Providing Feedback to Students. Can It Enhance the Feedback Experience for Staff and Students?" *Computers and Education* 58 (1): 386–396. Amsterdam, NL: Elsevier.

Delagrange, Susan. 2011. *The Technologies of Wonder*. Logan, UT: Utah State University Press. ccdigitalpress.org/ebooks-and-projects/wonder.

Flavell, John. 1979. "Metacognition and Cognitive Monitoring: A new area of cognitive–developmental inquiry." *American Psychologist* 34 (10): 906–911. doi.org/10.1037/0003-066X.34.10.906

Freire, Paulo. 2005. *Pedagogy of the Oppressed*. Translated by Myra Ramos. New York, NY: Continuum International Publishing Group.

Gee, James Paul. 2004. *What Video Games Have to Teach us about Learning and Literacy*. New York, NY: Palgrave Macmillan.

King, D., S. McGugan, and N. Bunyan. 2008. "Does It Make a Difference? Replacing Text with Audio Feedback." *Practice and Evidence of Scholarship of Teaching and Learning in Higher Education*, 3 (2): 145–163. N.p.

Lamb, James. 2018. "To Boldly Go: Feedback as Digital, Multimodal Dialogue." *Multimodal Technologies Interact* 2 (3): 49. Edinburgh, UK: Centre for Research in Digital Education, Moray House School of Education, University of Edinburgh.

Larson, Mindy Legard, and Donna Kalmbach Phillips. 2005. "Becoming a Teacher of Literacy: The Struggle between Authoritative Discourses." *Faculty Publications* 4: 13. digitalcommons.linfield.edu/educfac_pubs/4.

Martin, Dan. 2018a. "Interview 2." Interview by Joe Doe. April 24, 2018.

—. 2018b. "Interview 3." Interview by Joe Doe. May 6, 2018.

—. 2018c. "Interview 1." Interview by Roger Doe. January 8, 2018.

—. 2018d. "Interview 2." Interview by Roger Doe. March 6, 2018.

—. 2018e. "Interview 3." Interview by Roger Doe. April 20, 2018.

—. 2018f. "Interview 1B." Interview by William Doe. January 11, 2018.

—. 2018g. "Interview 2." Interview by William Doe. March 13, 2018.

—. 2018h. "Interview 3." Interview by William Doe. April 24, 2018.

McCarthy, Josh. 2015. "Evaluating Written, Audio and Video Feedback in Higher Education Summative Assessment Tasks." *Issues in Educational Research* 25 (2): 153–169. www.iier.org.au/iier25/mccarthy.pdf

Papaleontiou-Louca, Elanor. 2003. "The Concept and Instruction of Metacognition." *Teacher Development* 7 (1): 9–30. N.p.

Parkin, Doug. 2017. *Leading, learning, and Teaching in Higher Education*. New York, NY: Routledge.

Rosaèn, Cheryl. 2015. "The Potential of Video to Help Literacy Pre-Service Teachers Learn to Teach for Social Justice and Develop Culturally Responsive Instruction." In *Video Reflection in Literacy Teacher Education and Development,* edited by Evan T. Ortlieb, Mary B. McVee, and Lynn E. Shanahan. Bingley, UK: Emerald Publishing.

Rule, Peter Neville. 2015. *Dialogue and Boundary Learning*. Rotterdam, NL: Sense Publishers.

Salmon, Diane, Alan Rossman, and Vito Dipinto. 2012. "Knowing by Doing and Doing by Knowing: Developing the Metacognition of Middle School Science Teachers." *Science Scope* 35 (6). N.p.

Selfe, Cynthia. 2009. "The Movement of Air, The Breath of Meaning: Aurality and Multimodal Composing." *College Composition and Communication* 60 (4): 616–663. Champaign, IL: National Council of Teachers of English.

Smith, Anna and Katrina Kennett. 2017. "Multimodal Meaning: Discursive Dimensions of e-Learning." In *e-Learning Ecologies: Principles for New Learning and Assessment*, edited by Bill Cope and Mary Kalantis, 88–117. New York, NY: Routledge.

Sommers, J. 1989. "The Effects of Tape-Recorded Commentary on Student Revision: A Case Study." *Journal of Teaching Writing* 8 (2): 49–76. journals.iupui.edu/index.php/ teachingwriting/article/download/1012/998.

Sommers, Nancy. 1980. "Revision Strategies of Student Writers and Experienced Adult Writers." *College Composition and Communication* 31 (4): 378–388. Champaign, IL: National Council of Teachers of English.

Sommers, Nancy. 1989. "Between the Drafts." *College Composition and Communication* 43 (1): 23–31. Champaign, IL: National Council of Teachers of English.

Sommers, Nancy . 2012. *Responding to Student Writers*. New York, NY: Bedford/St. Martin's Press.

Ward, Irene. 1994. *Literacy, Ideology, and Dialogue: Towards a Dialogic Pedagogy*. Albany, NY: State University of New York Press.

9 Classical Education and Partnership Networks: A Model for Higher Education Innovation

Meghan Griffin

As an interdisciplinary field, texts and technology prepares scholars for new modes of production and collaboration in the humanities. I was trained to function as an early adopter of educational technologies and was equipped for the interdisciplinarity of the future. In such a forward-looking field, our interests and energies are focused on what's coming next. Professors, colleagues, and the giants of texts and technology scholarship maintain an expectant posture oriented toward the future. *New* never surprised me; innovation is what we do.

What I did not expect was to follow my studies in texts and technology into a community of classical educators. *Classical* refers to content—great books, art and architecture, history and geography, Greek and Latin—as well as method—memorization, Socratic discussion, and guidance by long-term trusted mentors. The model as old as Plato, Socrates, and Aristotle is rising in popularity and has been reformed to include technologies and modes of inquiry that bring classical education into the twenty-first century. The classical community's focus on truth, goodness, and beauty has become a creative and networked model of diverse learners and institution types that include service providers, universities, educational consultants, and public education networks. Clark and Jain wrote, "In an age which has embraced every novelty, the true rebel is the traditionalist" (2013). Classical education is not old-fashioned; it is endlessly adaptable across time.

Modern education from preschool to higher education is disorienting in its array of options and modalities for delivery. In our current economy of educational choice, families at the K–12 level are aware of options that include public, charter, private, and homeschools, as well as virtual, part-time, STEM, STEAM, Montessori, and other options within each delivery type. There is much to debate about school choice. Has it historically functioned as a public good, or does the education system further entrench inequality? How should public funding play into school choice options? Wherever those debates land, proliferation of choice requires families to navigate educational philosophies and options at the household—and individual student—level. This is especially true in light of the COVID-19 pandemic, where households are required to individually determine levels of comfort and safety balanced with wildly different state mandates for public school reopening and choice options. Given the constant presence of choice-making, humanists can be encouraged that families in some settings are, at least in part, returning to a classical, humanities-rich approach to educational foundations.

This chapter focuses on the resurgence of classical education models and then moves to apply those frameworks to a networked model of higher education. Educational networks of local communities, I will show, contribute to student thriving by providing psychological safety and student supports that aid in retention and persistence for nontraditional student populations. Networked educational communities also offer pathways of affordability and accessibility that result in enrollment growth, despite shrinking university enrollment pools and increased competition for higher education enrollment.

Finally, I will cast a vision for the intersection of family, higher education institutions, local communities, and global educational partners as a model for college credit education in the coming decades. Rhizomatic actants and activities across the home, local communities, and universities evince all of the intensities of a dynamic, living organism as students create assemblages to form their educational experiences. Rather than prescribed inflexible plans, experiences that allow for flexibility and self-defined, mentor-guided paths create a new model for educational pathways. In a networked education, an individual no longer organizes their education around a fixed set of outcomes but instead pursues a series of learning "discoveries" where the result is even unknowable and undetermined. In sum, this chapter describes a movement in education that can be explained through an actor network approach as a social pursuit of truth, goodness, and beauty across institution and organization types. I describe the implications for future delivery of college education in the humanities and related disciplines and invite other texts and technologies scholars to engage in these networked models of humanities education.

Classical Education: A Reemergence of the Humanities

Those who study rhetoric, the structure of classical education, will be familiar. Classical education is comprised of the trivium—grammar, logic, and rhetoric. In some classical traditions, those aspects of the trivium coincide with ages and stages of learning where we are taught the grammar of subjects in the elementary years, dialectic in the middle grades, and then finally rhetoric with deeper understanding of subjects at the high school level. Hallmarks of a classical education include Socratic discussion; working across ages and stages with long-term trusted mentors; exposure to primary sources; study of great works in art, music, literature, and architecture; and language study in Latin or Greek. Classical education is enacted in classical schools and academies, homeschooling communities, and hybrid cottage schools. Those interested in classical education will find a network of actors and affiliations that include the Society for Classical Learning, the Association of Classical and Christian Schools, Trinity Schools, the CiRCE Institute, publishers like Roman Roads Media and Classical Academic Press, and homeschool curriculum providers like Classical Conversations, Inc.

With these multiple pathways to classical education, the exact number of students pursuing this type of education is unknown. What we do see is the proliferation of a market for classical learning and increased enrollments in classical private schools, homeschool networks, and in international contexts as these providers work to quickly translate materials to keep pace with global demand. There is such movement within classical education that students and educators have petitioned US colleges and universities to accept scores from the Classic Learning Test as an alternative to standardized instruments like the ACT or SAT. The appeal of the Classic Learning Test is to measure skills in logic, reason, and reading through exposure to rich passages, where the test itself is worthy to be read. Indeed, there is such interest in classical education that colleges and universities have developed institutes and divisions to house students trained in this tradition. Calvin College, Hillsdale College, New College Franklin, St. John's College, King's College, and other institutions centered on a great books' curriculum are preserving the humanities while growing enrollment.

At Southeastern University, we work closely with the classical homeschooling community to provide college credit options through our Classical Conversations Plus partnership. Classical Conversations, Inc., enjoys an average annual growth rate of fifty-two percent, includes 125,000 students enrolled in 2,500 communities in the United States and thirty additional countries, and ships over half a million books and curricula to classically homeschooling families each year ("Fast Facts" 2018). Forbes magazine has referred to Classical Conversations as the first Uber-like disrupter in the education marketplace (Shlaes 2017). As an educator, my interactions with these students are heartening; sixteen and seventeen-year-old students enrolled in my Greek and Roman Literature courses read original texts and received feedback in Latin, memorized long excerpts, and read in depth the works only excerpted in my own undergraduate studies. Students interact in local learning communities and with professors online. As I share often on the classical education speaking circuit, parents who are concerned with college-readiness for their students ought to be more concerned about ready-collegeness; indeed, colleges anticipate inbound students from a progressive education system and are not building curriculum that presumes a rich exposure to great works of art, literature, or the ability to read primary texts in their original languages.

Educational choice means a rising percentage of students opting out of public school over the past thirty years, though all school enrollment continues to climb alongside population growth. In 2012, the National Center for Educational Statistics found that nearly three percent of the total student population of United States' school-aged children were homeschooled—a figure doubling estimates in the prior decade (Redford et al. 2012). We can expect those numbers to rise quickly in light of the COVID-19 pandemic, where inquiries for Classical Conversations enrollment outpace the prior year by forty percent. Even public-school enrollment has favored charters, magnets, and academies, rather than traditional neighborhood schools. Homeschooling is attractive to counter-cultural movements of all kinds, including multiple religious expressions. The unschooling movement is generally non-religious and avoids curriculum or instruction and instead models itself on child-led learning. University model homeschooling is typically non-religious and allows families to select courses from experts and tutors in a variety of fields. Virtual schooling at home is ideal for medically complex families or those concerned about peer bullying or school violence. Homeschooling is useful for families that travel together for business or lifestyle. Homeschooling today is incredibly diverse in terms of method, delivery, educational philosophy, and in religious expression—when religious at all (Kunzman 2010).

While parents of the past could opt for a neighborhood public school, a local private school, or the rare path of homeschooling, today's parents are offered countless choices in the education landscape, with each selection signifying some adherence to an educational philosophy. Every option is an ever-present option, and all parents are interpellated into opting into or out of traditional, public schooling. Choosing to do the most common thing—registering your child in their zoned public school—means choosing it among a set of many alternatives. Public school districts themselves now offer academies, charter options, and magnet programs, along with state and district sponsored full- and part-time online options.

All the while, classical education is growing as a proportion of home- and private schools due to its perceived fit for ages and stages of development, as well as its ability to expose students to the great works of Western culture while leaving room for individuation, learning differences, and unique student interests. Indeed, the popularity of classical education has spread to include public charter schools in Arizona, Texas, and beyond, with numbers growing each year (Miller, J. 2015). May it be an encouragement to humanities scholars that, given the choice, a growing and significant number of families are opting for humanities-rich, classical learning.

Classical education suffers from perceived elitism in that its focus on the life of the mind is sometimes misconstrued as divorced from economic and practical realities. When STEM skills and coding bootcamps are of immediate market value, learning Latin does not seem so essential, but the value of a classical approach is not an effort to create a gentry class divorced from practicality. Rather, "classical education encourages us that we are capable of becoming an Oxford don who builds bicycles, or a plumber who reads Milton, or a business owner who spouts theology" (Bortins 2010, 40). The aim of classical education is the renaissance person who demonstrates Greek *arête*—excellence, moral virtue—both in their trade and in conversation, who thinks broadly and deeply, and connects with fellow citizens on the most foundational aspects of humanity—our big questions, our hopes, our fears, and meaning-making throughout our lives.

We have established that classical education is thriving in the economy of educational choice, which is good news for the humanities, but what *about* classical education leaves space for continued investment in the humanities for higher education? Four approaches of classical education are described below, along with their implications for the future of the humanities within the academy.

Acceleration and *Festina Lente*

In the current higher education landscape, we benefit from a sustained—although eroding—belief that a college degree is the primary pathway to upward mobility. At the same time, higher education institutions face pressure to deliver pathways to degrees at a lower cost, with less student debt and with shorter time-to-degree. The understood value of a degree, coupled with a desire to drive down costs, results in a praxis that speeds college credit along, accelerates degree pathways, and doubles down on efficiency in courses and programs. Semesters have become sub-terms while courses have become sets of competencies to achieve quickly and cheaply. Students in middle school want to get a head start on high school foreign language and physical education, students in high school want to earn an Associate of Arts degree through dual enrollment, and college students fill 3+1 programs to accelerate completion of professional master's degrees. Everybody seems to be in a hurry to finish, partly in response to states' pressure to reduce time-to-degree as a matter of performance for public funding. In my Florida county, one new charter school will require fifth-grade students to declare a major toward a defined career pathway. I wonder how many of us are doing what we would have imagined at age ten.

Acceleration is not inherently bad, and it does offer financial benefit to students. Acceleration has its place where appropriate and at each student's discretion. In contrast to acceleration, however, classical educators operate with the maxim "*festina lente*," which translates to "make haste slowly." Popularized by Erasmus's *Adagio* in the sixteenth century, *festina lente* balances the concepts of urgency and diligence (Barker 2001). It points toward purposeful lingering over rich concepts and discussions about them. For me, *festina lente* serves as a tether tying learning to the pace of human agency. Work purposefully, in good conscience and with excellence. Learn to relish and to remember, not for short-term test performance.

The drive toward dual enrollment, early achievement, and degree acceleration is grounded in the desire to keep costs low and to get students into the workforce earning wages quickly. It teaches us to prize completion over excellence and turns learning into a transaction with measurable efficiencies. Classical education makes room for acceleration but only at the pace of understanding. Some things take time. *Ordo amoris*—shaping the affections—takes time. We linger over that which we love.

Outcomes and Exposures

In a traditional learning environment, practitioners and curriculum designers refer often to learning outcomes or, in more recent language, Common Core State Standards. Bloom and Krathwohl's *Taxonomy of Educational Objectives: The Classification of Educational Goals* (1974) has shaped such outcomes, and modern educators are adept at linking outcomes, assignments, rubrics, and assessments at the course and program level to measure student learning and enact continuous program improvement.

While classical educators may also rely on outcomes for syllabi and assessments, the priority and fundamental belief undergirding a classical approach is one that avoids over-engineering learning experiences and environments. Instead, classical education focuses on rich *exposures* in order to facilitate learning. In a classical model, repeated exposures may be best. How a text might impact students varies, but the goal of introducing students to Plutarch's *Lives* is not that each student might take the same thing away or that each student might hit the same objective. Rather, the goal is that each student is formed and shaped by an exposure to great works of literature and art, and that exposure might spark something permanent, shaping the soul of the student.

If I have learned one great lesson over the course of my education, it is that great dissonance between concepts yields even greater understanding. The trick is to yield to the angst of the not-yet-figured-out, the seeming impossibility of tension between ideas. If we can sit with that swirl of anxious malalignment long enough, something magical happens—the mind does its work by creating a *new* framework that pulls the dissonant parts into alignment. It is that "aha!" moment we academics live for. It is, indeed, "good practice to let the brain sort out confusion" (Bortins 2010, 101). The question underlying classical assessment, then, is not "at what level has the student met defined learning outcomes?" but rather, "Has the student wrestled with this text? Has it formed their inner life?" That may look like recitations, narrations, or written analyses, but it will not look very much like a test. The test comes many years later when students can recall and draw from the content of their foundational educational experiences.

ATTENDANCE AND ATTENDING

In homeschool circles, the question of instructional time is an ongoing area of contestation. Many public-school districts require registered homeschoolers to keep a record of attendance—as if the child had an option to be "absent" from home—and instructional hours. This practice makes good sense for accountability *if* you believe that time spent on instruction equates to learning. The same question arises when we consider clock hours and college credit in higher education, as opposed to competency-based models that eliminate the belief that time measures learning. Classical educators do not deny that time spent matters, but classical educators would not place value on "instructional time" on its own. Instead, classical educators want to see time spent *with* a text or an idea. Time spent reading deeply, time spent thinking through ideas, time spent pondering, and, with value placed on the times in our futures, we will harken back to these great works and how they have shaped us.

Progressive education on a mass scale measures time in attendance. Students can earn perfect attendance awards and violations are recorded as absences and tardies. One might consider this a life-skill for the workplace, if the workplace also measures time as a measure of engagement—which is increasingly not the case in modern, virtual workplaces. Rather than attendance for clock hours, classical educators think to the Latin *attendere*, from *ad*, "to" + *tendere*, "stretch," where attendance really means "to apply one's mind or energies to." In this conception, one might truly attend to their studies only part of the day, only occasionally, or only in long stretches as the mind moves. In a classical education, attending to literature and art is a sacred activity, not to be rushed or hurried or overscheduled. If we translate the concept to a Montessori education, this would be the stretches of "uninterrupted work time" for children to engage deeply in their work. If we translate this attendance to modern language, it would be *flow*. This deep time is so much more precious than time-on-task and cannot be dictated by an instructor alone.

What attending does require is an atmosphere that allows for deep engagement. Socratic discussion with a sense of psychological safety—a long-term trusted mentor who knows us well and with whom we share a rapport and a body of knowledge—allows for such work. Charlotte Mason envisioned education as "an atmosphere, a discipline, a life" (2017, *viii*). In Mason's imagination, education is a feast and educators set the table with the finest, most delectable, most nourishing foods. Children and students then choose what and how much to eat. It is indeed a liberal, generous education suitable for *liber*, the free man and woman.

School and *Scholé*

Each of these concepts—*festina lente,* exposures, attending—can be summed up in the classical approach to *scholé*, or restful learning. Developed in Joseph Pieper's *Leisure: The Basis of Culture*, *scholé* is Greek for *leisure*. Later used in Latin as *scola*, the root is evident in our English words "school," "scholarship," "scholars," "scholarly," "scholastic," and so on. In each of its modern usages, the connotation is hardly one of leisure.

Pieper traces how the leisure prized by Greeks has come to be identified with idleness and sloth in our competitive, commerce-driven, fast-paced culture. This conflation robs us of the richness of scholé in its original form. We know that "leisure is the free time, *literally* the free time, in which we are not enslaved by practical concerns that keep us from cultivating our higher powers of discernment. Leisure is the condition under which intellectual virtues can be acquired" (Pieper 2009, 4). *Scholé* leaves room for wonder, and, in deep wonder, time is irrelevant. To understand *scholé* is to have a recording of Jesus' apprenticeship model of learning where he issues the following invitation to *scholé*: "I'll show you how to take a real rest. Walk with me and work with me—watch how I do it. Learn the unforced rhythms of grace . . . Keep company with me and you'll learn to live freely and lightly" (Peterson 2016, 1120). The same was true of Plato and Socrates. Just *be with me* and learn. That model for teaching and learning allows for *scholé* and has been passed down through the classical tradition. We are creatures meant for action, but we are also creatures meant for rest. We are bold in reclaiming our humanity when we stop to *enjoy* conversation, reading, and learning without guilt or shame and without rushing.

PARTNERSHIPS, NETWORKS, AND STUDENT THRIVING

While groups of classical educators continue to favor contemplative, restful learning, we see similar shifts toward alternatives in higher education as a harbinger of what is to come for institutional survival in the twenty-first century. There is no doubt that the higher education sector has been rocked by forces from budget cuts to closures in the face of COVID-19. Fortunately, there is still enough public trust in education as the primary vehicle for social and economic mobility that public funding for student aid remains strong. Yet the higher education "marketplace"—as a humanist, forgive me for using the term—must reconcile seemingly insurmountable shifts in the landscape related to adjunctification in the gig economy, proliferation of for-profit providers, changes to regulations and accreditations, market impacts of student loan debt, increased cost of campus operations, dramatically reduced institutional funding, and abbreviated tenure for higher education leaders. Add to that the loss of auxiliary income from dormitories and meal plans as the coronavirus shut down campuses throughout 2020, and many institutions—particularly small private liberal arts colleges—are left scrambling for institutional survival.

For universities to remain relevant and solvent, we must reimagine the ways we reach, teach, and retain students. At Southeastern University, we have taken a networked approach to education that decentralizes the residential campus in order to empower and embolden networks of campuses across the country. Our Unrestricted Education division exists to expand the footprint and impact of Southeastern University beyond its traditional residential campus in Lakeland, Florida. Unrestricted Education houses the university's 175 extension site and regional campus partnerships throughout the United States. Unrestricted Education could just as aptly be named "Partnership Education," and you would have a general idea of what our division does and how we operate. If you are imagining the many state compliance and accreditation challenges for such an operation, if you are wondering how we maintain healthy relationships with traditional faculty and programs, and if you are wondering how it is possible to serve that many partnerships well, you are beginning to ask the right questions.

Despite its complexity, the beauty of higher education partnership is that it allows students to learn within the context of their communities, embeds them in a network of relationships, and provides real-world experience through practicum experiences and internships within their majors and local communities. Non-traditional students in this context have a higher median age, often work while in school, are more frequently under-prepared, and are more likely first-generation college students. Andrew Miller studied student-thriving at these networked campuses as compared to our traditional, residential campus. The Thriving Quotient, a reliable and valid instrument that measures students' academic, interpersonal, and intrapersonal well-being, provides important predictive information as to students' likeliness to engage in academic activities, develop academic plans, maintain healthy relationships, value civic engagement, and maintain a positive perspective of their collegiate experiences (Schreiner 2010).

In his analysis of students thriving across traditional and extension-site campuses at Southeastern University, Miller established that measures of thriving are actually higher among extension-site students and that "spirituality, faculty commitment to diverse students, and psychological sense of community represented the largest contributors to extension-site student thriving" (2019, *vii*). Particularly within the sub-scores related to psychological sense of community, we see the value of networked education and studying in a student's own, local context. The value of psychological safety has been well-established for students and for leaders, with the primary value described as a sense of confidence in belonging. In communities,

> It is easy to know when we are in the Circle of Safety because we can feel it. We feel valued by our colleagues and we feel cared for by our superiors. We become absolutely confident that . . . those with whom we work are there for us and will do what it takes to help us succeed. We become members of the group. We feel like we belong. (Sinek 2014, 29)

Those feelings of belonging are essential to student thriving and result in better communication with professors and peers, more innovation in solving problems, and a sense of confidence and resilience when facing the inevitable challenges of earning a college degree.

For traditional students on a residential campus, these feelings of psychological safety and belonging might be tied to institutional fit, Greek life, athletics, relationships with peers, and other aspects of the student experience. For nontraditional students, those opportunities to build a sense of belonging and community are largely absent. In a site-based model, the need for a psychological sense of community is thereby extended beyond the university proper and into a local context and community. Miller's research indicates this reality as a determining factor in student thriving and extension campus growth:

> Students' membership, ownership, relationship, and partnership in a community are the result of intentional programming at the local extension site. To ensure a sense of community within the extension site, it would be wise for the university to empower the local site leadership to create programs and experiences for students that build networks of interdependent relationships to meet students' needs across the duration of the student experience. Involving a variety of constituents, including local faculty, staff, and . . . personnel will communicate institutional integrity and commitment to student welfare that contribute significantly to thriving. (Miller, A. 2019, 318)

To translate these findings into the language of material-semiotic analysis, partnership education provides space for the artifacts of the university including transcripts, credits, learning outcomes, catalogs, syllabi, master course templates, rubrics, user interfaces, Learning Management Systems, and student-services support in admissions, financial aid, and advising. Beyond those nodes, the university incorporates the extension site's personnel, relationships, friendships, cultural values, adjunct and full-time faculty, practicum experiences, student life, faculty engagement, and peer-to-peer relationships as integral to the student's sense of belonging and their ability to thrive and, in turn, persist to degree completion.

In our partnership model, this means balancing regional accreditation and state compliance with a flexible mindset that values the roles partner-sites play in facilitating the student learning experience. Partner-sites are screened through an institutional approval process that includes a faculty vote through the Unrestricted Education Council, where faculty review partner-sites for mission-fit, facilities, impact on the institution, state compliance, academic credentials of partner-site leadership, and resources for growth. Once approved, programs and courses are delivered using a master course philosophy by the university but are contextualized by site-based, university-vetted faculty on-site with students. The university provides advising, financial aid, and academic and career services support. Extension sites develop their own cultures, student activities, and practicum programs that initiate students into work experience, with an online component graded by a professor. This dispersion of duties means that we hold responsibility for outcomes and learning assessment, but the local relationships add value in mentoring and student life that are just as important as the academics offered by the university. Sites are additionally approved by our regional accreditor, The Southern Association of Colleges and Schools Commission on Colleges (SACSCOC), as well as state boards of education as required.

A partnership approach shifts the work of higher education administration significantly. Rather than focusing on faculty and internal relationships, the work of Unrestricted Education is primarily to translate and mediate between the university and its partners, with special attention to relationships and contexts. Familiarity with networked knowledge production has been essential to thriving in my role. Essential to the mission are mindsets of collaboration, innovation, tolerance for ambiguity, and accountability. No other field but texts and technology could have prepared me for this work on the frontier of partnership educational delivery and design because the mental frameworks of rhizomatic, networked, material-semiotic approaches inform every action and activity within this model. Texts and technology anticipates change and foregrounds adaptations in real time; the perpetual "shifting-ness" within the field becomes a way of being, a way of approaching work creatively. Because the work of texts and technology scholars integrates technological, social, political, and creative concerns, the field is poised to contextualize and align seemingly disparate forces into new modes of production and models for activity.

A mental image of Deleuze and Guattari's assemblages and rhizomatic networks guide my thinking and decision-making process often. I bear witness to processes of deterritorialization and reterritorialization daily. I witness our networks grow, shift, branch, and take shape in constantly shifting ways and it is remarkable to behold. If you imagine a static, top-down, organizational chart as one mode of defining work relationships, the reality of partnership models is as far from it as one can imagine. Instead, the mental framework for such relationships is much more like a constellation—each body is in three-dimensional relationship to the others. In a constellation, power is less about one node's function and more about the gravity that pulls all units into relationship with one another. These frameworks for imagining the network of relationships have been invaluable as I offer academic leadership and oversight in such a dynamic constellation of interests.

Part of networked relationships include, of course, contractual obligations, enrollment targets, accreditation matters, and compliance with state and local entities, all of which are mission-critical and prerequisite to student thriving. But even in such a complex landscape, there remains room for the *scholé* of a modern humanist education and the beauty of the win-win, with mission-matched partners engaged in practical, higher education, emphasizing student growth, development, and engagement. Since 2010, the university's enrollment has grown by roughly 250%, with a vast majority of that growth housed within Unrestricted Education through network relationships. The partnership model works.

At Southeastern University, extension sites are housed primarily with large multi-site churches across a variety of denominational and non-denominational affiliations. While church partnerships would not make sense for universities that do not offer practical ministry degrees, institutions can engage the partner site model with K–12 schools, businesses, non-profit organizations, or any organization type that represents a mission fit for the university. At Southeastern University, each potential partner site is vetted through the Unrestricted Education Council, the university's administrative cabinet, the board of trustees, our regional accreditor, and pertinent state regulatory boards. Partner education sites are subject to all of the rules, regulations, and responsibilities as a university's central campus, and accreditation reaffirmation hinges on including off-campus instructional site operations and oversight central to the university's functioning at every level.

While networked partner-site education is innovative, including local churches among those partner-site locations as a hub for learning and community engagement is quite classical; in fact, the role of church networks cannot be overstated within a Christian context. Equipping the church to partner with universities for education makes use of one of the most long-standing social and formative institutions, making visible the role that human relationships, spiritual formation, and intentional education play in the making of a citizen. Of course, not *all* churches share humanist values and aims, so partner selection remains a crucial role in developing networks.

Rhizomatic Education in the Coming Decades

Classical education serves as a case study for the persistence of humanities in an economy of choice. Southeastern University's partnership education model shows that when universities are embedded in networks, programs grow and students thrive. With those examples as a foundation, I turn now to setting a vision for higher education that actuates the work of texts and technology and the material semiotic tradition to describe a new landscape for the humanities in the twenty-first century.

The nodes comprising higher education networks will include familiar institutions like the university, the home, the workplace, and community and civic organizations in fluid connections. What will be notable is the decentering of the university as dispersion of educational programming and credit-bearing opportunities extend more deeply into those networks and student contexts.

As we have already seen with online education and telework employment, the home is increasingly consequential as a central node for learning and for commerce. For most of the twentieth century, "going to college" meant literally *going*, translocating from one place to another, and joining a university, residential community. Leaving your hometown—or at least your home—meant discovering new worldviews, new cultures, and a new sense of self. Junior and community colleges filled accessibility gaps, even if "transfer" to university was the aim. The technological shift at the turn of the century changed the way we work, learn, and live, and many are rediscovering the home as a hub for all of life's activities. Increasingly, adults are pursuing home-based employment as entrepreneurs or teleworkers, which, in turn, makes home-based education more feasible for families. Leigh Bortins, founder of Classical Conversations, sees her work as a homeschooling entrepreneur as "a participant in this sociological return to home as a hub" (2010, 41). From telework to virtual school, online degrees to tele-docs and e-medicine, incentive to leave home has diminished. This may mean less exposure to the humanities in a freshman-level seminar, but thanks to the foresight of the field and efforts toward digitization, humanities have never been more accessible. The critical thinking developed through liberal arts and the ability to navigate all forms of humanities are essential for pushing back against similar digitization and accessibility of conspiracy theories, militia, and groups with mal-intent.

Like the home, the church will become increasingly important as a potential actor in networked education. The Pew Research Center has marked a decline in church attendance and denominational affiliation, so the "church" here is used broadly to include newer and more progressive church-like affiliation groups like spiritually minded community centers, nondenominational and independent churches, and new expressions churches and movements—like dinner churches, bar churches, and churches without walls. Western higher education developed out of the Academy and Lyceum in Greece and proliferated in the Western seminary system where influencers gathered. In early seminary education, professors would deliver notable sermons while practitioners cared for local congregations, leaving professors cloistered in the ivory tower and divorcing practical ministry from academic study. The partnership model at Southeastern University reunites education and praxis, through practical ministry and business training. Mission-matched partner organizations, like some churches, serve as a conduit for services across a wider network to include financial services, medical care, mental health services, food pantries, and ministries at every age and stage of life. Members work with one another in business relationships, referrals, and mentoring, much like a university's alumni network. As a place where students can experience rich relationships, a sense of belonging, and purpose, the church will remain an important potential actant for interested students as they pursue alternate educational pathways. These long-standing cultural institutions—churches, synagogues, mosques, and other cultural organizations—have long been harbingers of the humanities, offering language study, Latin, Greek, Hebrew, and Arabic; textual analysis, of foundational documents like scriptures; musical and liturgical history, with choirs, orchestras, performance opportunities; and arts education, design, dance, and art appreciation. Universities partnering with mission-matched community organizations will be well-placed for contextual delivery of innovative higher education programs that proliferate the humanities in daily life.

The university, of course, remains essential to driving knowledge-production and thought-leadership and ratifying sound ideas through peer review and processes of critical analysis. Universities must get clear, however, on identifying the areas where they truly add value. Regional accreditation bodies will continue to hold standards for student learning assessment, student support, faculty credentialing, and the shape and content of foundational curriculum and inclusion of topics like diversity, critical thinking, science education, and the like. However, compliance will be enacted through the university's engagement with networks; as one example, the traditional model of an on-campus tutoring center is enacted in partner-sites through an online tutoring vendor and coupled with local, on-site tutors at the partnership-sites where classes are held. Thus, tutoring is not delivered one-to-one, university to student, but rather, the university acts as a conduit, connecting the student with tutoring services. This is one among many potential examples of how the university will function as an affiliation network rather than a direct connection for some aspects of educational support.

As nodes in networked education are added, centers shift and new connections form. For any given student, their place within that network and their connection among nodes could potentially look different. If these networks form constellations, students will situate themselves within the networks uniquely. What future students are *not* likely to do is replicate an outdated model—finish high school, apply to a college, move to that campus, enter as a freshman with zero credits, select a major, and follow a 120-credit-hour degree plan through to completion in four years. That is, of course, a university's *ideal* student—a student for whom the model is designed, and whose dollar value yields the greatest return on institutional recruitment investment—but in a networked environment, why would a student stay in one place for four full years? Why learn in just one place from just one group of people?

The modern student we must anticipate will apply to campus with credit—dual enrollment, transfer, or certificate-program credit of some kind. Articulation agreements will be increasingly useful to define potential pathways from market-based learning experiences into the university system. Once enrolled, the student of tomorrow will assemble a degree from modular components like gap year programs, industry certifications, and academic immersions to craft a customized educational pathway—a pastiche uniquely suited to their interests. Disciplinary integrity will rest on defining which pathways work and how they should be shaped. For students going into professions like medicine, engineering, or law, there will always be an industry-driven, prescribed course of study, but for students pursuing the arts, learning to create their own niche in the job market and pursuing their passions, degrees will look more individualized. A student pursuing a degree in, say, digital media, could do a semester-long coding bootcamp outside the university, a semester of on-campus coursework with university professors, a semester of internship supplemented with online coursework, and a semester abroad at a partner institution. The outcome is a digital media degree that is much more personalized than completing two years of coursework from a catalog on campus.

In addition to multiple pathways within existing majors, modular degrees will be increasingly attractive for students who are accustomed to individuation, like the many students coming to institutions with an individuated K–12 experience—homeschooled or otherwise. As we design the programs of the future, we must think around certificates and intensives for these students. Tying modular degree components to workplace pathways is one way to ensure they will attract students. The nature of the student's work will depend entirely upon what the student wants to accomplish and what experiences are important to them. Many of the potential short-term study opportunities can be outside the university system; the university will need to learn how to incorporate such rich experiences for credit through articulations and concurrent credit models. This illusion of universities owning all learning has ceased, so we must learn to acknowledge, assess, and accredit learning that happens across our larger networks.

In the same way that student experiences will be flexible, so, too, will student assessments. Many universities have worked with portfolio models, but in a modular and flexible degree pathway, portfolio curation and storytelling become essential. The student will need to become a storyteller for both their university advisors and potential employers, curating the experiences of their degree to demonstrate their unique preparedness to solve a problem or enter a field. In sum, students will market their own degrees and their own "brands" as part of translating their learning into the marketplace. The humanities will be an essential place to hone the necessary rhetorical and creative skills to make such self-marketing possible and profitable.

In this networked model, workplaces, university systems, educational partnership organizations, families, and community networks all contribute to a student's education and coalesce to develop a customized experience unique to the student. Learning is not held only at the university but distributed in ways that allow for capturing credit in context. A student's primary role will be to pastiche a suitable degree and to tell the story of that degree and how it has prepared them to enter the workforce;

for the student, educational experience is always an assemblage of their own making within the nodal spaces of the network.

The single most important factor in an assemblage education will be that of the long-term, trusted mentor we recognize from the classical model. To navigate partnership education assemblages, students will require mentors who know them well, help the student select pathways, mediate for gaps, and help the student capitalize on the most fitting educational opportunities, given their goals and aims. Students who are successful in this model will require a sponsor to guide them through. They need their "walk with me and work with me" teacher, their Socrates. *That* relationship is the crux of an excellent education in any century, which continues to define the future of the professoriate.

Above all, administrators, professors, and students alike must recapture the meaning of *scholé*, and the humanities are the best place to encounter such relationships. For education to be integrated in our life, integrated into our networks, dispersed through our communities, and shaping the deepest parts of ourselves, education must be a *part* of life, rather than a four-year diversion from it. As educational leaders, may we model the value of a humanist education by living out the pace of *scholé*. It is through us that others will come to know the joy of a robust, rich, twenty-first century education.

References

Barker, William. 2001. *The Adages of Erasmus*. 2nd ed. Toronto, CA: University of Toronto Press, Scholarly Publishing Division.

Bauer, Susan Wise, and Jessie Wise. 2016. *The Well-Trained Mind: A Guide to Classical Education at Home*. 4th ed. New York, NY: W. W. Norton & Company.

Baudrillard, Jean. 1994. *Simulacra and Simulation*. 14th ed. Translated by Sheila Faria Glaser. Ann Arbor, MI: University of Michigan Press.

Bauerlein, Mark. 2018. "Is This the Hardest Course in the Humanities?" *The Chronicle of Higher Education*, March 25, 2018. www.chronicle.com/article/The-Hardest-Course-in-the/242896.

Bortins, Leigh. 1997. "Fast Facts | Classical Conversations." Accessed July 14, 2019. members.classicalconversations.com/christian/about/fast-facts.

Bortins, Leigh A. 2010. *The Core: Teaching Your Child the Foundations of Classical Education*. 1st ed.. New York, NY: St. Martin's Griffin.

Caldecott, Stratford. 2012. *Beauty in the Word: Rethinking the Foundations of Education*. Brooklyn, NY: Angelico Press.

Caldecott, Stratford. 2017. *Beauty for Truth's Sake: On the Re-Enchantment of Education*. Reissue ed. Ada, MI: Brazos Press.

Clark, Kevin, and Ravi Jain. 2013. *The Liberal Arts Tradition: A Philosophy of Christian Classical Education*. 3rd ed. Camp Hill, PA: Classical Academic Press.
Krathwohl, David R., Benjamin S. Bloom, and Bertram B. Masia. 1956. *Taxonomy of Educational Objectives: The Classification of Educational Goals*. Philadelphia, PA: David McKay Publications.
Kunzman, Rob. 2010. "Homeschooling and Religious Fundamentalism." *International Electronic Journal of Elementary Education* 3 (1): 17–28. Oslo, Norway: Kura Publishing House.
Latour, Bruno. 2005. *Reassembling the Social: An Introduction to Actor-Network-Theory*. Oxford, UK: Oxford University Press.
Mackenzie, Sarah. 2015. *Teaching from Rest: A Homeschooler's Guide to Unshakable Peace*. Edited by Dr. Christopher Perrin. 2.0 ed. Camp Hill, PA: Classical Academic Press.
Mason, Charlotte M. 2017. *A Philosophy of Education*. N.p.: Living Book Press.
Michael, Mike. 2016. *Actor-Network Theory: Trials, Trails and Translations*. Thousand Oaks, CA: SAGE Publishing.
Miller, Andrew E. 2019. "College Student Thriving: A Comparison of Innovative Extension Sites to the Traditional College Campus." PhD diss., Azusa Pacific University. pqdtopen.proquest.com/pubnum/13806693.html.
Miller, John M. 2015. "Back to Basics." *National Review*, October 19, 2015. www.nationalreview.com/magazine/2015/10/19/back-basics-2/.
Perrin, Christopher. 2005. *An Introduction to Classical Education*. 2.5 ed. Camp Hill, PA: Classical Academic Press.
Peterson, Eugene H. 2016. *The Message: The Bible in Contemporary Language*. Colorado Springs, CO: NavPress, Inc.
Pieper, Josef, and James V. Schall. 2009. *Leisure: The Basis of Culture*. 1st ed.. San Francisco, CA: Ignatius Press.
Plato. 2002. *Plato: Five Dialogues: Euthyphro, Apology, Crito, Meno, Phaedo*. 2nd ed. Edited by John M. Cooper, translated by G. M. A. Grube. Indianapolis, IN: Hackett Publishing Company, Inc.
Redford, Jeremy, Danielle Battle, and Stacey Bielick. 2017. "Homeschooling in the United States: 2012." *National Center for Education Statistics*, April 7, 2017. nces.ed.gov/pubsearch/pubsinfo.asp?pubid=2016096rev.
Sayers, Dorothy L., and CrossReach Publications. 1948. "The Lost Tools of Learning: Symposium on Education." *Hibbert Journal: A Quarterly Review of Religion, Theology, and Philosophy* 46. London, UK: E.T. Heron.
Schreiner, Laurie A. 2010. "The 'Thriving Quotient': A New Vision for Student Success." *About* Campus 15, (2): 2–10. doi.org/10.1002/abc.20016.
Sinek, Simon. 2014. *Leaders Eat Last: Why Some Teams Pull Together and Others Don't*. 1st ed. New York, NY: Portfolio.
Shlaes, Amity. 2019. "Hail The (Ed) Work-Around." *Forbes*. Accessed July 14, 2019. forbes.com/sites/currentevents/2017/04/18/hail-the-ed-work-around-2/.

10 Pedagogy of Play: Fluxus in the College Classroom

Marci Mazzarotto

Pedagogy of play is an understudied concept, particularly in its use within post-secondary education, as evident by the lack of academic publications on the subject. However, the positive effects of play are being studied by a team of researchers at Harvard University's Graduate School of Education, through an extensive and multifaceted project known as Project Zero (PZ). Harvard's PZ was founded in 1967 by Nelson Goodman, a professor of philosophy, who taught several famous contemporary theorists such as Noam Chomsky. PZ was created with the specific intent "to study and improve education in the arts. Goodman believed that arts learning should be studied as a serious cognitive activity but found that the general communicable knowledge about arts education was zero," hence the project's name (Newmann 2017).

While remaining grounded in the empirical and critical analysis of the arts within educational settings, the scope of PZ's research has expanded extensively over the past five decades, and in 2015, they began a dedicated "Pedagogy of Play," PoP project. PoP was initially deployed in elementary school classrooms in Denmark, 2015, and South Africa, 2017, and the research from both locations reveals the importance of purposeful play as a key element in a child's learning process and development. PoP's findings state that "by fostering engagement and stimulating sense making, play allows learners to build domain-related skills, content knowledge, and creative thinking" (Mardell 2016, 4). In January

2020, the PoP team began classroom observations in several Boston area schools, as researchers are interested in developing a better context and understanding of pedagogy of play in the US, as well as abroad.

The term pedagogy *of* play—rather than pedagogy *as* play—is utilized throughout this chapter, in order to more clearly align with the verbiage and experiments set forth via PZ's PoP research. There are three key ideas to note with relation to the ongoing dialogue surrounding pedagogy of play, particularly when considering PZ's contribution to the current research:

1. Empirically driven data about the efficacy of play as a form of pedagogy is limited. This is due in part to various factors, such as the relatively new academic interest in critically researching the topic, the lack of other well-funded projects beyond Harvard's PoP, and the partially subjective nature of the data that relies on qualitative analysis from methods like researcher observations and participant reflections.

2. The existing data, however, does demonstrate that forms of play, ranging from drawing to comedic improvisation, is effective in fostering student engagement in the learning process, that, in turn, aids in building the skills necessary for creative thinking.

3. The research conducted on pedagogy of play is focused primarily on young children—pre-kindergarten through middle school—although it is slowly branching into secondary schooling and beyond. While the current research only brushes upon higher education and adult learning, PZ's PoP data, nevertheless, indicates that play is an effective learning tool for both children and adults alike.

The need remains for continued discourse and additional research in deploying and assessing pedagogy of play in various learning contexts; however, at the center of PoP's research is the key notion that:

> *Play is a core resource for learning.* When people play they are engaged, relaxed, and challenged—states of mind highly conducive to learning. Through play, children and adults try out ideas, test theories, experiment with symbol systems, explore social relations, take risks, and reimagine the world. They develop agency, empathy, and their imaginations. (Krstich 2016)

Consequently, in addressing how artistic ideas inspired by Fluxus, an avant-garde art movement, are utilized in the college classroom to foster student engagement and creative thinking, this chapter seeks to contribute to the limited academic discourse on the role of pedagogy of play in higher education. It highlights defamiliarization as key to the process of learning and knowledge acquisition, Fluxus-inspired ideas as the tools encouraging defamiliarization to occur, and greater levels of student engagement and creative thinking as the by-product of playing with Fluxus in a pedagogical context.

The pedagogical ideas and sample assignments presented are methods of reinvention that have demonstrated success in fostering greater levels of student engagement and creating higher quality work. The success of such assignments was measured via formative assessments of ongoing student participation and enthusiasm with the subject matter inside the classroom, as well as the summative assessment of projects indicating higher quality of work conducted outside of the class (e.g., formal grades above the eighty percent range when assessed against a single-point rubric). It is important to note, however, that the concept of play as central to the learning process is anything but new, as many educators from Plato to John Dewey have

> extolled the virtues of play and playfulness in learning; however, playful learning has rarely been a prevalent approach in primary or secondary education. This is certainly the case in the last 150 years in Europe and the US, with the dominance of the industrial model of school. (Mardell 2016, 10)

The dominance of an industrial model of schooling remains; however, numerous progressive changes to education have been made throughout the decades, such as a greater emphasis on curriculum development that is student- rather than teacher-centered. As PZ's PoP research illustrates, employing play in the classroom is foundational to prepping the mind for learning.

Process: Defamiliarization

Historically, the experimental methods and creative practices of the avant-garde resided within the periphery of institutionalized art, thus making such practices—in their original contexts—"unfamiliar." The importance of presenting audiences with the unfamiliar, though often combined with the familiar, was to make way for a key moment in the learning process. In his 1917 essay, "The Art of Technique," Russian literary theorist, Viktor Shklovsky, discusses the defamiliarization process as follows:

> And art exists that one may recover the sensation of life; it exists to make one feel things, to make the stone stony. The purpose of art is to impart the sensation of things as they are perceived and not as they are known. The technique of art is to make objects "unfamiliar," to make forms difficult, to increase the difficulty and length of perception because the process of perception is an aesthetic end in itself and must be prolonged. Art is a way of experiencing the artfulness of an object: the object is not important. (2)

Shklovsky emphasizes the importance of changing perception as a way of changing experience, because "if the whole complex lives of many people go on unconsciously, then such lives are as if they had never been" (1917). That is, if we live only within the realm of what is familiar, then we cease to exist at all, as being exposed to new and unfamiliar perspectives and experiences help us break away from our comfort zones and allow for deeper personal growth.

Dewey, extending Shklovsky's work on defamiliarization, argues that familiar works only require "recognition" and "perception," meaning "that when we are familiar with a work of art, we do not perceive it so much as recognize it. This recognition can be a kind of anesthesia, a hinderance to perception and the experience of the work" (Marshall and Donahue 2014, 4). In content creation and distribution—artistic or otherwise—Fluxus seeks to defamiliarize both artist and audience, serving as a creative method that is adaptable and encouraging of students to think and understand beyond what is perceived as "known."

However, as Fluxus artist and scholar, Ken Friedman, points out, understanding the foundational context of the familiar is absolutely necessary to transition into discovering the unfamiliar, as familiar-unfamiliar share a symbiotic relationship. Friedman explains that

> the big question is contextual. . . . All education requires some sense of dialectical engagement. One can't be satisfied with given answers. To move beyond given answers always requires widening the inquiry. To widen an inquiry, however, one needs a set of reasonable skills and a grasp of [what has] been done to

date, what human beings have discovered so far. For this to be possible, one needs to engage fully in the dialectic—to know what has been known, and to work towards an unknown. The possibility of defamiliarization doesn't exist without a grasp of the familiar. (email to author, 2020)

Thus, encouraging students to engage in discourse with the familiar while using unfamiliar methods aids in shifting perspectives that then allow for knowledge acquisition. What does it mean to be human, in both a collective and individual sense? Within the avant-garde arts, such knowledge is produced almost exclusively via dialectical inquiry (e.g., creative experiments and exploratory research) versus data-driven, empirical inquiry.

Arts-based inquiry relates to Shklovsky's theory of defamiliarization, in that an art object is created and re-interpreted with the intent of shifting the audience's perspective. Art theorist and educator, Graeme Sullivan, argues the following:

> The process of making art and interpreting art adds to our understanding as new ideas are presented to help us see in new ways. These creative insights have the potential to transform our understanding by expanding the various descriptions, explanatory, and immersive systems of knowledge that frame individual and community awareness. These forms of understanding are grounded in human experiences and interactions and yield outcomes that can be individually liberating and culturally enlightening. (2005, 97)

What Sullivan describes above is intrinsic to avant-garde practices, as Fluxus sought to destroy the notion that life and art are separate; their aim was to reframe both as working in unison and, ultimately, as part of the human experience.

METHOD: FLUXUS AND THE AVANT-GARDE

Fluxus depended upon both artistic innovations and theoretical interventions to drive its principal ideas; thus, it was not uncommon to find both artist and theorist roles encompassed within the same person. Numerous Fluxus artists like Friedman, Joseph Beuys, John Cage, and Nam June Paik taught at the college level and brought their experiential artistic practices into their classrooms. The seemingly-natural fluency between artist and theorist is a unique feature to Fluxus, not because other avant-garde movements entirely lacked this dynamic but because it enjoyed a more defined presence within Fluxus. While some Fluxus artists sought to disrupt institutional practices by partaking in some of them (e.g., Cage teaching at established institutions like Mills College, The New School, and Chicago's Institute of Design), room remains for the re-invention and re-adaptation of Fluxus ideas into contemporary pedagogical situations. Not only are Fluxist methods of invention easy—as they require little practical skill—such methods center on transforming the familiar into something "new," therefore allowing for a renewed context of an old perspective.

While qualitative and quantitative methods remain key in various kinds of academic research, these methods do not preclude additional creative and inventive tools that provide a more dynamic inquiry process. Referring to the works of Sigmund Freud—particularly those related to the conscious and unconscious mind—André Breton, founder of the Surrealist movement, addresses methods of inquiry that move beyond the conventional. Breton's first *Surrealist Manifesto*, published in 1924, asserts,

> On the evidence of [Freud's] discoveries, a current of opinion is at last developing which will enable the explorer of the human mind to extend his investigations, since he will be empowered to deal with more than merely summary realities. Perhaps the imagination is on the verge of recovering its rights. If the depths of our minds conceal strange forces capable of augmenting . . . those on the surface, it is in our greatest interest to capture them; first to capture them and later to submit them, should the occasion arise, to the control of reason. The analysts themselves can only gain by this. But it is important to note that there is no method fixed a priori for the execution of this enterprise, that until the new order, it can be considered the province of poets as well as scholars, and that its success does not depend upon the more or less capricious routes that will be followed. (n.p.)

Breton argues that an artist or researcher is free to extend her investigation into the realm of the unknown and, should she deem it necessary or appropriate, can analyze the results of such inquiries using rational logic. Thus, Breton's main preoccupation was the *process*, even if it consisted of information primarily, if not solely, derived from a mental state extending beyond conscious logic. Breton's process was influenced by Freud's theory of free association; thus, the ultimate purpose was to unleash imaginative powers through automatic, unrestrained expression.

Fluxus, like the Surrealists, conducted experimental research as a form of creative expression and social communication that became central to their collective work as avant-garde artists; in turn, "Fluxus offered a research methodology for . . . 'networked ideas' and demonstrated the value of these ideas in various experiments. . . . These networks are based on an interactive model of art rather than on the traditional model of art as a one-way communication from sender to receiver" (Saper 1998, 136). Similar to modernist avant-garde movements, who also preferred exploring the social over the aesthetic, Fluxus was unique in that its creative explorations contained a pedagogical focus. Fluxus founder, George Maciunas, explains the movement's "objective was social, not aesthetic, and . . . [that] this social project specifically concerns the dissemination of knowledge—the social situation of pedagogy" (Saper 2001, 44).

Focused not only on new and creative means of production, avant-gardists also sought unique ways of distribution because they "shunned museums, theaters, and mainstream publishing houses and reached their audiences through alternative outlets" (Berghaus 2005, 14). By producing and distributing works within a multimedia space (e.g., blog, podcast, video) or even acting as a cultural critic when conducting peer-review, students, like avant-gardists, are encouraged to move beyond the accepted institutionalized methods of production and distribution. However, simply changing the medium is not sufficient, as there must be a greater shift away from the familiar towards the unfamiliar to allow for a renewed perspective.

In thinking about a re-interpretation of both content and apparatus, it serves to echo Marshall McLuhan's controversial and prophetic remark "the medium is the message." As exhaustively stated in existing media studies discourse, McLuhan did not believe that the message itself ceased to matter; it is that the medium has vast sociocultural impact on the manner that content is created, distributed, and received. McLuhan makes a key argument about the defamiliarizing qualities of technologies and the new environments they produce—he argues

> that any new medium "tends to create a new environment," and that "the arts and the sciences act as anti-environments that make us able to perceive the environment" even if they themselves tend to become our environment in the age of electricity;

this forces us to "create new strategies of attention and perception." (quoted in Citton, 2017, 294)

McLuhan believes that it is only the child and artist who have the ability to re-invent the environment with a renewed sense of perception. Without a constant renewal of perception, we remain stuck in outdated modes of thinking about the media environment that surrounds us.

Therefore, encouraging students to experiment with digital platforms functions as a way to defamiliarize them with the object so they perceive it as new. By engaging in passive consumption of online content, from binge watching a show to endlessly scrolling on social media, students are stuck in what Shklovsky terms as "habitual, automatic" perception, not conducive to engagement and, thus, ultimately failing to produce new knowledge. The automatic thinking patterns of the passive media consumer echo the Nobel prize winning work of economist and psychologist Daniel Kahneman. Kahneman states that the human mind is divided into two systems: "System 1" that is fast (e.g., unconscious, automatic, effortless) and "System 2" that is slow (e.g., conscious, deliberate, effortful).

Thus, the defamiliarization process should trigger System 2 to make us conscientiously reanalyze our heuristics, which are shortcuts (often biased) based upon a variety of individual factors and context. Some students shy away from engaging with experimental methods that allow for the re-invention of content—as they would prefer to remain in System 1; however, most students do take up the challenge and demonstrate a higher level of satisfaction in overcoming what they initially perceived as an obstacle—in turn, activating System 2.

Since the goal is to defamiliarize, students must learn that creating content in a fully digital format is different from creating in print. For example, if a student is composing and distributing an argumentative essay via a podcast on a topic that is entirely new to her, she will first need to learn how podcasting tools work from a production standpoint and then understand her potential target audience. A form of defamiliarization takes place in creating unfamiliar content on an unfamiliar platform, as this encourages students to perceive the information and the medium in a new way. Utilizing play in a pedagogical context contributes to the creation of the anti-environment, primarily preoccupied with promoting learning and knowledge acquisition through the defamiliarization process.

It is difficult to shift perspectives without adapting some level of creative and experimental research practices. Friedman explains, "Fluxus was a forum for experimentation. The commitment to experimentation and research was profound" (1998). Addressing the research orientation so inherent to the collective Fluxus attitude, he states:

> Most artists, even those who believe themselves experimentalists, understand very little about the way ideas develop. In science, the notion of collaboration, or theoreticians, experimenters and researchers working together to build new methods and results is well established. Fluxus applies this idea to art. Many Fluxus works are the result of numbers of artists active in dialogue. (1998, 93)

The scientific method itself, however, is employed in a variety of different ways and has been a topic of continued debate among scientists. Various schools of thought offer different perspectives regarding the process of scientific inquiry—from Aristotle's deduction-induction method to Thomas Kuhn's paradigm shifts. While there is no universally accepted version of the scientific method, it still offers key principles to the discovery process. Responding to the ongoing debate on climate change, for example, the National Center for Atmospheric Research provides a concise explanation of the continued importance of the scientific method, even with its apparent flaws:

> Science is a human activity, and no human is infallible. Science is also a community activity, and scientists rely on each other to question, challenge, and improve one another's work. When corrections are made, this is not a sign that the system is broken but rather that it's working as designed. (2015)

The scientific method functions as a simplified aid in organizing the discovery process towards the acquisition of new knowledge, and as addressed herein, refers to a continuous process focused on producing new knowledge and a different perspective about an existing body of knowledge. Experimenting with elements of the scientific method (e.g., a preliminary hypothesis or historical contextualization of a particular object) is another tool that assists in the process of defamiliarization and knowledge acquisition. While students are familiar with the basics of the scientific method, it is not a concept most non-science majors have ever directly experimented with, particularly within an arts and humanities classroom setting.

Discovery and Chance

In the process of defamiliarization, whether through a class assignment or an organization, the element of chance comes into play, but one must be prepared to welcome it. For example, in conducting research about an organization that is the focus of a culture jam piece, it is not unusual to discover unanticipated data, particularly when following specific links—explicitly associative or not—that lead to new information, such as the organization's political ties. Having a prepared mind and eye to decipher such instances is significant in that it alters our project in uniquely strategic ways, much like in the process of scientific discovery.

Alexander Fleming's accidental discovery of penicillin is one example of discovery through chance. In "Causal Thinking in Science: How Scientists and Students Interpret the Unexpected," psychology professors, Kevin Dunbar and Jonathan Fugelsang (2005), describe how serendipitous events are vital components in the process of scientific inquiry, particularly if the scientist is prepared for the unexpected. Expanding on Louis Pasteur's belief that "chance favors the prepared mind," Dunbar and Fugelsang's argument supports the notion that since nearly half, or more, of all scientific discoveries encounter an unanticipated element, scientists will benefit from being prepared to observe and embrace the unexpected when conducting their experiments (62–64).

A core part of the avant-garde process is its openness to the unanticipated element and the chance moment that occur in the mundane aspects of everyday life, often embracing the elements of play as well. Chance, however, is pre-planned and manipulated or occurs naturally and accidentally or, as Peter Bürger argues, is either *direct* or *mediated*. Avant-gardists employed the element of chance in both ways. For example, direct chance allows materials to develop naturally, with minimal interference; mediated chance carefully creates a situation, but results are often unpredictable, such as Allan Kaprow's "happenings" (Bürger 1984, 67). Central to Kaprow's mediated chance events is the notion of play as pedagogy, as he was "dismayed with the plight of humanities programs, the training of professional teachers and the attitudes of college-level art students" (Krstich 2016).

Ultimately, "Kaprow insisted that universities should establish experimental institutes to advance research and creation in the visual artists, as well as an artist-in-residence program that would serve the needs of the lower schools" (Krstich 2016). Kaprow, Friedman, and Paik are three artists, among many, who saw Fluxus as having a role in pedagogical reformation in the college classroom. Fluxus artists so often employed play and experimentation as tools to foster a progressive and collaborative learning environment, similar to the vision of educational reformists like Dewey and Paulo Freire.

Paying attention to chance events proves useful as, "human beings, in general, and scientists, in particular, appear to have a propensity to attend to the unexpected, have definitive strategies for sifting through these findings, and focus on the potentially interesting" (Dunbar and Fugelsang 2005, 73). Thus, scientists and artists employ chance events in developing their theoretical and artistic pursuits—scientists seeking empirical confirmation and artists seeking something else. Additionally, "using the trappings of the science experiment suggests a way to further displace the interpretation of Fluxus as an art movement. Building and interacting with their work, rather than passively appreciating it as a finished product, changes interpretation into a generative project" (Saper 2001, 137). Moving from an interpretive project to a generative one is key in promoting student engagement and creative thinking, particularly in a media-saturated society. Why? Because it functions to defamiliarize students from their all-too-familiar role in passively consuming media. Students understanding the basics of media production (e.g., storytelling and editing) helps move them from passive viewers into active producers as they form deeper knowledge about the ways that content is created, distributed, and consumed.

Similar to scientists re-developing an experiment based on initially unexpected results, Fluxus artists perceived value in the experimental process of trial and error, regardless of whether the process was complete or a finished product was achieved. Unlike the sciences, however, the unexpected results of a Fluxus experiment become part of the process itself, as artists may be more interested in the varying results of a particular experiment, rather than repeating the same experiment to gain a specific result. Two significant examples of Fluxus experiments include George Maciunas's development of a school curriculum focused on the practical components of an art-based education ("Curriculum Plan"), and more importantly, his Flux housing project ("The Fluxhouse Cooperatives of

SoHo"), that began the revitalization process of New York City's SoHo neighborhood and also helped to—for better or worse—set the stage for the regentrification of neighborhoods across the country.

Through its various activities, Fluxus was akin to a laboratory with large manufacturing concerns, as "they attempt[ed] to develop new products through endless rounds of experiments, failures and sharing of success among participants" (Saper 2001, 139). The classroom functions in a similar way—a place where information is presented, researched, and questioned, subjectively or objectively contextualized, and subsequently reinvented and placed into a different context. Creative experimentation, no matter how minute, greatly contributes to deepening a student's ability to think actively and critically. For example, a performance piece engages students in the creative process, while simultaneously fostering a space for collaboration, and automatic writing exercises or project journals aid in breaking away from more familiar modes of writing, like the five-paragraph structure. In the Fluxus experimental lab, performance and publications were foundational in the process of de-institutionalizing standard practices of the art world. However, what constitutes a performance or publication within a Fluxist context differs greatly from that of the mainstream, as the latter centers around maintaining an elitist reputation like a performance at the Lincoln Center or a publication on the *New York Times* best-seller list.

Nevertheless, Fluxus inspired performance and publication prove great activities to utilize in the classroom. Not only are these activities simple, as they require minimal talent and skill, but they also require little-to-no direct content knowledge. These activities also allow students an opportunity to play with the familiar in unfamiliar ways, such as students performing an activity rather than simply presenting it or creating a multimedia essay. The following pages discuss three types of activities—culture jamming, mail art, and performance—as forms of pedagogy of play in the college classroom.

Example: Culture Jamming

Culture jamming demands higher levels of defamiliarization because it forces both content creator and consumer to look at a familiar object (e.g., an Apple iPad) in an unfamiliar way—(e.g., contributing to poverty). The criticism of Apple as an inhuman, capitalist machine has been the subject of countless culture jam pieces, calling out the tech giant as a major contributor to addiction issues, poverty, abuse, greed, hunger, and narcissism—to name a few. More specifically, culture jamming uses "various forms of semiotic defamiliarization," as it "seeks to interrupt the flow of mainstream, market-driven communication—scrambling the signal, injecting the unexpected, jarring audiences, provoking critical thinking, inviting play, and public participation" (DeLaure and Fink 2017, 6). In an advanced theory course ("Mass Media & Social Issues"), a culture jam assignment provided students with the opportunity to play with an unfamiliar concept. The project was substantial in scope and begins with students selecting a media object to analyze and subsequently re-invent. The media object was anything from a specific consumer product to a major corporation. Students then manually outlined several creative ways that they would like to re-create the objects or message, eventually choosing the one that best fit their ultimate goal. After the object was re-invented, students must critically analyze their own defamiliarization or familiarization process to understand how and why we culture jam.

The final deliverables include a two-part write up, one describing the pre-process of contextualizing the object students chose to "jam," and the post-process, where students discussed and reflected on the intent within their "jamming" process. The remainder of the formal grading focused on the original jammed object that students created using Adobe Photoshop. None of the students had ever done such a project before and while they found it challenging at first, most reported feeling confident about their final submissions. In the first and only rendition of this assignment thus far, the benchmark set at the time was that eighty percent of all students in class must achieve at least a seventy percent on the final project. That was met and exceeded, as eighty-two percent of students received a grade of seventy-four percent or higher. These numbers are surprising considering the project's complexity, level of theoretical difficulty, students' lack of experience using graphic design tools, and their prior unfamiliarity with the process of culture jamming.

While culture jamming, as a practice, is not directly inherited from Fluxus, its core concepts relate to Fluxist ideals of play, humor, institutional dissent, and defamiliarization. Much like culture jamming strives to deconstruct the consumerist-driven agenda inherit within capitalistic ideology, "Fluxus strove to strip artistic expression of its significance and sensible qualities as part of a questioning of the established system of constructing and evaluating meaning" (Brill 2010, 124). By students actively engaging in the process of culture jamming, students play in an act of humorous dissent towards their chosen object, while unexpectedly shifting their previously familiar perspective of said object.

Example: Mail Art

Mail art was developed in 1940s New York by artist Ray Johnson and its popularity increased throughout the 1960s via Johnson's famed—and intentionally misspelled—The New York Correspondance School. It currently has a global stronghold through the International Union of Mail-Artists, an association created in 1988 by Dutch artist Ruud Janssen, as well as via social media outlets like Instagram. Since around the 1950's, "some artists and poets have sought innovative ways to reach their audience and collaborators. These artists have sought to circumvent the gallery system by means of direct mailings and alternative distribution networks" (Saper 2001, 129). Through mail art, artists can create and successfully distribute their own artwork without the financial or emotional burden of established markets. Friedman asserts,

> Fluxus approached mail art as an opportunity to experimentation, to communication and to interaction. At the beginning, Fluxus artists were part of that primary group of individual participants on a small network: at the end, the trenchant experimentation that Fluxus artists pursued, the paradigms they developed and proved redefined the medium (1984, 24).

It is important to note that Johnson's Correspondance School was inherently pedagogical in nature, just as much as it was Fluxist. Johnson's work, life, and even his death centered around play, experimentation, and the absurd. His long history of mail art objects used similar principles that ultimately fostered a practical application of art as a form of learning. Johnson's "pedagogical mailings destabilized traditional concepts of art and socialization and turned forms of communication and education into artistic media in personal letters, mass-produced flyers, absurd packages, and everything in between" (Kofodimos 2015). In turn, Johnson's mail art provides educators with a creative and re-adaptable collaborative media platform, as simple, creative exercises like collage, blogging, or photography allows students to experience the familiar in an unfamiliar way—particularly in the context of taking and sharing photos using a smart phone, like the ubiquitous social media selfie.

To use photography as a specific example, students in an introductory visual communication course spent part of class time wandering around campus, taking photographs on their phones. They were encouraged to get as creative as possible, with the only restriction being to take exactly four photographs—no more, no less. After thirty minutes, students gathered back together at our designated meeting spot—that class session was held outside that day. Students were then instructed to select their favorite photo and e-mail a copy to me and to at least one other student in the class. After completing this exercise, we debriefed on the process. Nearly all students reported the activity to fall somewhere on the spectrum of difficult or uncomfortable, and that initially made little sense, as all of them are comfortably accustomed to using their phones. However, having students engage with their phones in a new way—as part of a class activity—fundamentally changed how they handled the apparatus itself, as they naturally thought more critically about what they were going to photograph. While students are so accustomed to taking selfies and photos on a daily basis, they do so under their own parameters and not for a grade. I was stunned at how such a simple activity took students so far away from the familiar, but it did. Having to take only four photos, for a class, with the possibility of having to share them with one another, placed students in an unfamiliar space. Since students share such a familiar relationship with their smart phones—in that they use it hundreds of times of day to create and share information through photos, social media, messaging, etc.—when asked to participate in a graded class exercise, such an activity initiated the defamiliarization process, altering the familiar ways that students utilized their phones.

Due to ongoing technical issues in our computer lab at the time, the photos were unable to be printed. The ultimate goal for such an exercise is for it to occur in stages that mimic the entire process of a piece of Fluxus mail art. Nevertheless, even the initial photo-taking and sharing stage proved key in promoting student engagement and creative thinking through a simple defamiliarization exercise, allowing students a chance to play. Students, most of whom do not like public presentations, reported they were not comfortable sharing their photos with the class. Aside from those with a love of theater, the only activity more terrifying to students than a public presentation is a public performance.

Example: Performance

Fluxus performances function in a learning space, as they "teach how a process is part of content and content is the form of process: they present models of how the meaning of content is determined by the processes in which the substance of that content was formed, and by the ways it is received" (Jenkins 1993, 95). Fluxus performance sought to push the boundaries of acceptability, as they often included a wide range of activities, such as the mundane task of eating an identical lunch at the same time and place every day like Alison Knowles's *Identical Lunch*.

Knowles began her *Identical Lunch* project in 1968, and it was performed by various artists for a number of years after its initial debut. While the performance was meant to be identical every single time, in reality, it was not. Knowles ate a tuna fish sandwich on wheat toast with lettuce, butter and no mayo, accompanied by either a large glass of milk or a bowl of soup. She ate this lunch at the same place and at the same time every single day (Jenkins 1993, 89). Other artists set out to replicate Knowles's lunch routine, thereby transforming the piece from a solo project into a collective one. However, other artists could not possibly replicate an identical daily routine and consume the same lunch, at the same place, at the same time and for the same price. The reason for the break in continuity was simple: life is simply not that predictable. Kristine Stiles, art history professor at Duke University, argued that *Identical Lunch*

> offers a model of activities by Fluxus artists for the ways in which they negotiate the content and processes of life and infiltrate the social fabric with the ethos of Fluxus. It examines the sameness, unity, homogeneity—all aspects of individual identity unmitigated by the social—and simultaneously the foils of opposition, counterpoint, and heterogeneity that are characteristic of the communal. (qtd. in Jenkins 1993, 89–90)

The variations in *Identical Lunch* served as a collective experiment in chance operations, such as those provided by the Chinese Book of Changes, *I Ching*, which was famously used by Cage in creating his groundbreaking compositions. Fluxus experimentation embraces both sides of the research spectrum—the carefully pre-planned side and the side that allows for the element of chance to occur. On the one hand, performances such as Kaprow's happenings can appear deliberate and chaotic when in fact they were all carefully pre-planned with key event elements drafted ahead of time. On the other hand, performances are altered by random chance events unforeseen by the artists, such as changes in a restaurant's daily menu. Either way, it points to experimental methods of artistic creation.

Performance is adaptable into the classroom in a variety of ways, but perhaps the most powerful and pedagogically driven manner is to employ the avant-garde methods of Augusto Boal. Boal developed the Theater of the Oppressed, TO, an artistic adaptation and homage to fellow Brazilian scholar Paulo Freire's famous book, *Pedagogy of the Oppressed* (1968). While Boal's work is not directly Fluxist in nature, it is nevertheless democratic, participatory, and experimental, as it primarily seeks to break down boundaries of institutionalized art by giving power to the voiceless and the invisible. Foundational to Boal's work is the process of defamiliarization, particularly in what he termed "legislative theater"—the branch of TO specifically created to empower citizens to voice their opinions through the right to vote.

TO implicitly aligns itself with a Brechtian read of Shklovsky's work, as Bertolt Brecht interpreted "defamiliarization not just as a formal but also as a didactic technique that would promote his audience's better grasp of reality and would thus enhance its ability to fight for its political goals" (quoted in Pötzsch 2017). While TO is inherently political, it does not need to expressly deal with politics, as its multifaceted nature allows for a wide range of possibilities and adaptations, providing quite a bit of flexibility in its adaptation into a pedagogical setting. It should be noted that TO is relatively complex for students to understand, at least initially. However, in the times I have deployed TO in my classes, particularly when dedicated time is spent contextualizing exactly what it is, students have produced some powerful mini-plays—and some not-so-great ones, too.

This past semester in my intercultural communication class, students—working in partners—created a mini TO-inspired play based on their chosen topic, and the play was performed, recorded, and uploaded in a digital video format. The play was not a live class performance, per usual, due to the campus shutdown to prevent the spread of COVID-19. Since the class was forced to go virtual, students had to come up with new ways to collaborate remotely. One group did a phenomenal job in creating and performing a "Newspaper Cross Reading" piece in which each student, acting like a news anchor, took turns reading two news articles that were reporting completely different information on the exact same event. One student would read a line from an MSNBC article, the other from FOX News. Watching the video was purposely disorienting, as the incongruity in news outlets reporting the same event functions to defamiliarize the audience in recognizing mis- or disinformation, an absurd and dangerous type of "news" that has gained mainstream attention in recent years.

While it remains in the periphery of the professional theater world, TO is still widely practiced today and although it is not an initially easily understood practice by undergrads, it is nevertheless a powerful teaching tool in the classroom—particularly in politically charged content areas such as those related to gender, race, and media studies. With a bit of time and preparation—depending on the specific course and project goals—incorporating any style of performance, such as elements from the two aforementioned examples, acts as a pedagogical tool in which to creatively engage students with more difficult to understand content.

Closing Thoughts

This chapter sought to break ground in briefly illustrating a few ways that Fluxus-inspired methods aid in the learning process by fostering defamiliarization through pedagogy of play, specifically in promoting student engagement and creative thinking. Fluxus—as a global, collective movement—focused its creative efforts on producing and distributing art in ways that challenged that status quo of the familiar. One of the greatest benefits of using Fluxus in the college classroom is in its emphasis on creative collaboration and experimentation, simultaneously highlighting a model of content creation that is simple and requires minimal requisite skill, talent, or specific content knowledge.

While students must, at some point in time, be evaluated on a finished product (e.g., final exam or essay) teaching the importance of the process is crucial, particularly in allowing students to fail safely. Paik argued that "in a nomadic post-industrial time we are more experience-oriented than possession-oriented" (1993, 9). Paik's argument points to the need of shifting focus from the narrow lens of *product completion* to the wider lens of *creative process*, as the latter lends itself to a more significant interpretation of life and the acquisition of new knowledge that, at the very least, offers us a renewed perspective on art and life. It is worth reiterating Shklovsky's theory that shifting perspective is key to living a full life because "if the whole complex lives of many people go on unconsciously, then such lives are as if they had never been" (1917).

Additional room remains for further academic research, experimentation, and discourse relating to the numerous ways that instructors can introduce, adapt, and re-interpret avant-garde methods into the classroom—be it from Fluxus or any other movement. Since the defamiliarization process is foundational in the context of learning for both teacher and student, fellow academics are encouraged to experiment with adopting creative methods of play into their pedagogical practices and may do so by re-inventing any idea, activity, or project discussed herein.

References

Berghaus, Günter. 2005. *Avant-garde Performance: Live Events and Electronic Technologies*. London, UK: Palgrave Macmillan.
Beuys, Joseph. 1978. *Jeder Mensch ein Kunstler*. Tate.
Boal, Augusto. 1993. *Theatre of the Oppressed*. Translated by Charles A. and Maria-Odilia Leal McBride. New York, NY: Theatre Communications Group.
Breton, André. 1924. *Surrealist Manifesto*. Paris, FR: Éditions du Sagittaire.
Brill, Dorothée. 2010. *Shock and the Senseless in Dada and Fluxus*. Lebanon, NH: University Press of New England.
Bürger, Peter. 1984. *Theory of the Avant-garde*. Minneapolis, MN: University of Minnesota Press.
Caruth, Gail D. 2018. "Student Engagement, Retention, and Motivation: Assessing Academic Success in Today's College Students." *Participatory Educational Research*. 5 (1): 17–30. N.p.
Csikszentmihalyi, Mihaly. 1996. *Creativity: Flow and the Psychology of Discovery and Invention*. New York, NY: Harper Perennial.
Dary, Teri, Terry Pickeral, Rob Shumer, and Anderson Williams. 2016. *Weaving Student Engagement into the Core Practices of Schools: A National Dropout Prevention Center/Network Position Paper*. Clemson, SC: National Dropout Prevention Center/Network.
DeLaure, Marilyn, and Mortiz Fink, eds. 2017. *Culture Jamming: Activism and the Art of Cultural Resistance*. New York, NY: NYU Press.
Dunbar, Kevin N., and Jonathan A. Fugelsang. 2005. "Causal Thinking in Science: How Scientists and Students Interpret the Unexpected." In *Scientific and Technological Thinking*, edited by Michael E. Gorman, 57–79. Mahwah, NJ: Psychology Press.
Durozoi, Gérard. 2002. *History of the Surrealist Movement*. Chicago, IL: University of Chicago Press.

"The Fluxhouse Cooperatives of SoHo." 2014. *Fluxus Foundation*. fluxusfoundation.com/fluxus-as-architecture/essays/the-fluxhouse-cooperatives-of-soho/.

Freire, Paulo. 2018. *Pedagogy of the Oppressed*, 4th ed. Translated by Donaldo Macedo. New York, NY: Bloomsbury Academic.

Friedman, Ken. 1998. "A Fluxus Idea." *The Fluxus Reader*. West Sussex, UK: Academy Editions.

Friedman, Ken. 1984. "Mail Art History: The Fluxus Factor." *FLUE–Franklin Furnace Archive* 4, no. 3–4 (Winter): 18–24.

Jenkins, Janet, ed. 1993. *In the Spirit of Fluxus*. Minneapolis, MN: Walker Art Center.

Ken Dewey Collection, 1959–1972. 2020. New York Public Library Archives.

Kim, Jung-rak. 2011. *Diaspora: Korean Nomadism*. Seoul, KR: Hollym.

Krstich, Vesna. 2016. "The Pedagogy of Play: Fluxus, Happenings, and Curriculum Reform in the 1960s." *C Magazine* 131. N.p.

Kofodimos, Sofia. 2015. *The Open Curriculum of the New York Correspondence School: Ray Johnson's Pedagogical Mail Art*. YouTube. Video, 13:34. Mar 6, 2015. www.youtube.com/watch?v=dzEmEiRKog4.

Maciunas, George. 1968–1969. "Curriculum Plan." *George Maciunas Foundation Inc.*

McLuhan, Marshall. 1994. *Understanding Media: The Extensions of Man*. Reprint ed. Boston, MA: The MIT Press.

Mardell, Brian, Daniel Wilson, Jen Ryan, Katie Ertel, Mara Krechevsky, and Megina Baker. 2016. *Towards a Pedagogy of Play—Harvard Project Zero*. Boston, MA: Harvard University.

Marshall, Julia, and David M. Donahue. 2014. *Art-Centered Learning Across the Curriculum: Integrating Contemporary Art in the Secondary School Classroom*. New York, NY: Teachers College Press.

Nam June Paik. 2020. *The Monthly Review of the University for Avant-Garde Hinduism! (Postmusic). 1963*. New York, NY: The Museum of Modern Art.

NCAR. 2015. *Isn't There Still a Lot of Debate among Scientists?* Boulder, CO: National Center for Atmospheric Research—University Corporation for Atmospheric Research.

Newmann, Fred. 1992. *Student engagement and achievement in American secondary schools*. New York, NY: Teachers College Press.

—. 2017. *Our First 50 Years—Project Zero*. Cambridge, MA: Harvard Graduate School of Education.

—. 2019. "What We Believe about Learning through Play in Schools." *The Pedagogy of Play*, January 31, 2019. www.popatplay.org/post/what-we-believe-about-learning-through-play-in-schools.

Pijnappel, Johan. 1993. *Fluxus: Today and Yesterday*. London, UK: Academy Editions.

Pötzsch, Holger. 2017. "Playing Games with Shklovsky, Brecht, and Boal: Ostranenie, V-Effect, and Spect-Actors as Analytical Tools for Game Studies." *The International Journal of Computer Game Research*, 17 (2). København, DK: IT-Universitetet i København

Saper, Craig J. 1998. "Fluxus as a Laboratory." In *The Fluxus Reader*, edited by Ken Friedman, 135–51. West Sussex, UK: Academy Editions.

Saper, Craig J. 2001. *Networked Art*. Minneapolis, MN: University of Minnesota Press.

Sharp, William. 1969. "An Interview with Joseph Beuys." *Artforum International*, 8 (4): 40–47. New York, NY: Artforum International Magazine.

Shklovsky, Viktor. 1917. "Art as Technique." warwick.ac.uk/fac/arts/english/currentstudents/undergraduate/modules/fulllist/first/en122/lecturelist-2015-16-2/shklovsky.pdf.

Skinner, Ellen A., and Michael J. Belmont. 1993. "Motivation in the classroom: Reciprocal effects of teacher behavior and student engagement across the school year." *Journal of Educational Psychology*, 85 (4): 571–81. Washington, DC: American Psychological Association, Inc.

Sullivan, Graeme. 2005. *Art Practice as Research: Inquiry in the Visual Arts*. Thousand Oaks, CA: SAGE Publishing.

Temkin, Ann, and Bernice Rose. 1993. *Thinking Is Form: The Drawings of Joseph Beuys*, 1st ed. London, UK: Thames and Hudson.

11 Life in the Megapocalypse (Digital)

Kenton Taylor Howard

Engaging the value of interactive fiction games for addressing queer representation and discourse within the classroom, "Life in the Megapocalypse" is a playable, web-based game built in Ink, an open-source scripting language for writing games. Along with its framing introduction—which draws on lessons from existing limitations in queer play in games and frameworks for digital humanities critical making as pedagogical practice—the project demonstrates an activist approach to educational design, suggesting that scholars seeking to benefit from digital, playful pedagogy must build systems alongside and with their students and create moddable, shared spaces for creative work. Digital content creation is a skill that can be useful to almost any scholar of games who is interested in representation, and foundational systems like "Life in the Megapocalypse" that are designed to be easy to learn, easy to modify, and that have a clear focus on representation can provide a framework that such scholars can use to begin exploring their potential.

The notion that representation of queerness and marginalized forms of identity in visual media is important is relatively uncontroversial at this point—numerous mainstream media franchises, such as the *American Horror Story* television series, have included queer characters in prominent narrative arcs in the series, resulting in increased visibility for queerness in popular culture. Games are no different in this respect, though they perhaps lag behind other forms of visual media, such as television or film, in that there tends to be less inclusion of queer characters in mainstream, popular games. Calls for inclusion of marginalized identities in mainstream games have also been met with resistance—or in some cases, an outright hostility—that is not often seen when other forms of media portray queer characters. Reactions to characters like Tracer in *Overwatch* (Blizzard Entertainment, 2016), whose identity as a lesbian was revealed in a comic, are an example of this resistance—one fan meme mocked Blizzard by calling them "the JK Rowling of

Games" (Tamburro, 2019) in reference to the *Harry Potter* author revealing the queer sexuality identity of a major character after the book series ended.

As mainstream games handle queer representation poorly, rightly drawing attention for tokenism and reliance on narrative tropes, indie game making—informed by principles from serious game design and interactive fiction—offers more potential for meaningful engagement. Scholars have worked to document these lesser-known exemplars of queer play, including projects such as the *LGBTQ Video Game Archive*, the *Queer Game Studies* (Shaw and Ruberg, 2017) collection and *Video Games Have Always Been Queer* (Ruberg, 2019). This work draws on an adage from Mark Rosewater (2016), a long-time designer for *Magic: The Gathering*, who claimed that "restrictions breed creativity" in a Game Developers Conference (GDC) talk reflecting on twenty-five years of working on the game.

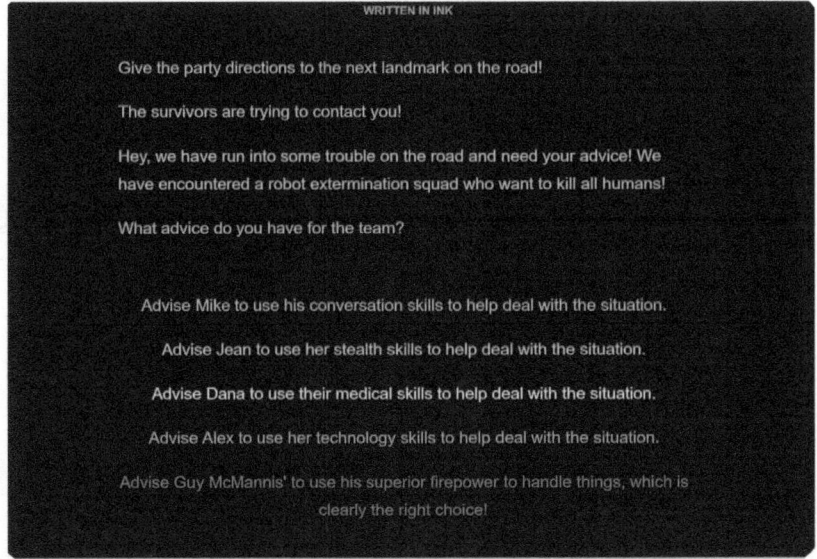

View Kenton Taylor Howard's "Life in the Megapocalypse" online at https://bit.ly/reimagining-humanities or follow the QR code.

SECTION THREE: EXPERIMENTING

12 The Cowboy/Gypsy Boot: The Wide Image as Method for Humanist Inquiry and Action (Digital)

David Matteson

How might the humanities lead us to a sense of justice? In the spring of 2019, this question served as my focus of inquiry after learning of the tragic deaths of Timothy Dean and Gemmel Moore, two black, gay men who fell victim to the predator Edward Buck. Dean and Moore both lethally overdosed on methamphetamine eighteen months apart in Buck's Los Angeles apartment. Despite a reputation for luring susceptible men to his home and paying them to "slam" the dangerous drug, Buck was not arrested after the second death. It was not until a third man nearly overdosed later that year that the US Attorney brought charges against Buck. The press claimed this delay in arrest was due to Buck's status as a Democratic donor and political influencer. It was a case where power imbalance had evident lethal consequences.

As this case unfolded, I was concurrently developing a wide image through the approach outlined by Gregory Ulmer in *Internet Invention*. I reflected on the formative institutions of career, family, community, and entertainment. Recognizing patterns that arise across these institutions led to my acknowledgement of an image of "widescope," or a representation of my metaphysical position, moral beliefs, and mood. Ulmer outlines various exercises that assist the mystorian, or explorer, as he divines this wide image. Many of these exercises rely on the study of images—what Ulmer identifies as electracy's primary mode of communication.

Through an analysis of family photographs, maps, community folklore, popular culture, and other personally significant media, I discovered that my image of widescope is a cowboy or gypsy boot. My understanding of this emblem relies on its protective function and its significance as an aesthetic symbol of identity—the modern cowboy dress boot is often custom designed and decorated to reflect attributes of the wearer's personality. Cowboys are not the only ones who wear these types of boots. During a subsequent exercise, I recognized that these are also worn by Stevie Nicks for Fleetwood Mac's "Gypsy" music video, in which the singer portrays an Americanized stereotype of a "gypsy" linked more so with bohemian aesthetics than with the cultural specifics of the Romani people. The boot is gender malleable, worn by two archetypes—the cowboy and the gypsy— who have seemingly opposite traits, but they are unified through the wearing of the boot. In recognizing what I reflexively entitle a "gypsy/cowboy binary," I intend not to validate reductive and pejorative stereotypes but to reflect on the cultural mood evoked through the representation or misrepresentation of these identities and to explore the gendered framework that these pejoratives evoke. My recognition of the gypsy and the cowboy's attributes inform my understanding of other oppositional individuals. In this case, it has guided my thinking about predator Buck and his victims Moore and Dean.

After identifying this wide image, I return to Dean and Moore's tragic case in the hope of greater understanding—recognizing that it is through empathy that we may lay the groundwork for justice. The investigation concludes with the application of this newfound perspective to my role as an educator who works with at-risk, LGBTQ+ youth. Overall, this process of self-recognition and discovery has further prepared me to shape community and inspire change.

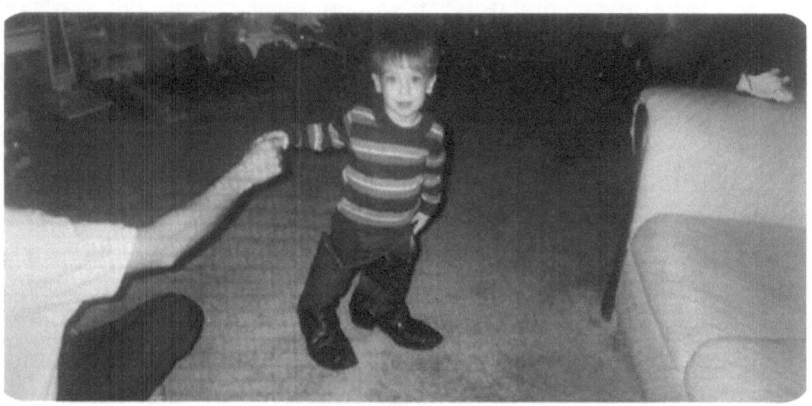

View David Matteson's "The Cowboy/Gypsy Boot: The Wide Image as Method for Humanist Inquiry and Action" online at https://bit.ly/reimagining-humanities or follow the QR code.

13 "The Deserters:" Activist Critical Making in Electronic Literature (Digital)

Laura Okkema

"The Deserters" is a text-based digital game based on the experiences of the author's family as refugees from East Germany. The player's objective in the game is to research a family's history by searching the game-world for authentic documents—including biographical writings, journal entries, photographs, and records—thereby retracing historical events through personal experience. "The Deserters" aims at inspiring a compassionate and empathetic stance towards immigrants and refugees today. The author reflects on the ethical, narrative, aesthetic, and technical choices she made throughout the creation process of The Deserters to create a critical activist game. The results of the analysis demonstrate that Twine offers a unique environment for composing politically impactful personal narratives.

Critical making is an approach to scholarship which combines discursive methods with creative practices. The concept has recently gained traction in the digital humanities, where scholars are looking for inclusive, empowering ways of integrating making into their research for marginalized populations. This dissertation explores how digital humanists can engage critical making as a form of activism in electronic literature, specifically in the interactive fiction platform Twine. The author analyzes the making process of her own activist Twine game, The Deserters, and embeds the project within digital humanities discourses on activism and social justice, hypertext, electronic literature, critical making, and hacker culture. From the project, the author derives best practices for activist critical making, which emphasize the importance for makers to imagine the needs and perspectives of their audience. The work expands digital humanities' theoretical and practical toolkit for critical making.

View Laura Okkema's "'The Deserters:' Activist Critical Making in Electronic Literature" online at https://bit.ly/reimagining-humanities or follow the QR code.

14 Citizen Curation (Digital)

Barry Mauer

Curating involves the selection of materials, either from archives or from new acquisitions, and their arrangement in an exhibition. Exhibitions can serve any number of purposes—from selling artworks to educating the public to glorifying a leader—but the process of archival research, selection, and production of an exhibition can be reimagined also as a process of attunement, of orienting to reality, and of promoting well-being for the community. A wise citizenry takes an active role in looking to its past so it can reason about its future.

The Citizen Curator Project assumes that curation is a form of writing, suited to an age of electronic multimedia that permits us to sample and remix virtually any texts. The project encourages ordinary citizens to begin the work of curating and to approach the task as a form of public policy consultation. Curating as activism requires that people assume the roles of uninvited consultants who witness catastrophe, deliberate about it, and wish to share their insights and recommendations with policy makers and other members of society. Because curating has been integral to the formation of community in the modern era—for example, museums arose with nation states and helped define national priorities—we encourage citizens to think of curating as another means of building and shaping community and as a means of increasing their agency within a more democratic public sphere.

In February 2017, the Citizen Curator Project invited community members, students, and artists to respond to the Pulse Nightclub attack by creating a series of exhibitions focused on the theme "Eliminationism and Resilience." This exhibition is documented in the online companion to this volume.

View Barry Mauer's "Citizen Curation" online at https://bit.ly/reimagining-humanities or follow the QR code.

15 Good Times Post-Pandemic: A Dyn-O-Mite Method?

Craig Saper

This essay began as a celebration in honor of the Texts & Technology Doctoral Program's anniversary of its founding more than two decades ago, and it was published later, as we were promised, to a post-pandemic "good times." In that sense, one might ask of this essay if it is possible that a theoretical perspective can produce a way of thinking through the unimaginable global suffering. Is there perhaps a school of thought, a shared focus of the research, that can help us think about these seemingly intractable problems? In academia, the Chicago school of economics, the Yale school of deconstruction, the MIT Media Lab, the Hopkins structuralist poetics, and many other school formations have suggested that programs often create loosely organized methodologies or approaches that become part of their identity in the marketplace of ideas. Certainly, in studies of cultural movements, the idea of a shared, aesthetic method and thematic concerns plays a prominent role. The names of groups like Bloomsbury, Dada, or Surrealists—and later the Beats, Fluxus, or Conceptual Artists—suggest an abbreviated umbrella term, handy to quickly gloss complicated relationships, shared or contentious visions, and a multitude of individuals. Each seemed set to think about a set of urgent questions; the Media Lab, for example, asked how we could incorporate interactive technologies into ways of managing information instantly before our eyes or at our fingertips, ways of bending technologies into human-like interactions and recognitions and make the dull tedium of code look fun and entertaining.

Often these names of schools of thought indicate a literal location and then encompass individuals who may not share any of the characteristics of the approach that the school's, or movement's, name signifies. So, Harold Bloom, for example, was not directly part of the deconstructionist group at Yale, but he published with them in the famous volume on the *Yale School* (Arac, Godzich, and Martin 1983; Bloom 2004; Redfield 2016; Edelman 2019). More directly related to the T&T academic program, located in Central Florida, were the discussions of the Florida School in the late 1980s in the introduction to a special issue of *Visible Language* on "Instant Theory" that I edited (Saper 1988, 371–97). Since its publication, the Florida School's shift away from traditional media studies toward new institutional practices (e.g., pedagogy, scholarship, publication, curriculum, and cultural change) continued and intensified; now, if there was a school of thought there, it has migrated north to Clemson University's Rhetorics, Communication, and Information Design graduate program. Similarly, the initial call for papers for this volume made clear "the projects within Texts and Technology . . . are experiments in method designed to reinvent contemporary humanistic practices" (Mauer 2018).

One imagines that the method would involve reading texts through media technologies as the necessary condition. That "reading" would, of course, involve technologies beyond, or at least not exclusively part of, print-literacy. These e-media technologies often have a networked and tele-visual component, and in our contemporary, cultural milieu, they favor situational narrative, music and sonic elements, and other entertaining and surface texts often previously rejected as insignificant in so-called serious print-literate scholarship (Havelock 1963; Ong 1982; Ulmer 2015).

If the now multiple Texts and Technology academic programs do suggest a school formation similar to those discussed above, then one should be able to produce work using that dynamic emerging method independent of the specific academic program based in Florida. Just as the Yale school spread throughout the United States and the world, one can imagine T&T—as method rather than simply a literal graduate program—becoming a shorthand indicator for specific approaches, methods, topics, and practices. The program itself was rarely referred to by its whole name, as Texts & Technology, and was almost exclusively pronounced in Central Florida as "TnT" with the "an" in "and" pronounced "en" and the "d" dropped. If TnT makes a claim as a school of thought, then one must also include its institutional context and machinations internally—in terms of its curriculum, alumni, current students, and faculty research—and externally—both institutionally at a large university and in relation to the socio-cultural systems in the United States and in the State of Florida. The TnT program embraced readings of and through electronic technology and media culture. Following that TnT style, one would not simply study, for example, the literary provenance of the inventor of dynamite, Alfred Nobel's prose play *Nemesis*. Instead, one would use Sisario's explanation about "The play, 'Nemesis,' printed shortly before [Nobel] died," which is "about 'violence, sex, torture, deceit, forbidden lusts, revenge and religious fanaticism,' according to the August Strindberg Intima Theater. It was considered so controversial by Nobel's relatives that they burned most of the manuscripts, but a few copies were spared, the theater said." Perhaps because of these themes in the play, it was not re-discovered and staged at the Intima Theater in Stockholm until 2005, a hundred and nine years after the death of Nobel, whose last will and testament, of course, initiated and funded his eponymous prize (Nobel 1896; Sisario 2005; Ardent 2019). In the TnT style of scholarship, one looks at dynamite and the Nobel Prize in terms of *Nemesis* through the play's explicit dramatization of forbidden lusts, revenge, and religious fanaticism set in the context of violence, sex, torture, and deceit, and the reasons the play was destroyed after Nobel's death.

In relation to a new type of media-culture reading, one might transport it to another electronic cultural context to get a new, applied perspective on an emerging TnT school of thought. Using the controversial figure of the character from the television program *Good Times* (*Good Times* 1974), J. J. Evans, and his famous tag-line, "Dyn-o-mite," this essay looks at the disciplinary question of school formation using a TnT *heuretic*—the neologism portmanteau word coined by Gregory L. Ulmer alludes to a number of terms including heuristic, heretic, and Eureka—approach. J. J.'s mother, Florida, had a vexed relationship with her son. The Central Florida region, famous as a vacation spot for "good times"—and the television program of the same name—might seem to have little to do with an academic program or the process of school formation, but the Dyn-o-mite method works at the register of the electronic shift in the sensorium.

The relation between the popular cultural references in this essay and the possibility of a disciplinary method depends on a Hypertextual linkage and on the platform-studies that would form another prong of the potential Dyn-o-mite! School formation. It is common knowledge that the development of the not-yet-named idea of hypertext as a platform began with Vannevar Bush's thought experiments. Vannevar Bush, in a 1945 *Atlantic Monthly* article, "As We May Think," proposed a "non-sequential" network of "lexias," or units of information content, forming a "docuverse" using ethernet-tethered computers. The actual terms hypertext and hypermedia were coined twenty years later by Theodor Holm Nelson, who built on Bush's "memex" plans of a platform that would solve two problems of the scale involved in large organizations. In the decades before and during the second world-war, the US government and corporations began photographically reproducing mountains of information onto microfilm, later microfiche, and started planning for the information to migrate to computers and digital storage. That process meant that storage and retrieval of large amounts of information—what would later be called an "information explosion" and what the Dyn-o-mite! School's name responds to—needed a new organizational system. Bush proposed a "machine-desk" reading machine that would merge the functions of an archival library and a home-based filing system. Instead of index cards as a storage, organizational, and retrieval system, Bush took the suffix "ex," combined it with the word memory, and created the neologism memex, suggesting a new way to remember information—a linked indexed memory, in the age of an information explosion or Dyn-o-mite! Thinking.

The memex would not simply store information in an electronic archive. The memex, more importantly, changed how we remember and how we "may think" in the future (as imagined in 1945) in terms of hypertextual associative thinking of branching paths of an inquiry that both mimicked human memory, thought, and imagination and changed it. Now, more than 75 years since that article appeared, the associative thinking of following the "hot links" is mundane. The possibility of a Dyn-o-mite! School depends on the platform study of texts and the "hot-links" made easier with computer technologies. Beyond that focus, the TnT agenda was built on this idea of textual connections, networked personal archives of information, and the associative thinking that the computer highlighted and intensified. In a literal way, the formation of the doctoral program responded to a need for trained professionals at the turn of the twenty-first century who could work with these new types of hyper-textual and other electronic forms of writing.

Given the associative logic programmed into the hypertextual system of composition, in a Dyn-o-mite system of thought or TnT school formation, the two registers of disciplinary knowledge and popular culture are hot-linked to think through the information explosion, not by ignoring its potential, but by following the associative logic made possible by a circuit connection at the surface of the two areas. Once we hyper-link the two areas, then we need to follow the thread of the associative links to the story of Dyn-o-mite's emergence as a tagline that we link to TnT as the locus of intersecting lines of thought around emerging hypertextual knowledge production. Dyn-o-mite now becomes, through an associative rather than analogous route, a different sort of tagline—as in creating hypertext links through tagging text—for an emerging or potential school of thought around the TnT academic program.

It is worth remembering how the term Dyn-O-Mite developed into a cultural phenomenon. First, the Norman Lear sitcom, *All in the Family* (1971), spun off other television programs—in fact, it created an entire industry as it spun off more TV shows than any other TV show did before and certainly after. Some were forgettable, including *704 Hauser* (1994), *Gloria* (1982), and even *Archie Bunker's Place* 1979), but some had a separate identity like *The Jeffersons* (1975), which was so successful that it in turn spun off the forgettable *Checking In* (1981). Another important spin-off from *All in the Family* was *Maude* (1972), which starred Bea Arthur in the eponymous role. *Maude* was set in a decidedly liberal household with a feminist role model and often included episodes with the housekeeper, Florida Evans—played by Esther Rolle—who poked gently at the contradictions of affluent liberalism and, more importantly, portrayed a smart and likeable African-American woman not played in minstrel-like mockery. The Florida character was so popular that eventually Esther Rolle moved to her own spinoff in *Good Times*, a situation comedy. The minstrel-like mockery was often considered "just a joke" even at the University of Central Florida during the early years of the T&T program; for example, UCF's then president, John Hitt, wore an Afro-wig and was widely condemned before apologizing and explaining that they—he and the Board of Trustee's chairman—"wore them to salute the [basketball] player," not to mock African-Americans. A 2019 Senior Thesis in art and film, "Of Martyrs and Minstrels" by Trevon Coleman, examined the links between Treyvon Martin's murder, about twenty miles north of UCF, and minstrels as an acceptable form of Black identity in a racist ideological frame.

The situation of *Good Times* is that Florida and her husband, James Evans, live with their three children at 921 North Gilbert Avenue, apartment 17C, a fictional address; the not explicitly named location and address is in the infamous Cabrini-Green projects—the Francis Cabrini Homes—shown in the opening and closing credits and located on Gilbert Ave. *The Bob Newhart Show* (1972) situation comedy was also set in Chicago around the same time in the 1970s and was only 1.2 miles away from the *Good Times* location but in a situation and world far removed from Cabrini-Green—rich, almost exclusively white, professionals, working in office towers, with humorous neuroses set within Newhart's group therapy sessions.

Reading the two situation comedies next to each other makes clear that the good times of Florida's world suggests, at least partially, an eye rolling irony about that situation. Eventually Rolle left the show because many perceived the title as part of a naively unironic, and even minstrel-like, celebration of good times with Florida and her family, especially in the character of her son with his tag-line "Dyn-o-mite" being particularly offensive. In later seasons, Janet Jackson joined the cast as Penny, a school-aged kid who was abused by her mother and did not want to leave the Evan's apartment as a safe space overseen by Florida. Penny had an elaborate backstory and her mother's abuse was revealed by the bandages to cover her wounds. Eventually, a neighbor adopted Penny to get her away from the mother. Janet Jackson went on to roles in "Diff'rent Strokes," as Willis Jackson's girlfriend, and "Fame," as an aspiring performer.

Children suffering from abuse later took on an even more ominous tone with Janet's famous brother being an alleged sexual child abuser. The *Good Times* formula was to deal with even the most serious sociopolitical issues, especially racism, sexism, poverty, unemployment, child-abuse, and gun violence—all in a way that was softened by the comedic situation. For the other actors, who saw the success of the program as an important and serious attempt to make a positive impact on American culture and for the civil rights struggle, the minstrel-like buffoonery of J. J. saying his tagline was disgusting, and worse, J. J.'s character began to eclipse everything else. Placing that tagline next to the history of an apparatus, or platform, theory of hypertext highlights the conjunctions on which the study of texts and technology depends.

Figure 1. Image of *Good Times*' character J. J. Evans (Jimmie Walker), "Dyn-O-Mite!" Digital Painting by the author, based on Refrigerator Magnet, personal collection of the Author, n.d. no copyright.

Gregory L. Ulmer (GLU) writes in an encyclopedia entry on hypertext:

> Hypertext is not only the result of a history of technology, but . . . it is useful to place its development in the context of the concept of the apparatus (social machine) commonly used in media studies. To say that hypertext is part of a new apparatus beginning to displace literacy as well as orality helps avoid the fallacy of technological determinism. Apparatus invention includes not only technology, but also institutional practices and human identity behaviors. . . . To have a term for the digital equivalent of literacy helps identify the full range of inventions in progress across the dimensions of the apparatus. This term is "electracy," combining "electricity" with "trace," used by Jacques Derrida to describe the operations of text. (2019)

As you can see from the image above, the danger of Dyn-O-Mite is that the associative joke-like playfulness obscured the seriousness of the situation—a comedy only because they persisted without ever winning the day. Each episode of *Good Times* ended with a stoic Sisyphean shrug—only for hopes to be raised and dashed in the next episode; racism, sexism, wealth inequities, and health disparities endured. This formula continued until the very last episode, when, through some forgotten *deus ex machina*, the entire family moves out of the projects and into the middle class with success in newfound employment, marriage, and economic stability.

Although based on the actor and writer Mike Evans' own life growing up in Cabrini Green, the program, once it was broadcast to a wide audience, serves as a useful allegory for the possibility of the TnT or Dyn-O-Mite Florida school. In each episode filled with hardships and serious social problems confronting the family, the central character, Florida, greets each travail stoically with a dry wit. As what Gregory L. Ulmer calls a "puncept," which connects different registers of communication—disciplinary knowledge and popular culture—Florida's character is dealing with swindles, cut-backs, unjust arrests, senseless violence, and obvious racial prejudice with a phlegmatic humor. If one were to simply list the misfortunes of Florida, it would make for a sad story filled with violence, racism, austerity, environmental disasters, drug addictions, and physical abuse. Given lemons, or perhaps sour oranges, Florida makes orangeade. The Dyn-o-mite method converts the catastrophic situation-comedy of tragic errors and missteps into creative intervention, even as it risks a more facile good-times and mockery.

Texts and Technology, as an associative way of thinking, examines and interrogates the foundational concepts of cultural texts, and specifically highlights the problems with translation, disciplinary boundaries, and norms of reading and writing. It also challenges definitions of all texts and communication modes in the context of the possibilities and disruptions of media technologies. On the one hand, Dyn-o-mite theory emerges from within the institutional home of an academic program. On the other hand, the theory has an uneasy relationship with their institutional homes precisely because it seeks to challenge—or explode—the foundation of a supposedly universal basis from which to compare texts, as if they were transcendent above the technological, pop culture, and other tightly-focused decontextualized notions of textual analysis. No, even the program's name, Texts and Technology, recognized that the consequence of an information explosion meant that there was a hyper-associative textual web. The risk to the method—and perhaps the school of thought—is that it is dismissed as mere clownish mockery.

The stand-up comedian who played J. J. had no serious acting experience or training, and the other actors, with much experience acting and a commitment to civil rights work outside of their work on television, movies, or the theater, were uncomfortable with the show turning into minstrelsy. Florida was increasingly uncomfortable with the popularity of the "Dyn-o-mite" line, and the actor who played the father would soon put down an ultimatum that he would quit unless the scripts were modified to have less buffoonery and less focus on J. J.'s jester act. What discipline could contain this theory, especially as the pandemic and social unrest challenged the sufficiency of disciplinary boundaries to solve or even address the multiple global catastrophes confronting our world and worldview? With students returning to campus with the promise of good times, perhaps with the Johnson & Johnson vax, one wonders if the old disciplines would expire.

In that sense, serious scholars might consider this theoretical approach as uncanny or the *unheimlich*—the strange within the home department. Scholars interested in the possibility of a TnT school formation could either confront this uncanny theory as a problem to control—for example, in designing technical communications to limit the disruptions—or a generative locus to cultivate—in an information explosion. The historical development of this continuing tension began in the late 1940s with the efforts to found interdisciplinary humanities programs in the States that would compare different types of texts. The "productive anxiety" increased in the 1970s and 1980s as poststructuralist theories both fueled the growth and importance of these types of programs and threatened their traditional foundation and goals to locate and pin-down the history and meaning of texts. The conflict shifted to questions about infrastructure. Universities scaled back resources for literature in favor of interdisciplinary programs in new media texts. TnT was at the locus of this struggle.

Poststructuralism had already found its way throughout the humanities, into the social sciences, and began appearing as an element within a number of new scientific disciplines. The transformations in studying texts and technology made networked hypermedia more important than singular decontextualized texts, but, nevertheless, the academic program at UCF—and the possibility of a school of thought—grew directly from an interdisciplinary English department and from the history of literary theory. Because textual and technological theory is both an institutional entity in TnT, as well as an often-contested disciplinary method, its relationship with scholarship is very often about institutional boundaries, interdisciplinary battles or conjunctions, and infrastructure. To appreciate this relationship, one needs to examine not just abstract ideas, but the people and institutions involved in implementing these theories. That is, in terms of TnT's importance for textual theory, the usually marginalized discussions of institutional issues become crucial. TnT grew from the idea of comparing texts within different modes of production—printed or electronic—and different impacts. The comparative aspects of studying texts and technology were crucial, and that's why the program grew from an English department with a wide interdisciplinary and comparativist scope.

The modern era of literary theory had emerged by the time René Wellek, in 1949, called for the formation of departments dedicated to this type of comparative study of texts. He built his conception of a modern, comparative literature on the rejection of the study of individual, national literature in the modern languages. He argued that Kant offered a philosophical basis to judge the aesthetics of literature across national boundaries. It was implicit in his argument—and in the formation of new departments—that literature was defined in terms of the Occident and excluded both other literatures and broader definitions of texts. So, a program focused on texts and technology pushed against the narrow definitions of texts and sought to expand, even explode, the idea of comparison of texts beyond the same print-literary mode of expression shared by all the literature compared; still the study of texts and technology does draw heavily on another model of comparative literature.

This initial use of the phrase "comparative literature" in the States intended to borrow the spirit of the German model, *vergleichende Literaturwissenschaft*, with its connotations of a science of literature. Theory became crucial to this formation as scholars looked for an appropriate universal basis from which to examine literature. In some ways, this model was opposed to the French model, *litterature comparée*, with its connotations of compared literature rather than a disciplinary science of literature. In England, the program titles comparative literature or humanities are often used interchangeably, but when programs adopt the former phrase, they usually depend on the universal theory model. Initially, modern comparative literature pushed against the previous approaches to literature that included studies of influence, genre, theme, aesthetic movements and periods, history of ideas, and a glance at the history of criticism. The primary task for comparatists was historical.

The modern movement wanted to challenge this approach, as well as look for a way to avoid studying national literatures as distinct and separate from each other.

Through the 1950s and 1960s, departments at Harvard and Yale dominated the scene in America. Later, the "Yale School" would challenge the older literary science models, including narratology, formalism, and structuralism. In general, modern comparative literature attempted to understand literature as a work of art rather than a symptomatic representation of a national or biographical history. The search for methods that could be applied to literature in general, and to the literariness and textuality of literature, led scholars to theory. The interest in theory also concerned an infrastructural problem for the new discipline. If students studied a wide variety of literary works, it was soon clear that no single cannon could accommodate all of these areas of study; as modern comparative literature grew, students looked for a common ground that all of them studied. If the literary and critical texts were different, then a general theory might function as the shared ground. This situation only intensified with the introduction of multiple platforms, modes, and technologies as ways to access, archive, produce, or read texts.

The need for a hyper-textual theory led to a search for meta-critical scholarship and a pushback against theory that continues today. By the late 1960s, theoretical concerns were pervasive throughout the discipline of literary and media studies, and these concerns were reflected in the meta-critical scholarship. Still, Harry Levin, for example, spoke for many scholars in the discipline when he confessed that he was less concerned with talking about comparative literature than with comparing literary texts. By the late 1970s, the two concerns were imbricated one upon the other because scholars, especially those interested in media technologies' impact on literary texts, had exposed that what it means to compare texts depends on what "texts" means in general; hyper-texts made a return to a singular printed-on-paper definition of the literary text increasingly difficult. Inevitably, literary theories noticed where the print-literacy of all texts seemed to break down or suggest an electronic mode that disrupted—or even exploded—the literate texts through the hyperlinks and infinite web of allusions. Parallel to that historical development, *Good Times* appeared on television.

The new modes of reading shifted the value of literary studies toward an exposure of the aporias in writing, including critical writing about text's definition. If Wellek based his foundation for a new discipline on

Kant's aesthetics, then Samuel Weber, and others later, noticed problems with even this philosophical basis. Weber noted that in Kant's philosophy there is no actual aesthetic realm that has an objective principle of taste precisely because, for Kant, aesthetics is the absolute specific. Textual theory, confronted by the idea of multiple ways to navigate—a hyper-navigation or hyper-reading—would allow for the absolutely specific reading, instead of the ideal reader and reading, but would also suggest ways to theorize literariness from the absolutely specific rather than the supposedly universal general norms. In essence, literary theory exploded the traditional humanist notion of a singular hermeneutic meaning to be pinned down definitively.

In addition to the problems with a general theory of literature, scholars also sought to expand the scope of literary studies. Wlad Godzich was one of the scholars who called for broadening the discipline to include "literatures," with the plural form meant to indicate both non-European literatures and other marginalized texts. Soon comparative literature became a locus for new areas of study, including multiculturalism, cultural studies, queer theory, and postcolonial literature. Within national literatures, comparatists found minority literatures and "minor literatures" with which to challenge the notion of a singular model of Literature. For example, Edward Said, Gayatri Spivak, and others introduced post-colonial strategies, later popularized throughout the humanities, as new strategies for comparatists. Another expansion involved new types of texts. One area of that dismantling of humanism's claim to a universalized reader concerned race and the primacy of whiteness.

George Lipsitz, Theodore Allen, and David Neiwert all began working on the issue of "whiteness," but decades earlier Leslie Fiedler, once recognized as a leader and innovator of the cultural essay form, had used personal analogies about his life as a Montanan, and their white faces, to examine literary and cultural issues around race, sexuality, and ethnicity: "one becomes a Montanan in strange ways" (Fiedler 1971b, 331; Fiedler 1971c, 337–42). His essays, widely regarded as the epitome of insightful and lively literary analysis, debunk the myths of innocence in American literature and culture. His most famous essay, "Come Back to the Raft Ag'n, Huck Honey," did not claim that Mark Twain had written this line or that Tom and Huck were even flirting with gay sexual encounters (Fiedler 1948, 664–71). Rather, Fiedler showed how the myth of nineteenth century American innocence made even the suggestion of a sexual encounter particularly unpalatable and scandalous in literary studies, and his somewhat parodical posturing also took aim at the stuffy sanctimoniousness of mainstream literary and cultural criticism.

Likewise, his three controversial essays on Montana attacked the myth of white Montanans as the protectors of a naïve American innocence. He worried that the "Montana face," blank and friendly, actually expressed xenophobia, and that his own "dark, nervous, over expressive *New York face*"—euphemism for Jewish—was distrusted by Montanans who demanded a more grounded literal interpretation of the world and expressed this in their faces. Fiedler later wondered—after many loud complaints from Montanans about his attack—if he should have called it the "Gary Cooper Face," as an analogy to unpack his own legacy of Montanan's knightly honor and smug simpleness. Montana was for Fielder, instead, "a by-product of European letters, and invention of the Romantic movement in literature" with a past "artificially contrived for commercial purposes" as a tourist's Frontier (Fiedler 1971a, 131). Fiedler looks at the "community pageant" that presents in "dramatic form" the perverse identification with the American Indians' predicament as if to replace them with a mythic-Montana in which the "corpse of Rousseau is still twitching" (Fiedler 1971a, 138–139). The other Montana, the *artificial myth* where the Noble Savage is a lie and Huck Finn went to die, came from the East. It came not from Gary Cooper's face, but from Fiedler, who died in 2003 at the age of 85, and was "the last—or rather the first—of the wild-man literary critics . . . the original chest-thumping extrovert of American criticism, and no one ever did it better" (Tanenhaus 2003).

Fiedler, credited by the OED with the first instance of someone applying the term "postmodernist" to literature, celebrated the demise of Modernism. Fiedler wallowed in hyperbole and his most famous pronouncement that the classic, white, male, American writer returns "in a compulsive way to a limited world of experience, usually associated with childhood, writing the same book over and over again until he lapses into silence or self-parody" (Tanenhaus 2003). I had the pleasure of attending a lecture by Fiedler, as part of a series organized by Gregory L. Ulmer at the University of Florida, and in around the same years in the 1980s, I attended another lecture by Ulmer, who gave a moving public lecture in which he talked about innovative forms of writing essays about architectural theory and legacies. During the entire talk he held a concrete block on his shoulder. He talked about working at his father Walter's gravel and cement mill and about key issues in architecture. The block, a central image in most Modern and contemporary buildings, sat there weighing on his shoulder. Finally, at the end of the talk, he talked about what to do with a legacy and he put the old block down. As migration and transience became a generalizable condition since the 1950s, the corresponding paranoid hostility toward otherness and outsiders appeared as a reaction; now the white face morphed into an ugly monstrosity. How does one apprehend the weight of the universalized humanist legacy? You put down white block-heads and walk away.

As an ironic indication of the shift in literary studies, many of these theorists were connected to the Wellek Library at the University of California at Irvine. In the States, a productive enthusiasm encouraged many new journals to begin publication, including *diacritics*, *Sub-Stance*, *Enclitic*, and others. These journals explicitly engaged in the changing formations in literary studies. They also marked an institutional shift away from previous centers to a larger network of departments including Cornell, Brown, Wisconsin, Minnesota, UC Berkeley, and others throughout the States. In England, these same debates about the theoretical underpinnings of literary study led to the public controversy surrounding the dismissal of Colin McCabe from Cambridge University and Raymond Williams's futile defense of his colleague. The debate raged around three general areas—the notion of a universal theory of literary comprehension, the clear separation between literary language and scholarly description, and the previous agreement about an appropriate cannon. Against the notion of universal norms of reading, even those norms that directed close readings, the new theories countered with the problem of diverse identifications, reading practices, and social contexts of reception. The notion of a universally correct form of reading—close readings, for example—became suspect because it effaced other possibilities, including a hypertextual reading. Problems with contingencies of translation, the structure of language, and social identity of readers and writers led scholars to express an ambivalence toward theories that promised a progress toward true universal understanding of literature or texts. Instead, they sought to embrace the impact of an information explosion, not wall off the texts from any border-crossing alien readings or allusions. In any case, one could not put the text back inside a sealed-up boundary. The lessening of theory's influence paralleled the demise of *Good Times*' creative effort.

Even though Mike Evans had appeared on two incredibly successful sitcoms, *All in the Family* and *The Jeffersons*, and written *Good Times*, he later faced a drought in job opportunities and roles for African Americans in the 1980s. In the late 1980s, he developed a crack cocaine addiction, had a series of medical problems, including strokes, and, over the next two decades, many financial problems. He eventually landed in an East L.A. homeless shelter and was living there until a few months before he died in 2006. He had converted his childhood traumas into situational comedies, with his mother Florida as the central character, and, analogous to those struggles, Central Florida had to deal with violence, election and real estate swindles, and environmental catastrophes threatening the good-times image of the area. *Good Times* has a deep and profound irony in its situation that has greater relevance today and especially for Florida. What seems like tragedy fuels the real methodological comedy and theoretical meaning of the situation-comedy on television and in academia. Every time the main characters get a big job opportunity, they will have the rug pulled out from under them.

Every time Florida's family has economic success and finds themselves with a little more money than expected, the cash and good fortune will disappear in a housing crisis. Every time one of Florida's children gets a lucky break—for example, J. J. gets a commission for his artwork, a prestigious sorority invites Thelma to join, or a magnet school offers Michael admission—something is going to go wrong, and the characters will not get out of a bad situation as the theme music and song "Good Times" plays over the credits. Parodic allegories do not offer solutions; they simply offer a defamiliarized view of a situation that we might not see except from a distance. The cast infamously did not get along, and years later Jimmie, wearing a t-shirt with Naples, Florida, printed on it, told the interviewer, "I can honestly say that I don't remember speaking a word to Esther the whole time we were there."

In terms of the examination of reading in textual studies, Paul de Man's influential work expanded the field to examine the whole concept of aesthetics and to expose the discipline's delusions. Unfortunately, one somewhat anti-Semitic editorial—for a collaborationist newspaper during World War II—not only besmirched his own reputation but also made postmodern theory a target of those arguing that the endless meta-critical examinations and textual explosions led to a politically pernicious solipsism. In that interpretation, de Man's previous affiliations were evidence of the problems with Derrida's theoretical work, despite Derrida himself being a persecuted Jew during the Second World War, and Derrida's work often referring directly to a Judaic tradition. The critics claimed that Derrida's philosophical attitude allowed him to be duped by de Man. Another aspect of textual studies was the widespread interest in interrogating the boundaries between literary aesthetics and scholarly distance. If these borders and boundaries were far from a scientific certainty, then alternative strategies of scholarship could highlight previously effaced aspects of reading and literature, especially given the increasing ability of search and retrieval, highlighted and hyper-intensified by computer technologies. Theories would no longer lead to a clear and simple truth about literature, but the textual theories would allow for a less totalizing response.

The strategies of the proto-Dyn-O-Mite theory included irony, pastiche, parody, and an interest in the play of surface structures using chance—coincidental links. This aspect of theory was, predictably, bitterly dismissed and attacked by those supporting the literary science model; even within the UCF Texts and Technology program, which includes approximately three dozen faculty members, there were and are those who think of the TnT project as firmly anchored by a scientifically-valid digital encoding initiative that definitively tags and links texts to a specific historical context of production and editions. Although there are important differences in approaches to using hypertextual tagging for either—on the one hand, presenting texts as linked to concordance-like annotations about a context of production, including all editions in a text's production, or, on the other hand, hyper-linking to potential contexts of readings—there is a similarity between the hypertext uses suggested by Dyn-O-Mite theorists, digital humanities scholars, and technical writers alike. They all stress the importance of alternative approaches to scholarly or technical-communication presentations and readings.

In the proto-Dyn-O-Mite theories, Geoffrey Hartman was among those who called for alternative approaches to scholarly presentation, and Ihab Hassan forcefully challenged the notion of a disinterested critic. Hassan explicitly called for new approaches in comparative literature that employed collage, montage, silence, and action. He cited Surrealism as a possible model. Gregory L. Ulmer and others connected theory to other experimental approaches, including "applied grammatology," and that approach became the locus of a mashup explosive style of presentation that some might associate with the experimental platform theory of the Texts and Technology doctoral program at UCF.

Finally, the borders and boundaries between elite, cultural production and popular culture became particularly important and contentious because literary studies usually focused on the classic works of European literature, rather than either world literatures or texts never considered as worthy of comparison to great works. This last interest opened an explosive floodgate for new areas of study that eventually led to a Dyn-O-Mite theory of textuality. Throughout the 1980s, the antagonism toward theory became stronger, and theorists suffered from these attacks, especially from those claiming that these theories were irresponsibly apolitical buffoonery, or that these theories were actually attacks on progressive political change whether from the left or right. The challenge to a universal science of literature was interpreted as a solipsistic impasse to creating universal political projects.

Significantly, Mary Russo exposed how these theoretical debates were often translated into decisions about infrastructure. She discussed two controversial reappointment cases at Hampshire College, well known for its openness to experimentation—and now known as a college threatened with closure because of a financial crisis. The cases depended on theoretical definitions of literary studies and conflicts over disciplinary boundaries. Russo opened the door for appreciating the institutional and infrastructural conflicts in terms of arguments about theory. The cases brought into public view a tension between those who sought to dictate progressive curriculum through the selection of particular types of authors and theorists who taught texts as models of investigation. That is, those who sought to include specific texts in curricula often instituted new universal norms. The expansion of the textual domain soon led to new types of film and media theory emerging from the conjuncture of these textual theories and media studies. Tom Conley, Mary Ann Doane, Robert Ray, Kaja Silverman, and Dudley Andrew also sought in very different ways to find the junctures between film theory and textual approaches. Andrew's guidance of the enormously influential film studies program at the University of Iowa, and Indiana's film studies program in a Comparative Literature department, helped to define the particularly international and poststructuralist qualities of contemporary film theory. It also served as a model for the formation of the niche program of Texts and Technology at UCF decades later.

In the mid-1990s, theory-inflected comparative literature as an institutional entity, and as departments and academic programs, was clearly under siege. Charles Bernheimer introduced the problem in infrastructural terms as a crisis in the job market for comparative literature students. He saw the current problems as part of the discipline's tradition that finds itself in perpetual crisis. Significantly, Bernheimer saw the tensions optimistically as producing a productive anxiety. The same generative possibilities that fueled the enthusiasm for theory might also produce new configurations of comparative literature, now confronting the expansion of the field to include multiculturalism and alternative texts including electronic texts. Marjorie Perloff noted that a problem continuing to haunt this expansion was that scholars focus on cultural politics at the expense of expanding the very notion of textuality and the literary text—again, to include literary electronic media texts. The pessimistic view of poststructuralism was perhaps more prevalent.

For example, in a meeting with administrators at the University of Pennsylvania, Lilliane Weissberg, the chair of the Comparative Literature and Theory program at that university, angrily bemoaned the fact that a proposed program in film studies—with a strong comparative dimension—would inevitably draw students and funds away from comparative literature. This type of program would also set a precedent for future programs seeking to expand disciplinary boundaries to include multimedia. These programs might compare narratives across the borders of print, electronics, performance, and other media. With few jobs available in comparative literature, it seems fitting that Weissberg, a Germanist, read the writing on the wall, as she seemed, in this reader's imagination, to echo Hegel's comment, according to Simone de Beauvoir's paraphrase in *Second Sex*, that "the birth of children is the death of parents" (de Beauvoir 1980, 162). Of course, I am using the quote in a very different way than either de Beauvoir or Hegel intended, and de Beauvoir is loosely paraphrasing an uncited passage from Hegel that lacks the pithy aphoristic quality and suggestiveness that de Beauvoir produces. My use of the quote suggests that dialectical process in which the Texts and Technology doctoral program, initiated in an interdisciplinary English department with strengths in technical communication, would eventually move outside of literary studies and technical communication into a completely interdisciplinary space; moving an offspring field away from a parenting department often initially creates tensions.

The analogy between J. J.'s tagline on *Good Times* and the T&T Dyn-O-Mite method allows for a dialectical apprehension of a *zeitgeist*—for example, a sunshine state culture, social setting or situation and a popular media meme. It allows for a simple tagline and media situational comedy in popular culture to describe something situationally, culturally, and institutionally complex; the analogy allows for a reading of a text through a media technology's viral tagline. It allows for an easily accessible comedic television program to illuminate a relatively obscure and philosophically abstract theoretical approach to texts and technology. Other related methods of comparison include historical analogy between two periods—for example, some commentators have controversially drawn an analogy between the effort to place permanent, immigrant detention centers in Central Florida in September of 2019 and the internment or concentration camps during the 1930s and 1940s. Another analogical type of comparison displaces political dynamics into personal drama. For example, in the news coverage of domestic violence, child abuse, and gun violence, especially including in Central Florida, the stories often individualize and medicalize issues to putatively help victims recover because it is politically safer than focusing on the larger social and cultural dynamics fostering a climate of violence. A fourth type of analogical comparison involves comparing blind obedience of "just following orders" to carry out atrocities and crimes against humanity and the Florida-based broadcasts that motivate "dittoheads" to commit mass murders: what Barry Mauer calls "deadly delusions" (2020). Part of the advantage of arguments by analogy and the almost parodic use of popular culture as a vehicle for an argument is that it avoids the censors' shutting down of negative antithetical criticism.

In that sense, and in light of that historical context, any theory or school of thought growing from UCF's Texts and Technology program will have a continuing, uneasy relationship with literary and media studies within a single disciplinary department. Yes, TnT has, in large part, grown from the institutional home base of literary studies; in fact, some critics might argue that it is a child of comparative literature's popularization of theory in American universities. Now, in its twentieth anniversary, TnT continues to threaten to de-center literary studies' importance, and English departments institutionally, as the theorization of texts in hyper-technologies inevitably justifies different disciplinary conjunctions beyond those contained in even the most elastic literature and rhetoric programs. Those who continue to see TnT theory, or a corresponding school of thought, as a threat or a buffoonish mockery of serious scholarship, will certainly continue to win many local battles, but the fate of this supposed war was decided long ago against those who cling to a *Literaturwissenschaft*. For those who appreciate Dyn-O-Mite's contributions, texts in the context of media technologies and electronic platforms may once again function as a locus for innovation in the humanities and throughout academia.

References

704 Hauser. 1994. Directed by Norman Lear and Jack Shea. Aired 1994, on CBS.
All In The Family. 1971–1979. Directed by Norman Lear. Aired 1971–1979, on CBS.
Arac, Jonathan, Wlad Godzich, and Wallace Martin. 1983. *The Yale Critics: Deconstruction in America*. Minneapolis, MN: University of Minnesota Press.
Archie Bunker's Place. 1979–1983. Directed by Gary Shimokawa, Joe Gannon, Linda Day, Carroll O'Connor, Paul Bogart, Peter Bonerz, Dick Martin et al. Aired 1979–1983, on CBS.
Arendt, Paul. 2005. "Nobel's raunchy anti-capitalist play gets world premiere." *The Guardian*, September 8, 2005. www.theguardian.com/culture/2005/sep/08/theatre.nobelprize2005.
Bloom, Harold, Paul De Man, and Jacques Derrida. 2004. *Deconstruction and Criticism*. London, UK: Continuum.
Checking In. 1981. Directed by Jack Shea. Aired 1981, on CBS.
de Beauvoir, Simone. 1980. *The Second Sex*. Translated and edited by Howard M. Parshley. New York, NY: Vintage.
Edelman, Lee. 2015. "The Yale School." *ESC: English Studies in Canada* 41, no. 4 (December): 5. muse.jhu.edu/article/619126.
Fiedler, Leslie. 1948. "Come Back to the Raft Ag'n, Huck Honey." *Partisan Review* 15, no. 6: 664–71.
Fiedler, Leslie. 1971a. "Montana; or The End of Jean-Jacques Rousseau." In *The Collected Essays of Leslie Fiedler* 1. New York, NY: Stein and Day.
Fiedler, Leslie. 1971b. "Montana: P.S." In *The Collected Essays of Leslie Fiedler* 2. New York, NY: Stein and Day.
Fiedler, Leslie. 1971c. "Montana: P.S.S." In *The Collected Essays of Leslie Fiedler* 2. New York, NY: Stein and Day.
Gloria. 1982–1983. Directed by Paul Bogart and Bob Claver. Aired 1982–1983, on CBS.
Good Times. 1974–1979. Directed by Gerren Keith, Herbert Kenwith, Bob LaHendro, Donald McKayle, and Perry Rosemond. Aired 1974–1979, on CBS.
Havelock, Eric. 1963. *Preface to Plato*. Cambridge, UK: The Belknap Press of Harvard University Press.
Maude. 1972–1978. Directed by Hal Cooper and Tony Csiki. Aired 1972–1978, on CBS.

Mauer, Barry. 2020. *Deadly Delusions: Right-Wing Death Cult*. Florida: The Governors of the State of Florida Press.

Nobel, Alfred. 1896. "Nemesis." Unpublished play.

Ong, Walter. 1982. *Orality and Literacy*. New York, NY: Methuen & Co., Ltd.

Redfield, Marc. 2016. *Theory at Yale: The Strange Case of Deconstruction in America*. New York, NY: Fordham University Press.

Saper, Craig. 1988. "Introduction." In "Instant Theory: Making Thinking Popular," edited by Craig Saper. Special issue, *Visible Language* 22, no. 4 (Autumn): 371–97.

Sisario, Ben. 2005. "Arts, Briefly." *New York Times*. www.nytimes.com/2005/11/25/arts/movies/arts-briefly.html.

Tanenhaus, Sam. 2003. "Fear and Loathing: How Leslie Fiedler Turned American Criticism on Its Head," *Slate*. slate.com/news-and-politics/2003/02/remembering-leslie-fiedler.html.

The Bob Newhart Show. 1972–1978. Directed by Peter Bonerz, Alan Rafkin, Michael Zinberg, Peter Baldwin, James Burrows, Dick Martin, and Jay Sandrich et al. Aired 1972–1978, on CBS.

The Jeffersons. 1975–1985. Directed by Bob Lally, Oz Scott, Jack Shea, Tony Singletary, and Arlando Smith. Aired 1975–1985, on CBS.

Ulmer, Gregory L. 2015. *Electracy: Gregory L. Ulmer's Textshop Experiments*. Edited by Craig Saper and Victor Vitanza. Boulder, CO: The Davies Group Publishers.

Ulmer, Gregory L. 2019. "Text/Hypertext." In *Blackwell Encyclopedia of Sociology*. London, UK: John Wiley & Sons, Ltd. Online Library. onlinelibrary.wiley.com/doi/10.1002/9781405165518.wbeost017.pub2.

16 The Hypertext Years? (Digital)

Stuart Moulthrop

I begin with an admittedly strange notion—that three and a half decades of recent history, 1985–2020—can be called the hypertext years, as if this technology has some explanatory power for the time in question. We could, of course, just as easily think of this period as the golden age of popular computing, as the heyday of cellular communication or of cable television, or maybe more obviously as the Before Times; but I want to try the virtue of perversity.

Calling out hypertext instead of Twitter, Web 2.0, or technoculture generally may look decidedly foolish, and there is plenty of folly in the record. The early hypertext years were not a good time for predictions. "Hypertext will help us with a great task of our time," wrote one tech commentator in 1987. Linked information would help in "judging what lies ahead, adjusting our thinking to prospects that shake the foundations of established worldviews. Hypertext will strengthen our foresight" (Drexler, 1986). These remarks were offered toward the end of a book extolling nanotechnology. Now, of course, we live in mortal dread of very small replicators. While our highly imperfect, hypertext system, the World Wide Web, arguably did strengthen scientific foresight ahead of the virus crisis, other communication technologies have made the situation worse. The inevitable judgment on "foresight" is not so much the arguably positive insurgency of Black Twitter, as expounded by André Brock and others, but what we might call its Orange counterpart—a potent vector of ignorance, denial, and risk.

Reading technology as text means examining the mediated emergence of meaning. This work may lead us to propose new rhetorics, as George Landow did foundationally for hypertext. We may have recourse to pattern language—as Mark Bernstein has memorably done in *Patterns*—or to the procedural rhetorics proposed by Ian Bogost in *Persuasive Games* and Mary Flanagan in *Critical Play*. We may be drawn, as I always am, to Espen Aarseth's notion of the ergodic—understanding discourse, narrative or otherwise, as a path chosen from a range of possibilities or the traversal of a graph or network (Cybertext).

This work—simultaneously essay, talk, and hypertext built in Twine—explores these possibilities in form and theory.

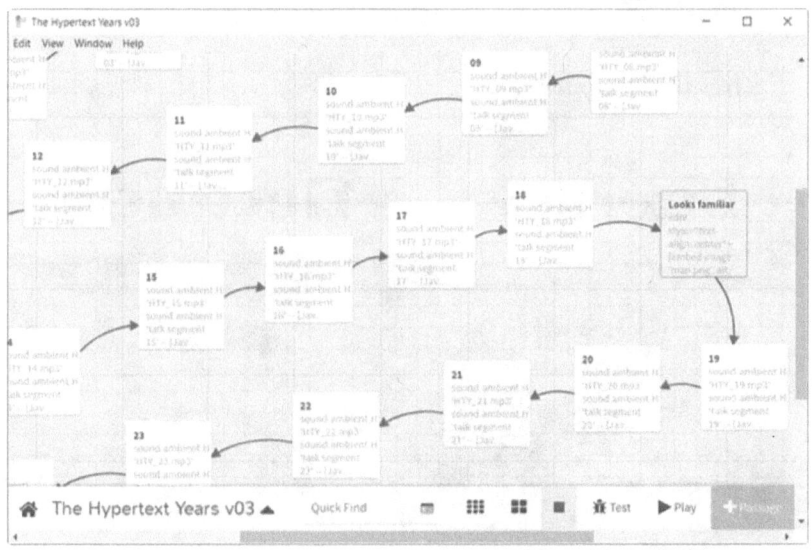

View Stuart Moulthrop's "The Hypertext Years?" online at https://bit.ly/reimagining-humanities or follow the QR code.

17 The Cheshire Diagrams

Gregory L. Ulmer

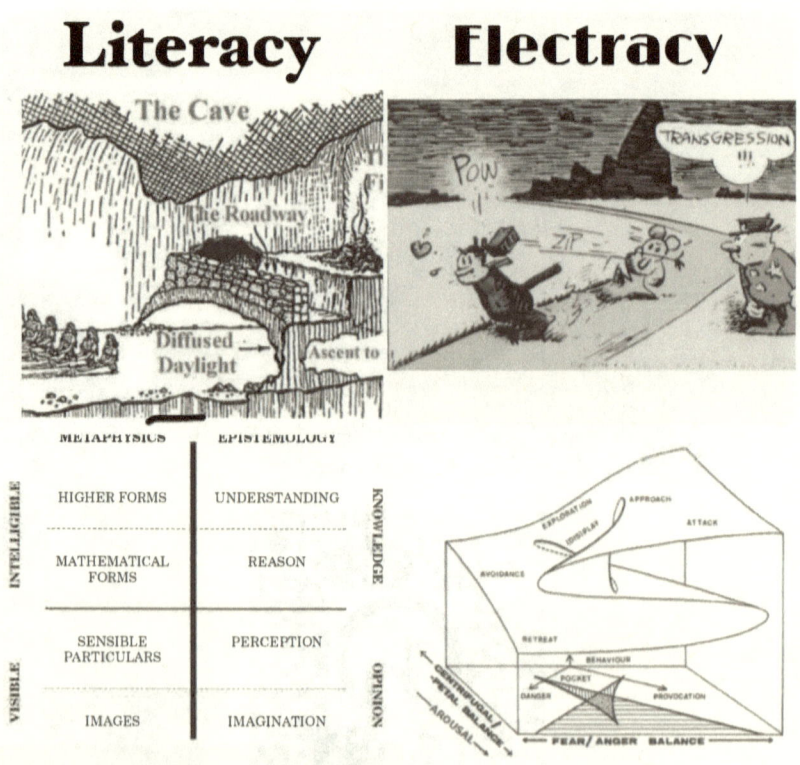

Figure 1. Diagram: Allegory with Analogy (Gregory Ulmer)

"Cheshire Diagrams" is an experiment in conduction—a mode of inference introduced in electracy, supported by digital technologies and vanguard poetics, to supplement the inferential procedures of abduction, deduction, and induction created within literacy. The Diagrams are posted on konsultexperiment.com, KE, a site devoted to the invention of education designed for electracy—the apparatus of digital civilization. The immediate goal of KE is to promote a transition from literate school into natively electrate practices. Primary partners for this collaboration are colleagues engaged in developing humanities curriculum and pedagogy addressing learning through digital media. KE approaches this project in terms of heuretics—the logic of invention. We do not assume that we know in advance the coming electrate education. We do know how it may be invented. The first step in transforming learning from literacy to electracy is to reimagine Arts and Letters curricula as resources for creativity, not only within the humanities disciplines but across the curriculum. Literacy remains relevant to all disciplines in this framing to the extent that writing and its related powers of reason and argument are a dimension of all learning. Electracy is similarly relevant to the extent that creativity is practiced as pedagogy across the curriculum.

KE's point of departure is the theory and practice of education Gregory L. Ulmer developed in a series of books and articles, beginning with the publication of *Applied Grammatology* (1985), including his collaboration with colleagues in the Florida Research Ensemble, FRE. The preliminary phase of KE invention involved a synthesis, update, translation, and remake of these publications into exercises, assignments, and projects—*textshop* pedagogy. The point of departure of the blog konsultexperiment.com is the book, *Konsult: Theopraxesis*, published in Parlor Press's Electracy and Transmedia Studies series (2019). This book develops the Theory register of the generative CATTt guiding KE. A basic heuristic is to invent electracy by analogy with the invention of literacy in Plato's Acade-

View Gregory L. Ulmer's "The Cheshire Diagrams" online at https://bit.ly/reimagining-humanities or follow the QR code.

my in Classical Athens. In brief, Konsult is to electracy what Plato's dialogue is to literacy. Plato's dialogue performed an interface event in which illiterate students encountered literacy, undergoing a transition from conversation to dialectic. Konsult similarly performs a transition from scientific consulting to conduction.

Heuretics

Konsult Experiment promotes heuretics as a pedagogy and research methodology. Heuretics applies theory to the creation of new forms, practices, and methods in the way that hermeneutics applies theory to the interpretation of extant works. The two operations are interdependent. The initial project is an experiment to invent a genre supporting learning in digital media. Through this specific invention, the operations of heuretics as a method are also articulated. We want to understand not only how to invent a genre of electrate consulting, *konsulting,* but how to perform heuretics in general—how to adapt it to other programs and experiments. All the terms of our experiment are open for testing, contesting, and alteration. Konsult is not first invented and then revealed to egents, or electrate learners; egents are introduced to electracy by undertaking the design and testing of a genre native to digital media. The proposal is that this project constitutes the core of digital education.

Poetics are generated by means of the CATTt. This generator first appeared as a pattern in the readings of a seminar on the history of theory—from Plato to the present. Each of the historical discourses on method were constructed using a Contrast, Analogy, existing Theory, a Target context, and a tale—tail of a cat—in which to communicate and demonstrate the new practice. Plato's dialogue method, for example, *Phaedrus,* the first discourse on method in the Western tradition, is the prototype: *Contrast* with Homer's epics; *Analogy* with medical diagnosis or seeking a "diagnosis" of moral ills; *Theory* is Socrates, representing a Pythagorean tradition; *Target* is the new institution of School; *tale* is the dialogue form itself, a dramatized conversational interface within which one is introduced to dialectic as a mode of reason native to alphabetic technology. The CATTt may be used to analyze existing works. Any hermeneutics may be translated into a heuretics, meaning that the features identified by analysis may be refunctioned as *instructions for production.*

The CATTt slots function like a spread in Tarot reading or in any generative template— the slot itself is active and inflects any resource it receives. The syntax of CATTt begins with the articulation of a problem—Contrast repels; Target attracts. Contrast is the extant metaphysics of literacy being constrained relative to its apparatus. Target is the Internet soliciting a native metaphysics. The Contrast and Target are kenotic, emptying out, opening a site for invention. The procedure is to inventory the respective resources to understand the terms of the problem, both what is being rejected—that for which an alternative is sought— and the affordances of the new condition. *Solution* is generated from an inventory of Analogy and Theory. Analogy is an extant related practice suggesting possibilities of the new discourse; Theory identifies the principles structuring the invention as a whole—the What of the enterprise. The heuristic produces four inventories, four lists, each list inflected by its slot. A pattern of correspondences emerges in the intertext created by the juxtaposition of lists. This pattern is configured into a poetics, a formula or recipe of instructions for composing—in our case—an electrate metaphysics. The blog medium as tale supports and organizes this process of collection, inventory, and correlation. The articulation requires some art and some craft, since the intertext does not produce an algorithm, but a pattern. The resulting poetics is valid, which is not true: the validity is authenticated by the formal coherence among the readings. "What resembles, assembles" (Jakobson). The basic CATTt for konsult developed in the book and blog is the following: Contrast = Plato's Republic; Analogy = Vanguard Arts; Theory = Poststructuralism; Target = Internet; tale = Game design (?). Egents are invited to test other versions of the CATTt.

TERMS: *ELECTRACY*

Electracy, like literacy and orality before it, names an *apparatus*, meaning that it is a social machine—part technological, part ideological, part metaphysical. An analogy with the invention of literacy guides our experimental approach to electracy. The Classical Greeks invented alphabetic writing, like the vowel, signs recording the spoken word, the material support for inscription; school and its practices, like the Academy, the Lyceum, in which were invented the categories, method, concept, logic—in short: science; individual and collective identity-behaviors, like selfhood, democratic city state. The question is: what are the electrate equivalents of the literate institutional practices and identity formations?

Despite all the explicit statements made by leading commentators rejecting technological determinism, much of the best theorizing of new media and digital technology in general today neglects the insights of *apparatus:* that the Internet is an emerging institution that is to electracy what school was to literacy; that the categorial, logical, and rhetorical practices needed to function natively in this institution must be invented, and, moreover, that the invention of an image metaphysics—the equivalent of what Aristotle accomplished for the written word—has its own invention stream, independent of the features of modern recording equipment. A shorthand version of what KE proposes is to enact the electrate equivalent of essence. Literate category formation, or metaphysics, functions by means of definitional determination of essence—that without which a thing may not be what it is. This categorial operator was used to organize every aspect of literate civilization, including the social construction of identity in terms of essences. The movement away from essential identities in contemporary culture is not due to some emancipatory politics; or rather, emancipatory politics, breaking free from essentialism, is a symptom of the mutation in the apparatus, from lettered metaphysics to image metaphysics.

TERMS: *EVENT*

Konsult supports thinking from the position of event, rather than from the position of subject and object, the prototype of the latter being that of the Cartesian *cogito*—hence the shift from "agent" to "egent." Deleuze and Guattari wrote

> The concept is obviously knowledge—but knowledge of itself, and what it knows is the pure event, which must not be confused with the state of affairs in which it is embodied. The task of philosophy when it creates concepts, entities, is always to extract an event from things and beings, to set up the new event from things and beings, always to give them a new event: space, time, matter, thought, the possible as events. (1996)

The thought of event is that of a collective, a group that is not one but multitude. The imperative to construct this capability comes from Paul Virilio, his description of the society of the spectacle as a *dromosphere*—a condition of dimension collapse due to light-speed technologies. The Internet General Accident is one that happens everywhere simultaneously, as a possibility of an information economy. Virilio warns that the dromosphere reduces time to *Now*, disjoined from here or there. In such conditions, the established rubrics of rhetoric—practical reason, the logical means of ethics and politics and of decision—are made problematic, to the extent that they concern one or the other dimension of time: Forensic, determine what was true in the past; Epideictic, praise or blame in the present; Deliberative, decide on a future action. Prudence, Phronesis, is a time-image, a wisdom of temporality, gathering up the three orders of time into an act of judgment. Electracy requires the introduction of a fourth order of rhetoric, capable of ethical and political reasoning *Now*, in the Moment, *Augenblick*. In *Heuretics* (Ulmer 1994), the practice of event reasoning is developed as *flash reason*. *Event* names this fourth order, as an invitation for further invention—the construction of concepts enabling this collective rhetoric. Forensic, Epideictic, Deliberative, *Eventive*. The Cheshire Diagrams are eventive.

Terms: *Choragraphy*

Choragraphy is generated by updating the historical term *chorography*—a mapping design combining mimetic depiction and geographical measure— to include Jacques Derrida's reading of *chora* or *khora* in Plato's *Timaeus*. In his collaboration with the architect Peter Eisenman on the design of a *folie* for the Parc de la Villette in Paris, Derrida proposed chora as the *idea* or *parti pris*. In *Heuretics*, Ulmer generated *choragraphy* using a CATTt in which the Derrida/Eisenman *folie* served as Theory. The hypothesis was that chora is to electracy what Aristotle's topos was to literacy. GPS is topical: Existential Positioning System, EPS, is choral. Konsult correlates existential experience with everyday life materiality. For an environment to be intelligent, the apparatus needs to manage not only physical location, GPS, but EPS, which requires tracking not only presence but absence or *différance*. If conventional wayfinding gives coordinates showing "You Are Here," existential coordinates engage a more complex displaced mediated orientation: "I think where I am not, therefore I am where I do not think" (Lacan 1977, 166). Fredric Jameson put it this way: "We can say that if individual experience is authentic, then it cannot be true; and that if a scientific or cognitive model of the same content is true, then it escapes individual experience" (1992).

A *Visit* is an event of encounter between egents and places, both of which involve dimensions that are not phenomenal, not present, without presence and not presentable. Thoreau's *Walden* concludes with a figure that provides an emblem for EPS:

> What was the meaning of that South-Sea Exploring Expedition, with all its parade and expense, but an indirect recognition of the fact that there are continents and seas in the moral world to which every man is an isthmus or an inlet, yet unexplored by him, but that it is easier to sail many thousand miles through cold and storm and cannibals, in a government ship, with five hundred men and boys to assist one, than it is to explore the private sea, the Atlantic and Pacific Ocean of one's being alone. (321)

Inspired in part by Jameson's cognitive mapping, chorography as ontology takes up this question of coordinating material and spiritual wayfinding, exploring the shifting borders and thresholds between inner and outer identity formations. Thoreau's passage is emblematic because it uses global exploration and mapping as a metaphor for self-knowledge—the kind of knowledge and the mode of expression within the cognitive jurisdiction of Arts & Letters disciplines informing konsulting on Well-Being. The challenge of EPS chorography is that the spacetime for which it is responsible is a second-order construction—figurative rather than literal—a fictional and fantasy order emerging through aesthetic formal manipulation of media associated with the visceral appetites rather than with reason. But the promise of konsult is to create an interface convergence of literal and figurative dimensions of human experience, taking up the program of surrealism and the vanguard arts in general. "Cheshire Diagrams" concern the dimension of reality opened through aesthetic indirection, which is—like Plato's chora—beyond both thought and perception, operating a third order of generation.

Assignment

KE's framing project, within which Cheshire Diagrams is one episode, is to invent, or design and test konsult, the genre in which egents, or literate agencies becoming electrate, transition from literacy to electracy. Konsult is the "dialogue" of the digital apparatus. Assuming that the point of departure is within school—the primary institution of literacy—this project appropriates and reframes the archive of world culture as a resource for creativity. Most of the existing school curriculum remains relevant, but the pedagogy changes. Egents consult within a situation of Disaster. The

Disaster includes not only some irreducibly complex hyperobject—the threat to humanity posed by the Anthropocene in multiple variations for example—but also an existential crisis of one's own being. What is *Life-Death* today? The premise is that the resources of the disciplines available within literate schooling—a redundancy, including the egent's major and minor fields of study—are stumped, at impasse, or aporia, becoming themselves part of the problem. The disciplines require *revolutionary science* (Thomas Kuhn).

Electronic Monuments: EM (Ulmer 2005) originally was intended to be the concluding section of *Internet Invention* (Ulmer 2003). Internet Invention adopts the three-act structure of a narrative adventure tale to introduce the pedagogy of mystory to compose an *image of wide scope* or Wide Image. Mystory (Ulmer, *Teletheory,* 1989) is a version of cognitive mapping applied not to hermeneutics, as in Jameson, but to heuretics. The conceit is that the Wide Image functions allegorically for students in the manner of the magic tool acquired by the hero in a classic folktale, earned by undergoing three trials—the popcycle exercises testing theopraxesis. The assignment is to design the Wide Image, which was completed at the end of the second act. Due to considerations of length and complexity, the book stopped at the second act, and EM was published separately. In terms of the narrative frame, the assignment in EM is to "confront the Plague (monster, obstacle, opponent)" of the tale, which for konsult is some public policy disaster that triggers—sting, *punctum*—egents' sense of injustice. The original assignment was to treat the Wide Image as the source of an original hypothesis, applied to the configuration of the disaster by means of diagram design. This plan was abandoned so that EM could stand alone, and the emphasis was shifted to the *MEmorial* genre, as an electrate alternative to traditional monumentality, and anti-memorial, as support for a new global public sphere emerging as a "fifth estate" in digital media. The original plan is revisited in KE, which undertakes the design of Wide Image as resource for original hypotheses applied to hyperobject impasses.

Avatar Emergency: AE concerns Classical Prudence, or Phronesis— good judgment, the capacity to make the right decision spontaneously, intuitively, in the middle of crisis action—updated for dromosphere (Virilio) conditions of dimension collapse created by Real-Time speed-of-light feedback loops in digital civilization. Phronesis is mythologized in American values as *The Right Man with a Gun*—embodied in the Westerns starring John Wayne, and now informing the ideology of the

National Rifle Association. In *Miami Virtue* (Ulmer et al. 2012) this "fast-draw" myth was countered by the mythology of blues jazz improv as a model for Real-Time decision—the western relative of Buddhist *No Mind* adopted by Beat artists such as Jack Kerouac. AE takes up this question of the need for cultural practices of instant judgment, drawing on millennia of epiphanic experience documented in the archive. AE draws upon this history of revelation in religious and arts practices to formulate *flash reason*—"reasoneon." The assignment running through the book is organized as a remake or adaptation of Titian's *Allegory of Time Governed by Prudence*, 1565. The painting commemorates an important decision Titian made late in his life. Selecting Titian as relay was inspired by seeing Francesco Clemente's "encounter" with Titian's *Allegory* in *Smile Now, Cry Later*, 1998, included in the collection of updates or remakes, *Encounters: New Art from Old,* Richard Morphet, reporting on an extensive set of such projects by famous artists. The chapters in AE included recurring discussion of Ulmer's mystory remake of the *Allegory* respecting an important decision in his life by discovering the relevant allegorical animals after Titian. This theme of flash reason for Real-Time decision continues in Konsult, introducing *theopraxesis—theoria praxis poiesis* integrated within Moment.

Konsult Experiment

Konsult Experiment takes up the project and program introduced in the book, *Konsult: Theoprasesis* (2019). The ambition of the book is to update and articulate Justice for digital civilization, given that konsult is to electracy what dialogue is to literacy. The literate concept of Justice was invented by Plato in *The Republic*, so what better way to undertake a transition from literacy to electracy than by updating Justice? The motivation is guided by the *capabilities* approach to economic development advocated by Amartya Sen, winner of the Nobel Prize in Economics, 1998. The first part of konsultexperiment.com provides instructions and rationale for the invention of an electrate equivalent of dialogue, to be included in the curriculum and pedagogy of digital humanities or any program committed to developing education for online learning native to digital civilization. The premise is that Arts and Letters curriculum— and all disciplines in principle—begin the shift to electracy or digital apparatus by reframing learning as heuretics or the logic of invention— on making rather than meaning. To konsult, egents generate from their image of widescope an original hypothesis, revolutionary science, that is applied to the policy impasses of some irreducible disaster emotionally important to the egent. The application is by means of allegory in cognitive mapping. To formulate this hypothesis, egents must compose a mystory to find and design their unique Wide Image—disposition of imagination, cognitive map. Ulmer taught mystoriography in his undergraduate Hypermedia course for several decades at the University of Florida. The exposition of Wide Image design draws upon that experience, including support materials for the course and numerous blogs and websites, extended by the synthesis and integration of retrospection. The first benefit of this process is to make explicit that mystory is pedagogy developing a practice of theopraxesis—thinking, willing, imagining; knowing, doing, making— integrating the *capabilities*, the intellectual virtues whose themes constitute an underlying dynamic of the Western Tradition. Mystory actualizes the potentiality of human capability documented and dramatized in the archive of civilizations—*Dunamis* into *Energeia*. The narrative of heuretic education borrows from the *hero's quest*; such is the structure of *Internet Invention*: human capital is the negentropic force of well-being against disaster or the Anthropocene.

THEOPRAXESIS

What resources are available to egents in their practice of konsult? Egents design their Wide Image in the context of the curriculum, as a reminder of the resources of the archive of Arts and Letters traditions available for *retrieval* or *reoccupation* in the project of invention. In addition to heuretics and mystory as a genre for composing Wide Image against Disaster, egents are introduced to their own capabilities as these have been dramatized, augmented, and explored in the tradition. The entire archive is reconfigured according to this pattern, which is consistent from Plato's *Republic* to Alan Kay's Graphical User Interface, GUI. These capabilities—powers, virtues—constitute the intellectual virtues in Aristotle's account: *Theoria, Praxis, Poiesis*. The portmanteau *Theopraxesis* in the subtitle of the book affiliated with KE refers to these powers with the new term signaling the need for integration of capabilities in the dromosphere. In becoming electrate, egents expand thinking into theopraxesis.

Capabilities: The argument of *Konsult: Theopraxesis* is that Justice updated for electracy makes capability a human right (Amartya Sen). The heuretics curriculum samples the status and relationships among the capabilities or virtues historically. Rubens' *Judgment of Paris* typifies the many works that visualize, in this legend, the quarrel or conflict inherent in the relationship among these powers, both within an individual person and in their institutional extensions. The quarrel is among three goddesses, associated with the respective powers, as to which one is more desirable: Athena, wisdom and war; Hera, wife of Zeus, political power and worldly action; and Aphrodite, beauty and sexual fertility. The mortal Paris is asked to judge by awarding a Golden Apple to the One. Each Power tries to bribe him, and Aphrodite wins by promising Helen as prize, the most attractive mortal woman. Paris took the bribe and the rest is Epic. Hubert Damisch, in his book on this topos, notes the challenge of visualizing the three powers. In this medium, Aphrodite has the advantage. This tripartite distribution of powers at every level of an apparatus is reconfirmed today in Alain Badiou's *conditions* of existence: Science, Politics, Art, plus the fourth condition—Love—which in our version is the embodiment—organic and social—of the virtues in the forces of attraction and repulsion.

Modality: The mystorical imperative always is to recognize these histories as *belonging to me*. What is my experience of these three virtues in my own embodiment, personally and institutionally? Modality in grammar is the speaker or writer's attitude towards the world—disposition. Literacy grounded its invention of a metaphysics of true or false in the neutral modality of the written, declarative proposition. Electracy grounds its invention of a metaphysics of attraction and repulsion in a feeling of ability and disability—to be able and unable, capable and incapable, potent and impotent—addressing the disjunctive conditions separating elements from their system, the displacements of orientation and disorientation between experience and truth—cognitive map and choragraphy.

In Plato's *Republic*—Contrast in the CATTt generating Konsult as genre—the three powers are articulated in a microcosm and macrocosm structure, imagining social institutions as collective realizations of human virtues: Head as Rulers; Heart as Guardians; and Viscera as Workers. The pattern continues in modernity in Kant's critiques of pure reason, practical reason, and the judgment of taste. Hannah Arendt attempted to update Kant's *Critiques* for a post-Holocaust civilization, leaving the project unfinished at her death. This history is relevant to understanding the challenge of electrate learning—to integrate in one performance the powers of thinking-doing-making and knowing-willing-imagining. Alan Kay designed c with this history in mind, providing three inputs interfacing human capability with the digiverse—*keyboard, mouse, image*.

Pedagogy: The practical import of this reconfiguration is as guidance for transition from literacy to electracy. The quarrel among the virtues underlies the dispute among the traditions of Philosophy, History, and Literature as to which one is closest to Truth. Philosophy declares what is; History documents what happens; Literature imagines possibilities. The shift in orientation in electracy is away from the information of the archive to the capabilities of the egent; the goal is not objective coverage of history, but egent empowerment. This shift is supplemental, complementary, and integrative—the goal of theopraxesis being full possession of collective capability. Refunctioned in electracy, the three powers overcome the conflicts, keeping them at odds in literacy. Electracy integrates the visceral dimension of capability into education. Visceral education is undertaken by infants discovering how to control their bodies. The experience of *being able* that drives infant behavior is taken up in Husserl's phenomenology, who replaced Descartes's "I think," with "I can"—*ich kann*—to express intentionality. The force of poststructuralist Theory in Konsult's CATTt is focalized in the problematic of modality, for which Herman Melville's story, "Bartleby, the Scrivener: A Story of Wall Street," has become the emblem, dramatizing the attitude that Aristotle identified as privative, "I would prefer not to," framed today as a stand of resistance.

Cheshire Diagrams

This review of the *Konsult* program—book and website—contextualizes one experiment, "The Cheshire Diagrams," demonstrating heuretics applied to electracy. The experiment tests the inferential practice of conduction, navigating information archive using the aesthetic relationships of dream work. Composed as images—nine diagrams consisting of twenty-two emblems—the Diagrams themselves in principle could be published in print like any other illustration, but their native existence as emblems, text and image constructions, designed using collage poetics, appropriation, visual poetics, allusion—the resources of aesthetics in short—becomes practical for general education in the digital apparatus. They were created to test the possibility of slides to stand on their own, apart from the lecture they conventionally illustrate in such software as

PowerPoint or Keynote. The lectureless slide is identified as such with the name *zlide*. "The Cheshire Diagrams" demonstrate conduction testing the zlide form.

The book, *Konsult: Theopraxesis*, theorized the generation of an electrate genre of education, equivalent of dialogue for digital equipment. The website, konsultexperiment.com, takes up where the book leaves off, shifting away from theory to practice and to theopraxesis. Using Plato's *Republic* as template relay to generate an electrate genre, the Theory proposed the historical city of Venice, Italy, as a resource for imagining the social place in electracy that Plato outlined for literacy as an ideal Republic. Venice was selected to figure this new dimension for numerous reasons, beginning with its contemporary status as an actual place transforming into fantasy, as in Italo Calvino's *Invisible Cities*. The current threat to the city posed by the overwhelming number of tourists is a symptom of what recommends it to represent the "Mecca" of electracy. This reflection on imaginal Venice is to be extended in the experiments into the more properly electrate order of theme parks, specifically in the casinos of Las Vegas, the Venetian Casino in particular.

Within the larger frame of the ideal city, Plato articulated his metaphysics in the Allegory of the Cave, perhaps the best-known fragment of philosophy in all of literacy. An ongoing experiment for konsult is to devise an equally effective allegory of electrate metaphysics. *Konsult*, the book, nominated the exiled Russian poet Joseph Brodsky's *Watermark*—a memoir of his annual visit to Venice during the high-water month of December—as basis for an *Allegory of the Wave*. Venice and *Watermark* are transitional entries, useful for introducing the project, inviting a collaborative engagement with this challenge—imagining the place and practices of the dimension of reality under construction in electracy. Such may be an assignment organizing an entire curriculum.

"The Cheshire Diagrams" take up this challenge in a modest way, moving beyond the book and the *Allegory of the Wave*, performing rather than discussing electrate metaphysics. Within electracy proper the equivalent of Plato's *Republic* is Walt Disney's Disneyland or Disney World, prototype of theming. Mickey Mouse is our Socrates in this scenario. The Diagrams experiment began with the hypothesis that an allegory of electrate metaphysics—attraction and repulsion as fundamental cause—already existed in the chase genre of Cat & Mouse animation (Tom & Jerry et al.). It is the reality of predation troped into a figure of insatiable desire and anxiety. This line of inquiry led to George Herriman's Krazy

Kat as the most eloquent dramatization of drive energy as minimum system—Krazy, Officer Pupp, Ignatz, Brick—and finally to the Cheshire Cat in Lewis Carroll's *Alice in Wonderland*. The series of emblems uses the inferential process of conduction, dada bachelor machine logic, to explore a cat-mouse joke in *Alice*—the *gag* is to konsult what *dialectic* is to dialogue. The joke is based on a macaronic pun—*la souris* in French means "smile," "mouse," and "girl" in slang. The discovery of the experiment is that the Cheshire Cat's grin functions as an equivalent in theopraxesis for category in literate reasoning: the syntagma of a grin without a cat separates from its context to circulate through information as a support for inference by means of aesthetics—Kant's reflective judgment. A first response to this discovery, conduction as a mode of inference navigates information passing from the known into the unknown, is that there are other such primary images and texts already extant, modeling a poetics for creative metaphysics. "The Cheshire Diagrams" models an operation for itself but also as an invitation and call for collaboration.

References

Deleuze, Gilles, and Félix Guattari. 1996. *What Is Philosophy?* Translated by Hugh Tomlinson and Graham Burchell III. New York, NY: Columbia University Press.

Jameson, Fredric. 1992. *Postmodernism, or, the Cultural Logic of Late Capitalism*. Durham, NC: Duke University Press.

Lacan, Jacques. 1977. "The Agency of the Letter in the Unconscious or Reason since Freud." In *Écrits: A Selection*, translated by A. Sheridan, 146–178. New York, NY: W. W. Norton & Company.

Thoreau, Henry David. 2004. *Walden: 150th Anniversary Edition*. Edited by J. Lyndon Shanley. Princeton, NJ: Princeton University Press.

Contributors

Barry Jason Mauer is Associate Professor of English at the University of Central Florida, and is the author of *Deadly Delusions: Right-Wing Death Cult* (2020) and co-author, with John Venecek, of *Strategies for Conducting Literary Research* (2022).

Anastasia Salter is the Director of Graduate Programs and Associate Professor of English for the College of Arts and Humanities and author of seven books that draw on humanities methods alongside computational discourse and subjects. These include most recently *Twining: Critical and Creative Approaches to Hypertext Narratives*, Amherst College Press 2021 with Stuart Moulthrop; *Portrait of the Auteur as Fanboy*, University of Mississippi Press 2020 with Mel Stanfill; and *Adventure Games: Playing the Outsider*, Bloomsbury 2020 with Aaron Reed and John Murray.

James Paul Gee is a Emeritus Presidential and Regents Professor at Arizona State University, where he taught literacy studies, learning theory, discourse analysis, and media and technology. He is the author of published books and papers in all these areas.

Kirk St.Amant is Professor and the Eunice C. Williamson Chair in technical communication at Louisiana Tech University, where he serves as the Director of Louisiana Tech's Center for Health and Medical Communication, CHMC. He is also a member of the University's Center for Biomedical Engineering and Rehabilitation Science, CBERS, and serves as a co-director of the University's Technology and Society Research Lab. Additionally, Kirk is an adjunct professor of health and medical communication with the University of Limerick in Ireland and a research fellow in user experience design with the University of Strasbourg in France. He researches how cognition affects usability and design with a focus on international health and medical contexts and international online education.

Dr. Jennifer Wojton has taught humanities and communication in higher education for nearly two decades at Embry-Riddle Aeronautical University in Daytona Beach, Florida. Jen writes about the intersection of digital culture, identity, and fandom and is grateful for the—often unsung—contributions of so many creators and fans to the rich tapestry of digital content and community, upon which her work depends. She is the co-author of *Sherlock and Digital Fandom: The Meeting of Creativity, Community, and Advocacy*. Her current interest in contributing to the shaping of methodology for digital culture studies has culminated in her contribution to this volume.

Dr. Sandy Branham is Assistant Professor of Humanities and Communication at Embry-Riddle Aeronautical University in Daytona Beach, Florida. Sandy's research focuses on veterans' studies, digital literacy, and social networking technologies, and she is interested in the ways in which social networking technologies equip users with digital literacies and how these digital literacies can be leveraged in the higher education. Sandy earned her PhD from the University of Central Florida's Text and Technology program, and she is the co-author of "Women Veterans' Advocacy Use of Social Networking: Curating and Responding to Trolling."

Carissa Baker is an assistant professor of theme park and attraction management at the University of Central Florida, where her primary focus is narrative in the theme park space. She uses her interdisciplinary background in her pedagogical, scholarly, and industry engagements.

Erik Champion is an Enterprise Fellow in Architecture, Creative, at the University of South Australia. He currently holds honorary research positions at the Australian National University, the University of Western Australia, and Curtin University and was a past UNESCO Chair. Trained in architecture and philosophy, he taught game design at the University of Queensland and the University of New South Wales and ran game design workshops in Australia, the United States, Italy, Poland, Finland, and Qatar.

Dr. Nathan S. Snow is a 2018 graduate in the Texts and Technology program and Assistant Professor of Film and Media Studies at Dixie State University in southern Utah. His dissertation offers historically contextual definitions for different forms of animation and explains the critical significance of the shift from traditional to 3D computer-generated techniques in terms of its effect on the spectator. As such, his research focuses on film history and animation specifically as they relate to theories of genre and spectatorship, identifying and expounding on the intersection between viewer and viewed. Additionally, Nathan has worked in video and animation production for over ten years and has published professional film and video game criticism for over eight years. He recently contributed a book chapter on how new media can be used to make higher education more effective for non-traditional students.

Jessica Kester is Professor of English in the School of Humanities and Communication and the Quanta-Honors College at Daytona State College. Her research has appeared in *Across the Disciplines* and *Currents in Teaching and Learning*.

Jessica Lipsey is Assistant Professor of English in the School of Humanities and Communication and the coordinator for the WAC/WID Program at Daytona State College.

Dan Martin is Assistant Professor and Director of Composition and Writing in the Disciplines at Central Washington University, where he teaches writing courses and studies digital rhetoric, multimodality, and composition theory. His current research investigates mentoring, feedback, and composition theory, and he has published articles in the *Journal of Multimodal Rhetoric*, *The Journal of Curriculum, Teaching, Learning and Leadership in Education*, and several edited collections on multimodal writing and composition and rhetoric.

Meghan Griffin, PhD, is Professor of Humanities and Provost at Southeastern University in Lakeland, Florida, an institution with more than two hundred extension campuses and international partner locations. She has published on classical education, embodiment philosophy, and gender in the workplace.

Marci Mazzarotto holds a PhD in Texts and Technology from the College of Arts and Humanities at the University of Central Florida and is Assistant Professor and Coordinator of the Digital Communication

Program at Georgian Court University in New Jersey. Her interdisciplinary research interests center on the intersection of academic theory and creative practice most often with a focus on media studies—film and television—as well as avant-garde art and critical pedagogy.

Kenton Taylor Howard is a full-time instructor in the Games and Interactive Media program at the University of Central Florida, where he teaches game programming and design. He has published articles in *Transactions of the Digital Games Research Association*, and his work has appeared in conference proceedings such as the Association of Computing Machinery Conference on Hypertext and Media and the International Conference on Interactive Digital Storytelling.

David Matteson is the Associate Curator of Education and Outreach at the Orlando Museum of Art, where he develops and facilitates programs for diverse audiences of all ages, backgrounds, and abilities. He is also a PhD candidate in the Texts and Technology program at the University of Central Florida. His research broadly focuses on digital curation, public history, and museum education.

Laura Okkema holds a PhD in Texts and Technology from the University of Central Florida, 2019, MS in Rhetoric and Technical Communication from Michigan Technological University, 2014, and BA in English and physics from Technische Universität Dortmund, Germany, 2011. Laura is interested in activist critical making, which combines academic research with social activism, creative expression, and technology. She currently works as a German lecturer at the University of Michigan, Ann Arbor.

Craig J. Saper is Professor at UMBC, where he teaches cultural and media theory in a doctoral program. His publications include *Artificial Mythologies*; *Networked Art*; *The Amazing Adventures of Bob Brown*; and, under his pseudonym, dj Readies, *Intimate Bureaucracies: a manifesto*. He has co-edited scholarly collections on: *Electracy*; *Imaging Place*; *Drifts*; and *Mapping Culture Multimodally*; and edited and introduced six critical editions, including five with Roving Eye Press: *The Readies*; *Words*; *Gems*; *1450–1950*; and *Houdini*. In 2020, Saper co-edited, introduced, and annotated the contributors' section of the 1931 *Readies for Bob Brown's Machine: A Critical Facsimile Edition* with Edinburgh University Press. He has published chapters and articles on digital humanities and print culture and built readies.org. He co-curated Type-

Bound—on typewriter and sculptural poetry—and was the co-founder of folkvine.org. Recent chapters—both in November 2020—appear in *The Contemporary Small Press and in Big Data: A New Medium?* Saper published in two other Parlor Press essay collections, *Florida* in 2015 and *New Media/New Methods* in 2008.

Stuart Moulthrop is Distinguished Professor of English at the University of Wisconsin-Milwaukee. His digital fictions in the 1990s and early 2000s were instrumental to cybertext theory and have been assigned to the "golden age" of electronic writing. He was a founding board member of the Electronic Literature Organization in 1999 and continues as part of that community. Between 2003 and 2010, Moulthrop helped build programs in digital design at the University of Baltimore. In Milwaukee, Moulthrop is co-PI of the Digital Cultures Collaboratory, a joint project of faculty, staff, and graduate students supporting the Serious Play live streaming channel on Twitch.tv. He has collaborated with Dene Grigar on *Traversals* from The MIT Press in 2017, concerning the preservation of early electronic literature, and with Anastasia Salter on *Twining* from Amherst College Press in 2021, a combined critical and creative exploration of the Twine writing tool. With Salter, he is co-editor of the book series *Electronic Communities of Play*, also from Amherst.

Gregory L. Ulmer is Professor Emeritus, English and Media Studies, University of Florida. He is coordinator of the Florida Research Ensemble, FRE, (see *Miami Virtue*, www.academia.edu/1352468/Miami_Virtue_Chorography_of_the_Virtual_City) and Joseph Beuys Chair at the European Graduate School in Saas Fee, Switzerland from 2000–2009. His most recent books are *Avatar Emergency*, 2012, *Electracy*, 2015, and *Konsult: Theopraxesis*, 2019. Ulmer's current project is a creative collaboration, *Konsult Experiment* (konsultexperiment.com/) hosted by the Electracy and Transmedia Studies series by Parlor Press, developing a pedagogy native to the digital apparatus. His CV is located at users.clas.ufl.edu/glue/vita.html.

Index

3D, 87, 90–92, 98, 100–107, 109
3D models, 104

Abbott, H. Porter, 74–75, 86
academy, xvi, xviii, 119, 150
access, xviii, xx, 7, 23–29, 31, 33, 34, 39, 40, 49, 57, 94, 100, 108, 115, 207; to ideas, 25–26; to participation, 25–27
accreditation bodies, 160
Acropolis, 96
actor-network approach, xxii
Adobe Atmosphere, 98
advocacy, 45, 46, 51, 59
aesthetics, xviii, 70, 191, 206, 208, 211–212, 231, 233
algorithms, 115
Alice in Wonderland, 79, 233
All in the Family, 201, 210
Allegory of the Cave, 232
Allegory of the Wave, 232
Allen, Theodore, 208
ambient rhetoric, xxi, 118, 120, 122
American Horror Story, 186
Andrew, Dudley, 213
animal communication, 10
animals, 7, 10, 228
animation, xx, 109–110, 232

Anthropocene, xxv, 229
anthropology, 44
anti-misogynist, xiv
anti-racist, xiv
Aphrodite, 230
apparatus, xv, xvii, xxv, 122, 171, 179, 202–203, 221, 223–226, 228, 230–231
apparatus theory, xv
Apple, 176, 230
Arabic, 160
Archive of Our Own, 58
Arendt, Hannah, 216, 230
arête, 150
art, xx, xxiii, 3, 13, 15–16, 33, 44, 58, 74, 83–84, 86, 92–93, 95, 96, 100, 103–104, 145, 147–148, 151, 152, 160, 167–169, 171, 173–176, 178, 180–182, 201, 207, 209, 223
art history, 92–93, 180
assessment, 34, 58, 60, 135, 152, 157, 161, 167
Association of Classical and Christian Schools, 147
Athena, 230
audience, xxi, 32–34, 36–38, 40, 58–59, 61–63, 69, 82– 83, 85,

241

116, 135, 139, 168, 169, 172, 178, 181–182, 194, 204
augmented reality (AR), 90–91, 93, 105–106
authors, xi, xv, xviii–xix, xxi, 5, 14, 44–45, 48–49, 56–57, 59–62, 91, 213
authors versus human subjects, 44
avant-garde, xvi, xxii, 167, 169–171, 174, 181, 183
avatar, xxv, 6, 87, 88
Avatar (film), 67–68, 82, 87–88
Azaryahu, Maoz, 71, 75, 76, 83, 89

Babel, 98
bachelor machine logic, 233
Badiou, Alain, 230
Baird, Davis, 117, 124
Baker, Carissa, xiv, xix, 67, 184
Bakhtin, Mikhail, 70, 75, 128, 130, 142
Bal, Mieke, 70, 71, 75, 84, 85, 86
Barthes, Roland, xvi, 71, 74, 78, 86
Beats, 197
Benjamin, Walter, xiv, 164
Berger, Adam, 81, 86
Bernheimer, Charles, 213–214
Bernstein, Basil, 7, 20
Bernstein, Mark, 219
Beuys, Joseph, 169, 183, 185
Bezemer, Jeff, 141–142
Bible, The, 11, 164
bibliographies, xv
Biden, Joseph, xiv
big data, xvi
bi-narrative structure, 68, 80, 82
biofeedback, 100, 106
Birmingham School, xxv
Black Lives Matter (BLM), xiii
Black Twitter, 218
Blake, William, 13, 16, 113, 124, 126

Bloom, Harold, 151, 164, 198, 216
Boal, Augusto, 181, 183, 185
Bob Newhart Show, The, 202, 217
Bobley, Brett, 105, 108
Booth, Paul, 51, 65–66
Borgias, 102
born-digital, xvi, xxiii
Bortins, Leigh, 149, 152, 159, 163
Branham, Cassandra, xviii, 44, 46–47, 52–55, 59–61
Brecht, Bertolt, 181, 185
Breton, André, xxii, 170–171, 183; *Surrealist Manifesto*, 170, 183
Brock, André, xiv, 218
Brodsky, Joseph: *Watermark*, 232
Buber, Martin, xxii, 127, 129, 141–142
Buck, Edward, 191–192
Buddhist, 228
Burke, Kenneth, 6
Bush, Vannevar, 200
Busse, Kristina, 51

Cabrini Green, 204
Cage, John, xxiii, 169–170, 180
Campbell, Breanna, 128
Campbell, Charles P., 30, 34–38
Campbell, Joseph, 81
capabilities, xxi, 83, 228–231
Carroll, Lewis: *Alice in Wonderland*, 79, 233
Carson, Don, 76, 86–87
case study, 46, 53–55, 131, 159
Cashman, Joe, 68
Catholicism, 11–12, 17, 18
CATTt (contrast, analogy, theory, target, tale), 221–223, 225, 230–231
Cervantes, Miguel de, xv
Champion, Erik, xx, 90, 94, 98–101, 107–108
change, xiii, xxv, 3–4, 11, 29, 34, 39, 40, 44, 46, 52, 54, 102, 104,

120, 123, 157, 173, 192, 198, 213
Chartres Cathedral, 93
Chatman, Seymour, 70, 72–73, 77, 87
Cheshire Diagrams, The, xxv, 220, 225–226, 231, 232, 233
chimpanzees, 8
Chin, Bertha, 62, 65
Chomsky, Noam, 12, 165
chora, xxi, 113, 114, 118–123, 225, 226
choragraphy, xxv, 225–226, 230
Christians, 17
chronotope, 69, 70, 75
Churchill, Winston, 4
CiRCE Institute, 147
Circle of Safety, 155
Citizen Curator Project, xxiv, 195
citizenship, xv, 150, 181, 195
civic engagement, xxii, 155
Classic Learning Test, 147
Classical Academic Press, 147, 164
Classical Conversations Plus, 148
Classical Conversations, Inc., 147–148
classical education, xxii, 145–152
Clemente, Francesco: *Smile Now, Cry Later*, 228
climate, xiii, 173, 215
co-constructing authority, 114, 116, 118–119, 121–123
coding, 33, 92, 149, 162
collaboration, 7–9, 90, 93, 95, 98, 105, 115, 123, 145, 157, 173, 176, 181–182, 221, 225, 233
college education, 147
Collins, Harry, 117, 124–125
comedy, 201–204, 211, 215
comic books, 71, 73, 80, 84, 88
Comic Life, xxiv
community, xv, xviii, xxii, xxiv, 22–40, 44–46, 48–49, 52–53, 55, 57–58, 61–63, 68, 90, 103, 122, 145–148, 155–156, 158–160, 162–163, 169, 173, 191–192, 195, 209
community discourse, 35
community engagement, 39, 90, 158
comparative literature, xxv, 206, 207, 208, 212–215
complex systems, 3
Compton, Kate, xxiii
computer-animated films, xx
computer-animation, xx, 109
conceptual artists, 197
conduction, xxv, 221–222, 231–233
Conference on College Composition and Communication (CCCC), 64–65, 124
Conley, Tom, 213
consulting, xvi, 222
Cooper, Gary, 209
COVID-19, xiii, 146, 148, 154, 181
creative thinking, 165–167, 175, 179, 182
creativity, 92, 105, 187, 221, 226
critical making, xiv, xxiv, 186, 193–194
critical race theory, xiv
critical thinking, xv, xx, 29, 31–32, 34, 118, 159, 161, 177
critics, xv, xix, 72–73, 86, 95, 209, 212, 215
cultural artifacts, 44, 49
cultural heritage, 90–91, 97, 104
cultural studies, 44–45, 70, 84, 208
culture jamming, 176–178

Dada, 183, 197
Damisch, Hubert, 230
dance, 71, 160

dark ride, 68, 80ç81
de Beauvoir, Simone, 214, 216
de Man, Paul, 211–212
Dead Poets Society, 14
Dean, Timothy, 191–192
decoding, 29, 30, 128
defamiliarization, 167–169, 172–174, 176–177, 179, 181–183
Delagrange, Susan, 133, 142
Deleuze, Gilles, xxii, 157, 224, 233
Derrida, Jacques, 203, 211–212, 216, 225
Deserters, The, xxiv, 193–194
deterritorialization, 157
Dewey, John, 167–168, 175, 184
diacritics, 210
dialectic, 129, 147, 169, 222, 233
dialogic pedagogies, 127–129, 132, 136, 141
dialogue, xxv, 54, 72, 81, 127–129, 132, 134, 137–138, 141, 166, 173, 222, 226, 228, 232–233
Dickinson, Emily, 13, 16–19
Diderot, Denis, xv
diegesis, 69
différance, 225
digital: culture, 44–48, 50, 53–55, 57–58, 62, 64; humanities, xv, 193; literacy, 22, 47, 52, 58, 95; media, xv, xviii, 55, 95, 161–162, 221, 222, 227; rhetorics, 44; scholarship, xi–xii; writing research, 44, 56, 58, 60–61, 63, 64
digital humanities, xiii–xiv, xvi, xxiv, 47, 90–95, 97, 102–103, 105, 114–115, 117, 123, 186, 193–194, 212, 228
Digital Media Experience Lab (MIT), 117
disaster, xiv, xxv, 3, 227, 229
disciplines, xii, 54, 56, 64, 69, 91, 114, 122, 153, 205, 207–208, 211, 214

discourse, xiii, 7, 29, 35, 39, 44, 62–63, 69, 70, 74, 77–78, 84, 116, 121, 130, 166–167, 169, 171, 183, 186, 219, 222–223
disinformation, 182
Disney, 68, 78–82, 84, 86–89, 232
distant reading, xvi
distribution access, 28
Doane, Mary Ann, 213
dominant narratives, xxv
Dreyfus, Hubert, 104–105, 107
Dryden, John, 5–6
Dunbar, Kevin, 174–175, 183
Dyn-o-mite! School, 200

educational apparatus, xv, xxvi
Efteling: Droomvlucht or Dreamflight, 79
egents, 222, 225–227, 229
Eisenman, Peter, 225
Elahi, Shirin, 76, 89
electracy, xxv, 95, 108, 191, 203, 221, 222–226, 228–229, 231–232
electrate age, xv–xvi, 100
electronic literacy, xv
Electronic Monuments (Ulmer), 227
elite culture, 5, 9
elitism, 6, 9, 16, 20, 149
Ellison, Ralph, 6
embodiment, 91, 97, 102, 105, 230
empathy, 51, 166, 192
Enclitic, 210
England, 4, 183, 206, 210
Enlightenment, The, xv, 51
environmentalism, xix–xx, 68, 72, 76–80, 87, 90, 98, 204, 211
epideictic rhetoric, 225
epidemics, xiii
Erasmus, Desiderius, 150, 163
ethics, xviii, 56, 70, 225
ethos, 116, 180

event, xxv, 17, 75, 181–182, 222, 224–225
eventive rhetoric, 225
examined life, 3
Existential Positioning System, EPS, 225
experimentation, xii, xvii, xxiii
expertise, xvii, 48, 54, 115, 120–121
eye-tracking, 106

fabula, 69
Facebook, 40, 46, 52–53, 59, 115, 125
familiarity-form-function relationship, 40
fan: culture, 46, 51, 62; fiction, 49, 58–63; scholars, 51
fandom, 51, 55, 63
fans, xviii, 46, 48–50, 55, 58–59, 61–63, 68, 72, 83
fascism, xiii
Father Busa, 93
feedback, xxi, xxii, 52, 57, 64, 127–129, 131–141, 148, 227
Feldman, Ann, 128
feminism, xxiii, 45, 47, 50–51, 116, 201
feminist theory, 45
Festina Lente, 150
Fiedler, Leslie, 208–209, 216, 217
fifth estate, 227
film, xx, 28, 68, 71–72, 74, 77, 79, 81–82, 186, 201, 213–214
film studies, 213, 214
film theory, 213
financial collapse, xiii
Flanagan, Mary, 219
Flavell, John, 129, 133, 142
Fleming, Alexander, 174
Florida Research Ensemble (FRE), 221
Fludernik, Monika, 70, 85, 87

Fluxus, xxii, xxiii, 165, 167–171, 173, 175–180, 182–185, 197
focalization, 68–69
Foote, Kenneth, 71, 75–76, 83, 89
footnotes, xv
forensic rhetoric, 225
Forester, C. S., 13
formalism, 207
fossil fuels, xx, 91
foundational knowledge, 32
Framework for Success in Postsecondary Writing (CWPA), 113, 124
France, 4, 228
Frawley, Jessica, 95
free association, 171
Freire, Paulo, 125, 129–130, 142, 175, 181, 184
Freud, Sigmund, xxiii, 170–171, 233
Friedman, Ken, 75, 87, 168–169, 173, 175, 178, 184–185
Friedman, Susan Stanford, 75, 87, 168–169, 173, 175, 178, 184–185
Frost, Robert, 13
Fugelsang, Jonathan, 174–175, 183

gag, 233
Gallon, Kim, xiv
game studies, xix, 85
games, xix, xxiii, xxv, 6, 73–74, 76, 79, 85, 90, 92, 97, 99, 103, 105–106, 186–187, 193
gameworlds, 76
Gardner, Jared, 71, 73, 87
Gee, James Paul, xvii–xviii, 3, 22–24, 33–35, 40, 41, 141–142
gender, xiv, xvii, 55, 63, 182, 192
Genette, Gérard, 68, 69, 82, 87
genocide, xiii

genre, xxiv, 35–38, 40, 68, 73, 77, 79, 105, 115, 206, 222, 226–227, 229–230, 232
geographic information systems (GIS), 97
George Landow, 219
gestures, 8
Gibson, Blaine, 77
gift economy, 62
Ginsburg, Carlo, xxi
Global Attractions Attendance Report, 86, 89
Gloria (TV show), 6, 201, 216
Godzich, Wlad, 198, 208, 216
Goethe, Johann Wolfgang von, 4
Goldsmith, Oliver, 5
Good Times (TV show), xxiv, 197, 199, 201–204, 207, 210–211, 214, 216
Goodman, Nelson, 165
grammar, xv, 10, 136, 147, 230
grammatology, xv, 107–108
graphic novels, 71
Great Books, 6
Griffin, Meghan, xxii, 145, 163
group identity, xxiv
Guattari, Felix, xxii, 157, 224, 233
GUI (Graphical User Interface), 229
Guidelines for the Ethical Conduct of Research in Composition Studies (CCCC), 64–65

Hampshire College, 12, 16, 213
hardware, 27, 90
Harry Potter, 74, 80, 88, 187
Hassan, Ihab, 212
Haunted Mansion (ride), 79, 80
Hayles, N. Katherine, 114–115
head-up displays (HUDs), 104
Hebrew, 160
Hegel, Georg Wilhelm Friedrich, 19, 214

hegemonic structures, xiv
hegemony, 4
Heidegger, Martin, xx, 96–97, 103, 107
Helen of Troy, 42, 230
Hellekson, Karen, 51
Hench, John, 77, 81, 86–87
Hera, 230
Herman, David, 88
hermeneutics, xvi, 105, 222, 227
heuretics, xv–xvi, xxv, 199, 221–222, 227–231
heuristics, 172
hierarchy, 6, 19
High Culture, 14
High in the Sky Seuss Trolley Train Ride, 79
high literature, 4–5
Hills, Matthew, 51
history, xx, xxii, xxv–xxvi, 3, 8–9, 15, 21, 44, 56, 70, 79, 85, 91, 98, 122, 132, 145, 160, 178, 193, 202–203, 205–207, 218, 222, 228, 230–231
Hockey, Susan, 91–93, 108
Homer, 6, 222
homeschooling, xxii, 147–149, 159
hooks, bell, 119, 124
Hopkins, Gerard Manley, 13, 87–89, 107, 125, 197
Horace, 12
Howard, Kenton Taylor, xxiii, 186, 187
HTC Vive (display), 99
human capital, 229
human subject formation, xv
humanities, xi–xx, xxii, xxiii, xxv, 3–5, 7, 9, 13, 20–21, 85–86, 91–94, 97–98, 100, 102–103, 105, 108, 110, 115, 117, 145–150, 159–160, 162–163, 174, 187, 191–192, 194, 196, 205–206, 208, 216, 219, 221; education,

xvi, 147; future of, 3, 150; print-era, xviii; publishing, xi
hypermedia, 200, 205
hyperobject, 227
Hyperrhiz, xii
hypertext, xiv, xvi, xxiv, xxv, 194, 200–203, 210, 212, 217–219

I Ching, 180
ideology, xiii, xv, 70, 84, 122–123, 177, 228
I-It relationship, 129–130
indexical reality, 109
industrial model of schooling, 167
information technologies, xv–xvi
informed consent, 44–45, 58, 59, 60, 64
innovation, xxv, 92, 145, 155, 157, 216
Instagram, 46, 59, 115–117, 178
Institute of Design (Chicago), xxiii, 170
Institutional Review Board (IRB), xix, 57–58
institutions, xiii, xv, xvii, xviii, xix, xxii, 7, 20, 57, 104, 122, 128–129, 146, 148, 150, 154, 158–160, 162, 170, 191, 206, 230
interdisciplinarity, 92, 145
interdisciplinary approaches, xix, 85
intermediality, 72
Internet General Accident, 224
Internet Invention (Ulmer), 113, 126, 191, 227, 229
intersectionality, xvii
interviews, 46, 54, 116, 131–132, 138
invention, xv, xxv, 98, 119, 170, 172, 203, 209, 221–225, 228–230

IRB (Institutional Review Board), 57, 58
I-Thou relationship, 127–129, 136, 139, 141

Jackson, Janet, 202
Jameson, Fredric, 225–227, 233
Janssen, Ruud, 178
Jenkins, Henry, 7, 31, 41, 48, 51, 65, 73, 76–77, 88, 180, 184
Jenstad, Janelle, 115–116, 124
Johnson, Ray, 178, 184, 205
justice, xxiv–xxvi, 191–192, 194

Kahneman, Daniel, 172
Kairos (journal), xi
Kant, Immanuel, xviii, 206, 208, 230, 233
Kaprow, Allan, 174–175, 180
Kay, Alan, 80, 88, 229, 231
Kerouac, Jack, 228
Kester, Jessica, xxi, 113
Keynote, 232
Knowles, Alison, 180
Knox-Williams, Charlotte, 114, 120, 124
konsult, xxv, 223, 226–229, 232–233
Konsult: Theopraxesis (Ulmer), 221, 229, 232
Krazy Kat (George Herriman), 233
Kress, Gunther, 141–142
Kuhn, Thomas, 173, 227

labor and exploitation, 44
labor fatigue, xi
Labov, William, 70
Lamb, James, 128, 143
Langlois, Henri, xx
Las Vegas, 232
Latin, 12, 145, 147–149, 152–153, 160
Laure-Ryan, Marie, 71

248 *Index*

Leap Motion, 99
Lear, Norman, 201, 216
Learning Management System (LMS), 156
Levin, Harry, 207
LGBTQ Video Game Archive, 187
LGBTQ+, xxiii–xxiv, 192
Limouzy, Agathe, 99, 100
Lipsey, Jessica, xxi, 113
Lipsitz, George, 208
literacy, xv, xviii, xxiv–xxv, 14, 22–34, 36, 38–42, 58, 94–95, 113, 115, 117, 130, 198, 203, 207, 221–226, 228, 231–232; alphabetic, xv–xvi, xxv; definition of, 25
literacy ecosystems, 28
literature, xxiv, 3–7, 12–16, 93, 97, 106, 147, 148, 151–152, 193–194, 205–210, 212–215
Little Mermaid, The, 74
logic, xxi, xxiv–xxv, 12, 85, 95, 147, 170–171, 201, 221, 223, 228
love, xvii, 14, 16, 18, 48, 151, 179
Lovelace, Ada, 93
Lukas, Scott, 77, 88
Luna Park, 81
Lyceum, 160, 223

Maciunas, George, 171, 175, 184
Mad Tea Party, 79
Magic: The Gathering, 187
mail art, 176–179
maps, 76, 191
marginalized identities, 186
Martin, Dan, xxii, 87, 96, 107, 127, 129, 142–144, 163, 198, 201, 216–217
Martiniere, Stephan, 68, 88
Marxism, 70
Mason, Charlotte, 153, 164
mass extinctions, xiii

material access, 28
Matteson, David, xxiii, 191–192
Maude (TV show), 201, 216
Mauer, Barry, xiii, xvii, xxiv, 122, 125, 195, 196, 198, 215, 217
Mazzarotto, Marci, xxii–xxiii, 165
McCabe, Colin, 210
McCarthy, Josh, 137, 143
McKee, Heidi, 44, 47, 56–58, 60, 64–66
media studies, 51, 171, 182, 198, 203, 207, 213, 215
Melville, Herman, 13, 231
memex, 200
MEmorial (Ulmer), 227
memory, xv, xvi, xxiv, 79, 86, 95, 200
Menabrea, Luigi Federico, 93
metacognitive activity, 132
metaphors, 77, 103
metaphysics, xviii, 223–224, 230, 232–233
Miami Virtue (Ulmer), 228
Mickey Mouse, 232
microfilm, 200
Miller, Andrew, 25, 35–37, 42, 95, 107–108, 149, 155–156, 164
Mills College, xxiii, 170
Milton, John, 6–7, 149
mimesis, 69
mirror neurons, xx
misinformation, 182
MIT Media Lab, 197
Mittel, Jason, 72
mixed reality, 90, 97–98, 103, 105–106
Moby Dick, 13
modernism, 209
Moffat, Stephen, 49
Montaigne, Michel de, xv
Montessori, 146, 153
Moore, Gemmel, 191

Moore, Marianne, 13, 42, 113, 124–125, 191–192
Morphet, Richard: *Encounters; New Art from Old*, 228
Mother Goose, 11
Moulthrop, Stuart, xiv, xxv, 218–219
movies, xx, 79, 82, 205, 217
MSNBC, 182
multimedia, xx, 92–93, 132, 171, 176, 195, 214
multimodal feedback, xxii, 128
multimodal texts, 56
Murray, Janet, 73, 88
museums, 71, 76, 104, 171, 195
music, 15, 71–72, 79, 81, 92–93, 100, 147, 191, 198, 211
Myst, 105
Mystic Manor (ride), 72, 79
mystory, xxv, 122, 227–229
myths, 77, 121, 208

narrative, xiv, xvi, xxiv, 46, 68–86, 93, 186–187, 193, 198, 219, 227, 229; schema, 74; theory, 68–69, 71, 72–74, 78, 83–86
narratives: functional, 78; indicial, 78; temporal, 76
narratology, 69–75, 77, 79, 83, 85–86, 207
National Center for Atmospheric Research, 173, 184
National Rifle Association (NRA), 228
Naylor, Gloria, 6
Neiwert, David, 208
Nelson, Theodor Holm, 165, 200
Nemesis (play), 199, 217
networked: education, 146, 155, 160–161; relationships, 158
new media, xix, 22, 72, 85, 119, 205, 224
New School, xxiii, 170

Nicks, Stevie, 191
Nobel, Alfred, 199
novels, 11, 69, 80
nuclear war, xiii

Okkema, Laura, xiv, xxiv, 193–194
online education, xiii, xxii, 159
online spaces, xviii, 53, 56
oppression, xvii, xxiv
orality, xv, xvi, xxv, 203, 223
Overwatch (game), 186
ownership, 45, 156

Paik, Nam June, 169, 184
painting, xx, 71–74, 79, 99–100, 228
pandemic, xi–xii, 86, 146, 148, 197, 205
Papaleontiou-Louca, Eleonora, 132, 134, 138, 143
Paradise Lost (Milton), 7
paratexts, 63
Parc de la Villette, 225
Paris, 42–43, 183, 225, 230
Pasteur, Louis, 174
patriarchy, xiii, 6
pedagogy, xiv, xvi, xxii–xxiii, 108, 114, 122–123, 128, 129, 132, 136, 138, 141, 166, 167, 171, 174, 176, 182, 186, 198, 221–222, 227–229
peer review, 57, 160
performance, xxiii, 69, 71, 74, 90, 118, 150–151, 160, 176, 179–182, 214, 231
performance art, 71
Perloff, Marjorie, 214
Peter Pan, 81
Pew Research Center, 115, 125, 160
Phaedrus (Plato, 222
Philips, Deborah, 77, 89

philosophy, 12–13, 149, 157, 165, 208, 224, 232
photorealism, 102
photoreality, xxi, 109
Pieper, Joseph, 153, 164
place, xvii, 12, 18, 23, 25–27, 39, 45, 58, 76–77, 80, 82, 92, 95, 97–98, 105, 114, 118, 120–123, 128, 150, 152, 159–163, 172, 176, 180, 203, 215, 232
Plato, xvi, 119, 125, 145, 153, 164, 167, 216, 222–223, 225–226, 228–230, 232
play: pedagogy of, xxiii, 166–167, 176, 182
Plutarch, 151
poetics, xvi, xx, xxv, 109, 197, 221, 223, 231, 233
poetry, xviii, 12–16, 19, 68
poiesis, 228
political scrutiny, xi
politics, 8, 181, 214, 217, 224–225
PoP, 165–167
popcycle, xxii, 122, 227
popular culture, 55, 186, 191, 201, 204, 213, 215
Poseidon's Fury (ride), 79
positionality, 46, 49–50, 55, 62, 64
poststructuralism, 70, 214
power relations, 63
Pradl, Gordon, 74, 89
praxis, 86, 150, 160, 228
Prensky, Marc, 95
primary access, 26
Prince, Gerald, 69, 84, 85, 89
print literacy, xv, xvi, xvii
print technology, xv
privacy, xix, xx, 45, 58, 59, 61, 90, 131
private schools, 147, 149
privilege, 45, 48, 130
procedural literacies, 117

production, xi, xvi, 33–34, 50, 56, 69, 96, 118, 120, 145, 157, 160, 171–172, 175, 195, 201, 206, 212–213, 222
Professional Knowledge for the Teaching of Writing (NCTE), 113
Project Zero (PZ), 165, 184
propaganda, 4
Protestant Hymnal, 16, 17
psychoanalysis, 70
public schools, 146, 148–149
public versus private spaces, 44
Pulse Nightclub, xxiv, 195
punctum, 227

qualitative: analysis, 46, 166; research, 44, 47, 50–51, 53–55, 56, 61, 64
Queen of England, 11
queer: play, 186–187; representation, xxiii, 186–187
Queer Game Studies, 187
Question Concerning Technology, The, 102, 107

race, xiv, xvii, xxiv–xxv, 5, 70, 182, 208
race theory, 70
racial hierarchies, xvii
RAD scholarship (replicable, aggregable, data-supported), 53
Rallis, Sharon F., 50–51, 66
Ramus, Peter, xv
Ratatouille (film), xxi
Raven, Paul Graham, 76, 89
Ray, Robert, 213
realism, 102, 109
recipes, 37
Reformation, xv
rehumanization, 70
remediation, 72, 131

replicable, aggregable, and data-supported (RAD), 53
Republic (Plato), 228
Republicans, xiv
research, xiii, xv–xvii, xix–xx, 20, 40, 44–47, 50–64, 83–85, 90–93, 97–98, 103, 113, 115, 117, 127–129, 156, 165–167, 169–171, 173–175, 180, 183, 193, 195,197, 199, 222
reterritorialization, 157
rhetoric, xvi, 47, 53, 64, 118, 147, 215, 225; types of: deliberative; epideictic, 225; eventive, 225; forensic, 225
rhetoric and composition, 47, 53
Rich, Adrienne, 13, 43
Rickert, Thomas, xxi, 118–120, 122, 125
Rohde, Joe, 68, 82
Rolle, Esther, 201–202
Roman Roads Media, 147
Rosaen, Cheryl, 136
Rose, Frank, 5, 21, 74, 89, 185
Rose, Jonathan, 5, 21, 74, 89, 185
Rosewater, Mark, 187
Rossman, Gretchen B., 50–51, 66, 131, 143
Roy, Arundhati: *The God of Small Things*, 75, 87
Rubens, Peter Paul: *Judgment of Paris*, 230
Rule, Peter Neville, 128, 143
Russian formalism, 70
Russo, Mary, 213

Said, Edward, 208
Sales, Nancy Jo, 116, 125
Saper, Craig, xvii, xxiv–xxv, 171, 175–176, 178, 185, 197–198, 217
scholé, 153, 158, 163

schooling, 7, 13, 123, 149, 166, 227
science, xxii, 10, 18, 22, 76, 98, 102, 161, 173, 175, 206–207, 212–213, 223, 227, 229
science fiction, 76
science literacy, 22
scientific method, 173
sculpture, 71–72, 93
Second Life, 105
secondary access, 26
Sekiguchi, Sachiyo, 98, 107
selective augmentation, xxi, 109–110
Selfe, Cynthia, 128, 143
self-reflexivity, 50
semiotic defamiliarization, 177
Sen, Amartya, 229
sensitive versus non-sensitive information, 44, 56
service, xvi, 6, 130, 145
Sexton, Anne, 13
sexual orientation, 59
sexuality, 63, 116, 187, 208
Shakespeare, William, 5–6, 14
Sherlock (TV show), 46, 48, 49, 66
Shifman, Limor, 116, 125
Shilton, Katie, 45, 57, 64, 66
Shklovsky, Viktor, 168–169, 172, 181–182, 185
sjuzet, 69
smart phones, 179
Smith, Mary, 5–7, 14, 20, 141, 143, 217
Smithsonian Institution, xiv
Snapchat, 115, 117
Snow White (film), 81
Snow White's Scary Adventures (ride), 81
Snow, Nathan, xx–xxi, 109
social media, xiv, xviii, xxi, 45, 48–49, 54, 57–58, 60, 61, 115–116, 125, 172, 178–179

social networks, 46
social sciences, 205
Society for Classical Learning, 147
Socrates, 145, 153, 163, 222, 232
Southeastern University, 148, 154, 155, 158–160
Southern Association of Colleges and Schools Commission on Colleges (SACSCOC), 157
spatial thinking, 75
specific universal, 19–20
spelling, xv
Spivak, Gayatri, 208
Splash Mountain (ride), 78, 81
St.Amant, Kirk, xviii, 22–23, 25, 30–31, 33–34, 36, 40, 43
standing-in-reserve (Heidegger), 97
Stanford University, 3
Star Wars (film), 80, 82
statistics, 53
Steam (gaming platform), 105
STEAM (Science, Technology, Engineering, Arts, and Mathematics), 146
STEM (Science, Technology, Engineering, and Mathematics), 146, 149
Stephens, Wallace, 13
Sterling, Bruce, 77
Stevenson, Taylor W., 129
Stiles, Kristine, 180
Stonehenge, 9, 10, 19
storytelling, xix, 68, 70, 72, 76–80, 83, 84–85, 87, 162, 175
storyworlds, 75, 82
structuralism, 70, 207
student engagement, 166–167, 175, 179, 182, 185
student-centered learning, 114
stylistics, 13–14
subject position, 47, 50, 51, 54, 63, 114, 120, 123, 130
Sub-Stance, 210

Sullivan, Graeme, 47, 50, 65, 66, 169, 185
Surrealism, xxiii, 212
Swiss Family Treehouse (ride), 79

Takeda, Joseph, 115–116, 124
Taoism, 99
Taoism Touch Screen, 99
Taxonomy of Educational Objectives: The Classification of Educational Goals (Krathwohl, Bloom, and Masia), 151, 164
teaching, xii, xiv, xvi–xvii, xxi, 74, 94, 98, 118, 120, 122–123, 127–132, 134, 136, 141, 153, 170, 182
teaching spaces, xxi
technē, xx, 90, 103
technoculture, 218
technologies, xii–xvi, xviii, xxii–xxiii, 22, 23–25, 28, 30, 33–36, 38–40, 56–57, 67, 91, 93–95, 97, 100, 103, 105–106, 109, 113–115, 119–122, 145, 147, 171, 197–200, 204, 206–207, 212, 215–216, 218, 219, 221–222, 224
technology studies, xiv
TEI (Text Encoding Initiative), 91, 103, 106
Teletheory (Ulmer), 95, 107, 108, 227
television, xxv, 28, 46, 48–49, 55, 71, 186, 199, 201, 205, 207, 211, 215, 218
Temple of Fire (ride), 79
Text Encoding Initiative (TEI), 91, 103
texts and technology, xvi, 22, 114, 145, 202, 205–206, 215
Texts and Technology PhD (University of Central Florida), xvi, xxiv, 198, 202–206, 212–215

Textshop Experiments, xii, 217
textuality, xv, 207, 213–214
Theatre of the Oppressed (TO), 181–183
theme parks, xiv, xix, 67–69, 71–84, 86, 232
theology, 11, 149
theopraxesis, xxv, 227–229, 231–233
theoria, 228
theorizing, xii, xvii, 49, 224
theory, xv–xvii, xix–xxi, xxiii–xxiv, 12, 69, 72, 75, 85, 94–95, 114, 118, 122, 129, 130, 169, 171, 177, 182, 202, 204–215, 219, 221–222, 232
therapeutic counseling, xiii
Thoreau, Henry David: *Walden*, 226, 233
Thriving Quotient, The, 155, 164
Titian, 228; *Allegory of Time Governed by Prudence*, 228
TnT, 199–201, 204–206, 212, 215
Tom & Jerry (TV show), 232
topical knowledge, 33
Toronto School, xxv
transdisciplinarity, xv
transmedia, xiv, 72, 80, 83
transmedial narratology, 71–72, 75, 83
transmedial theory, xix
Trinity Schools, 147
trivium, 147
Trowbridge, Scott, 82
Trump, Donald J., xiv
truth, xxii, 145, 147, 212, 230
Tumblr, 49
Twine, xxiv, xxv, 193, 219
Twitter, 25, 40, 46, 49, 59, 116, 218
typography, xv

Ulmer, Gregory L., xv, xxi–xxv, 95, 107–108, 113, 118–120, 122–125, 126, 191, 198–199, 203–204, 209, 212, 217, 220v 221, 225, 227–229; *Applied Grammatology*, 221; *Avatar Emergency*, 227; *Electronic Monuments*, 227; *Heuretics*, xv, 125, 222, 225; *Internet Invention*, 113, 126, 191, 227, 229; *Konsult*; *Theopraxesis*, 221, 229, 232; *Konsult Experiment*, 222, 228; *Miami Virtue*, 228
United States, xxii, 11, 115, 148, 154, 164, 198, 199
University of California at Santa Barbara, 3, 12
University of Central Florida (UCF), xvi, xxiv, 117, 201, 202, 205, 212–213, 215

Vanhoutte, Edward, 93, 108
Venetian Casino, 232
Venice, 232
veterans, xviii, 46–47, 52, 53, 55, 59
veterans studies, 46
video feedback (VF), 127–129, 131–141
video games, 6, 71, 73, 76, 79–80, 82, 84
Virgil, 12
Virilio, Paul, 224–225, 227
virtual environments, xx, 90–91, 103, 106
virtual heritage, xx, 90–91, 100–103, 106
virtual reality (VR), xx, 79, 90–92, 96–97, 99, 100, 104,–108
virtual worlds, xx, 91, 94, 98, 102–106
virtuality, 104, 106
Visit (Ulmer), 88, 225

visualization, 90, 94, 97
visualization literacy, 94

Wagner, Richard, 4
Wang, Neil, 99, 108
Ward, Irene, 128, 144
Wayne, John, 228
Web 2.0, 66, 113, 218
Weber, Samuel, 208
Weissberg, Lilliane, 214
wellbeing, xiii
Wellek, René, 206–207, 210
white supremacists, 20
white supremacy, xiii
Whitman, Walt, 13
Williams, Raymond, 13, 30–31, 43, 120, 183, 210
Wilson, Woodrow, 4, 7–8, 21, 184
Wizarding World of Harry Potter (ride), 77

Wojton, Jennifer, xviii, 44, 46, 58, 60–61, 63
Woolf, Virginia, 13
World War II, 93, 211
World Wide Web, 93, 218
WPA Outcomes Statement for First-Year Composition (CWPA), 113, 124
writing studies, 56–57, 113–114, 116, 117

Yale School, 198, 207, 216
Yancey, Kathleen Blake, 113, 115, 123–124, 126
Yeats, William Butler, 13
Yi-Fu Tuan, 118, 120
YouTube, 115, 184

Zeus, 23

About the Editors

Barry Jason Mauer is Associate Professor of English at the University of Central Florida, and served as director of the Texts and Technology doctoral program from 2016 to 2019. He researches citizen curating, which aims to bring ordinary people into the production of exhibits, both online and in public spaces, using archival materials available in museums, libraries, public history centers, and personal collections. Mauer publishes comics about  delusion and denial, particularly as they affect politics and is the author of *Deadly Delusions: Right-Wing Death Cult* (2020) and co-author, with John Venecek, of *Strategies for Conducting Literary Research* (2022). Mauer is also a songwriter and recording artist. He lives in Orlando with his wife, Claire, his two dogs, and his cat.

Anastasia Salter is Associate Professor of English and Director of Graduate Programs at the University of Central Florida, where they also coordinate the innovative interdisciplinary Texts and Technology doctoral program. Their research draws upon humanities methods alongside computational discourse and subjects. They have authored several books, including *Twining: Critical and Creative Approaches to Hypertext Narratives* (with Stuart Moulthrop, Amherst College Press,  2021), *Portrait of the Auteur as Fanboy* (with Mel Stanfill, University of Mississippi Press, 2020), and *Adventure Games: Playing the Outsider* (with Aaron Reed and John Murray, Bloomsbury, 2020). They are co-editor of the Parlor Press Comics and Graphic Narratives series.

www.ingramcontent.com/pod-product-compliance
Lightning Source LLC
Chambersburg PA
CBHW021657230426
43668CB00008B/654